Developments in the Study of
Criminal Behaviour

Developments in the Study of Criminal Behaviour

Volume 1

The Prevention and Control of Offending

Edited by
Philip Feldman
University of Birmingham

JOHN WILEY & SONS

Chichester · New York · Brisbane · Toronto · Singapore

Library of Congress Cataloging in Publication Data:
Main entry under title:

Developments in the study of criminal behavior.

  Includes index.
  Contents: v. 1. The prevention and control of offending.
   1. Criminal behavior, Prediction of—Collected works. 2. Juvenile delinquency—Collected works. 3. Violence—Collected works. I. Feldman, Philip.

HV6035.D48   364.3   81-21946
ISBN 0 471 10176 1 (v. 1)   AACR2

British Library Cataloguing in Publication Data:

Developments in the study of criminal behaviour.
  Vol. 1: The prevention and control of offending
  1. Crime and criminals
  I. Feldman, Philip
  364   HV6025

  ISBN 0 471 10176 1

Photosetting by Thomson Press (India) Ltd., New Delhi and Printed in the United States of America.

The Contributors

RON CLARKE — *Senior Principal Research Officer, Home Office Research Unit, London.*

PHILIP FELDMAN — *Reader in Clinical Psychology, University of Birmingham.*

KEVIN HEAL — *Research Psychologist, Home Office Research Unit, Longon.*

MIKE HOUGH — *Research Psychologist, Home Office Research Unit, London.*

EUGENE OSTAPIUK — *Senior Psychologist, Glenthorne Youth Treatment Centre, Birmingham.*

DEREK PERKINS — *Principal Psychologist, HM Prison, Birmingham.*

MARY ANN PRESTON — *Senior Psychologist, Glenthorne Youth Treatment Centre, Birmingham.*

IAN REID — *Programme Director, Glenthorne Youth Treatment Centre, Birmingham.*

IAN SINCLAIR — *Director of Research, National Institute for Social Work.*

SUSAN SPENCE — *Lecturer, Department of Psychology, Institute of Psychiatry, University of London.*

NORMAN TUTT — *Professor of Social Administration, University of Lancaster.*

Contents

Preface

There is general agreement that conventional penal methods, particularly those involving confinement, are largely ineffective in reducing re-offending and may even increase it. Psychology based alternatives are increasingly in evidence. They have drawn on the two main strands of clinical psychology, the psychotherapeutic and the behavioural, the latter being a more recent development. This book collects together a number of approaches to offender care and rehabilitation, both community and institution based, within the behavioural tradition. Three chapters remind us that innovative programmes have to exist within a framework determined by politicians and civil servants, that police practices are relevant both to prevention and intervention and to re-offending, and that the present interest in the behavioural approaches is not the first 'new look' at the care of young offenders.

Chapter 1, by Norman Tutt, describes the pressures on policy makers concerned with young offenders, and the resulting legislative context provided for those directly concerned with offender care. In the second chapter, Mike Hough and Kevin Heal discuss both conventional policing methods and more recent developments, such as community policing, which aim to reduce police/juvenile conflicts. In chapter 3, Ian Sinclair and Ron Clarke take us through less recent attempts at reforming juvenile offenders in institutional settings. They provide some salutory lessons for the current generation of innovators.

The remaining five chapters all describe programmes of behaviour change. Ian Reid outlines the early days of an institution established for particularly difficult young offenders and emphasizes the necessity for comprehensive planning of all aspects from the design of buildings through the selection and training of staff to the planning, execution and generalization of the programme of change. Susan Spence takes a detailed look of one specific aspect of such a programme, namely social skills training. The chapters by Eugene Ostapiuk and Mary Ann Preston move from institutions into the community. The former emphasizes the use of local resources and provides valuable data on both costs and effectiveness. The latter outlines Intermediate Treatment, a current attempt to maintain juvenile offenders within the community, and describes how she tried to introduce a more systematic approach for this section of young people.

In chapter 8 Derek Perkins reviews a quite different group, that of sex offenders, and describes a long-term programme being carried out at Birmingham Prison.

In the final chapter I have brought together some of the key themes concerning intervention and then moved on to discuss the possibility of prevention through large and small scale social plannings.

I hope that this book will be of interest to social science students, to policy planners, and to professionals concerned with the management of young offenders and sex offenders. I am most grateful to all the contributors for their skill and patience both in their professional work and in the writing of this book.

PHILIP FELDMAN, 1982

Developments in the Study of Criminal Behaviour
Volume 1: The Prevention and Control of Offending
Edited by P. Feldman
© 1982, John Wiley & Sons, Ltd.

1

An Overview of Intervention with Young Offenders: The Political and Legal Contexts

NORMAN TUTT

Any overview of a complex social problem such as juvenile offending has to consider at least three major issues. First, the formal context of the problem: in this instance, the formal context will be the stated policy objectives of central and local government in Britain, as articulated in legislation and administrative guidance. Secondly, the informal context of the problem. The formal declarations of policy may have little impact, or even an unpredicted impact, on the actual practice pursued in the social policy arena. An obvious example in the field of adult offenders is the way in which successive Home Secretaries have stated the dangers of over-crowded prisons and the policy objective of reducing the prison population. This objective is supported, in principle, by the Lord Chancellor and through him by the judiciary and magistracy, and yet despite this consensus the number of adults in prison continues to rise. The informal context, then, is what actually happens within the juvenile justice system. Thirdly, there are the significant developments in research and practice. Often research or good models of practice illustrate ways forward for policy, but, even if the ideas win political backing and are taken up into the policy field, there is an inevitable time lag between the appearance, dissemination, acceptance and possible ultimate introduction into policy of research findings and there is then a further time lag before the policy affects future practice. Obviously the interaction of these three facets produces changes and governs developments; for example, the formal policy context to some extent determines what research will be funded. Nevertheless, for the purposes of this chapter, it is intended to look at the three aspects separately and to examine changes in each over the part decade.

The formal context

The major legislation covering the prosecution, disposal and treatment of juvenile offenders in England and Wales is the Children and Young Persons Act (1969). Legislation in Scotland and in Northern Ireland is not only different in kind but in effect, so that the United Kingdom has three markedly different systems of juvenile justice. The Children and Young Persons Act (1969), hereafter referred to as the 1969 Act, had as two of its objectives:

(a) To shift the emphasis in dealing with juvenile offenders away from a system based on the magistrates courts' power to determine what disposal a child should receive. Instead an increase in formal cautioning by the police would, it was hoped, divert children from the courts. Those children found guilty by the court would be committed to the care of the local authority and specific decisions about the child's placement and treatment would be made by professional social workers.
(b) To replace the traditional institution-based programmes of approved schools with more community-based programmes which would lead to a greater integration of the child, his family and the community.

The sections of the 1969 Act which were agreed by Parliament for implementation finally came into effect in January 1971. Formerly, juvenile magistrates could make, among other dispositions, an approved school order, which ensured the child was placed in an approved school for a minimum of 6 months and a maximum of 3 years. The judicial model, although required to act for the welfare of the child, was replaced in 1971 by a more overt treatment model; now, after a finding of guilt, the only course of action available if the juvenile bench wishes to sanction the removal of the child from home, short of sending him to detention centre or recommending his committal to borstal, is to place the child into the care of the local authority. The actual placement of the child is determined by officers of the local authority, normally social workers. The placement may be in any one of a range of residential facilities, in a foster home, or in exceptional circumstances back in the child's own home.

Prior to 1971 the approved schools, although receiving the majority of their funding from the Home Office, were in the main managed by various voluntary bodies or locally recruited managers. The 1969 Act transferred responsibility for these institutions from the managers to local authorities, and in the process the approved schools were renamed Community Homes with Education (CHE). It was hoped that they would not only be more publicly accountable but would become integrated into the range of children's facilities already managed by the local authority. In addition, the 1969 Act provided statutory powers for the introduction of Intermediate Treatment (IT) which was 'treatment intermediate between a supervision order and the removal of the child from home' (Home Office, 1968; p. 9). Intermediate Treatment was to provide a range of community-based activities which would enable the young offender to be supervised and helped without necessitating his removal from home.

It is equally important to indicate those sections of the 1969 Act which were not implemented in 1971 and still remain unimplemented. Critical sections unimplemented are those which: (a) would have made consultations between police and social services compulsory prior to the decision to prosecute (Section 5); and (b) would have raised the age of criminal prosecution (Section 4). It was originally proposed that the age at which a child could be brought before a juvenile court to face criminal charges should be raised to 14 years other than in cases of homicide. This remains unimplemented and a child of 10 can still face criminal prosecution. It was also envisaged that the age at which a young person could be sentenced for Borstal training would be raised from 15 years to 17 years of age (Section 7(1)). This section also remains unimplemented and young people from the age of 15 can be sentenced to Borstal training. The 1969 Act also envisaged that expansion of Intermediate Treatment facilities organized by local authority social services departments would eventually replace the need for Attendance Centres (organized by the police on Saturday afternoons) and Junior Detention Centres, specialist Prison Department Establishments to which a young person aged between 14 and 17 years can be committed by a Magistrates court for a sentence of 3 or 6 months duration (Section 7(3)).

Almost immediately after the partial implementation of the 1969 Act there were claims that it was not 'working'. The House of Commons Expenditure Committee established a Sub-Committee in December 1973 to begin an enquiry into the workings of the Act (Expenditure Committee, 1975). At this time the act had been implemented for just under 2 years; indeed the system of Community Homes was only fully established in 1973, and yet the act was already under severe attack. The Sub-Committee, although chaired by a Labour MP and investigating a piece of legislation very much identified with and supported by Labour administrations, appeared to base its investigation on the assumption that the act was not working, an assumption for which there was no evidence except hearsay evidence, rumours and beliefs. The Sub-Committee were not unaware of their lack of evidence and commented in their report of 1975 that:

No figures are yet available to show whether recidivism figures have altered since the Act was passed, but in any case it is open to question how far the Act could have been expected to influence juvenile offending. The rise in juvenile crime has almost exactly paralleled the general increase in crime. (Expenditure Committee, 1975; p. viii)

In spite of these reservations the Sub-Committee went on to make forty recommendations for the 'improvement' of the workings of the 1969 Act. Two of these recommendations are of specific interest since they represent a train of thinking throughout the seventies that is now coming to fruition. The Sub-Committee obviously felt that the magistrates had lost powers under the 1969 Act, and that they, not social workers, should have the major voice in deciding the disposal of juvenile offenders. The two recommendations were:

That when a juvenile already the subject of a care order appears before a court charged with an offence, the court shall have the power to make, if it thinks fit, a 'secure care order' requiring the local authority to place the juvenile in secure accommodation for a period not less than that specified in the order. (Expenditure Committee, 1975; p. xlix)

That:
(a) when making a supervision order the court shall have the power to specify conditions with which the subject of the order must comply (such conditions being similar to those attaching to a probation order);
(b) for a breach of any of these conditions the supervisor shall be able to bring the juvenile back to court which shall have the power to deal with the matter, if it thinks fit, by way of a fine or an attendance centre order, whilst continuing the supervision order. (Expenditure Committee, 1975; p. li)

The Expenditure Sub-Committee were not completely agreed about 'toughening-up' the 1969 Act since they also recommended 'that the practice of remanding young persons to adult prisons should cease forthwith' (p. xlix).

The government responded to the report of the Expenditure Committee with a White Paper (Home Office et al., 1976) which, whilst rejecting the idea of a secure care order, accepted the phasing out of remands to prison and the introduction of conditions in supervision orders.

Following consultations with local authority associations, an Order was laid before Parliament under Section 34(7) of the 1969 Act which came into force on 31 March 1977, ending such remands of 14-year-old girls. A similar Order ending such remands for 15- and 16-year-old girls was laid on 24 November 1978 and came into force on 1 March 1979. A further Order under Section 69 of the Children Act (1975) restricting the circumstances under which certificates of unruliness could be issued came into force on 1 August 1977. In the 12-month period after the Order came into effect the number of certificates issued dropped by 28 per cent compared with the corresponding period before 1 August 1977 (DHSS, 1979).

Similarly, after consultation with local authority associations, Section 12 of the 1969 Act was amended by Section 37 of the Criminal Law Act (1977). This amendment gave courts the power to impose requirements on a juvenile when making him subject to a supervision order in criminal proceedings and to impose sanctions on him for breach of these or any statutory requirement.

By the end of the decade, the country was faced with a general election and 'law and order' became an overtly political issue. It had always been an issue which divided the major political parties; after all, at the beginning of the decade it had been a new Conservative government which refused to implement fully the Act passed under the previous Labour government. The Conservative manifesto for the general election in 1979 made specific mention of the intention to restore powers to the magistrates by the introduction of 'residential and secure care orders'. By October 1980 the decade was over and with unintended symbolism the government issued a White Paper outlining its proposals for dealing with Young Offenders (Home Office, 1980a). An analysis of that White Paper indicates the ways in which policy has shifted substantially over the decade.

There are several features other than the content of the Young Offenders

White Paper worthy of comment, since they indicate certain substantial shifts in thinking and policy. First, the very title is significant. In the 1960s White Papers were issued with the titles, *The Child, the Family and the Young Offender* (Home Office, 1965), and *Children in Trouble* (Home Office, 1968). Both titles indicate a view of juvenile offending, in which what is stressed is *the child*, with its connotations of immaturity and reduced individual responsibility. The title of the earlier White Paper hints at an underlying causal relationship between the child and his family and subsequent delinquent behaviour. The later White Paper plays down delinquency and uses the less emotive euphemism of 'trouble', i.e. trouble at school, trouble with the police, emotional troubles. Both these White Papers referred continually to children and stubbornly refused to pander to public concern about juvenile crime. Thus, from the 1968 White Paper: 'Much misbehaviour by children is part of the process of growing up, but some has more deep seated causes' (p. 16, para. 49). The 1980 White Paper not only devotes its first ten pages to the Young Adult Offender, but when discussing children it continually refers to juveniles, juvenile crime, and juvenile offending. The image of children misbehaving has gone; instead, 'The Government shares the general public concern about the level of juvenile offending' (p. 11 para. 34).

These features are extremely important. In the early seventies, when responsibility for Children's Services was transferred from the Home Office to the Department of Health and Social Security, consistent attempts were made to erode the division between the 'deprived and depraved'. Juvenile offenders were seen first as children with the same personal, social and educational needs as all other children; they were only secondly offenders who might need control. The emphasis on their immaturity has now been abandoned. The very fact that the current White Paper deals both with the young adult offender and the juvenile offenders without any clear differentiation suggests that offending is now the main focus rather than childhood.

Indeed Ministers have gone even further in public debate, so that at a conference on Intermediate Treatment held in Sheffield in July 1979, Leon Brittan, Junior Minister at the Home Office, stated

> There is a *very real difference* between the many young people who slip into offending as a reaction to the emptiness, boredom and sometimes brutality of their own lives and those who deliberately commit violent or totally uncaring crimes. ... We agree that for the great majority of young offenders a flexible range of treatment should be provided to meet their developing needs and to prevent them leaving home or being placed in custody unless it is absolutely essential. We also believe that it *is possible to identify* the relatively small minority for whom a deterrent sentence makes sense. (Brittan, 1979a) (author's italics)

Thus the deliberately depraved delinquent has been rediscovered.

The rediscovery of the delinquent and the subsequent policy of control is one of the major themes of the 1970s: the 1980 White Paper merely officially recognizes it. The tightening-up of the supervision orders in 1977, referred to above, was an earlier official recognition of this shift. The supervision order was created for juvenile offenders in order to align those young people with the children in need of care and protection supervised by the Children's Department rather than identify them with the offenders by expanding the Probation Orders. The changes in supervision orders in 1977, with the introduction of the possibility of a fine or attendance centre as a sanction for breach of the order, firmly re-established an element of control.

A second major theme which has rumbled through the decade and been recognized in the 1980 White Paper is the power struggle between the judiciary and the executive. *The Child, the Family and the Young Offender* (Home Office, 1965) proposed the abolition of the juvenile court and its replacement by a Family Council. Persistent lobbying behind the scenes and more publicly in the correspondence columns of *The Times* succeeded in removing this proposal from *Children in Trouble* (Home Office, 1968). Interestingly, in Scotland, where the juvenile courts had never been well established, it proved possible to push though a reform similar to that envisaged in the earlier White Paper. 1969 Act barely eroded the powers of the magistrate. They still had all their previous powers with the exception of two new orders which did not guarantee that the child would be removed from home in the case of a care order and did not allow magistrates to specify what intermediate treatment activity the child would undertake. This marginal erosion of magisterial power became a 'cause celebre' over which the Magistrates Association kept up a persistent and effective lobby both of the Home Office and in Parliament.

The Home Office were swayed by the pressure of the magistrates and proposed in the 1980 White Paper 'that where a juvenile [sic] already in the care of a local authority as an offender is found guilty of a further imprisonable offence [sic], power should exist for the courts to add a "residential care order", with the effect that for a fixed period not exceeding six months he is not to be allowed to remain at home' (p. 1, para. 1(f)). Assuming this proposal will eventually reach the statute book it represents a victory for the judiciary over the executive.

The third major strand of policy development has resulted from the inconsistent stance which the Home Office has been forced into accepting. The major criminal policy issue facing the Home Office is the need to reduce the adult criminal population. A number of changes—e.g. parole, suspended sentences and community service orders—have been intended to reduce the proportion of adults receiving custodial sentences, although the increased use of fines seems to be the major factor in the reduction which has actually occurred. However, these changes have had little impact on the young adult offender between 17 and 21 years of age. The Home Office have been eager to reform this end of the custodial system but are continually bedevilled by the fact that the fastest-growing proportion at the lower age range are the 14- or 15- to 17-year-olds in junior detention centres and borstals. Leon Brittan neatly illustrated the problem:

Let me start by putting the problem into perspective. There is no doubt that recorded crime among juveniles has increased substantially during the past twenty years. But, contrary to the impression usually given, it has not increased more than adult crime. The proportionate increase in the number of offences by juveniles has been about the same as for adults: both have approximately tripled. Nevertheless, serious crimes and offences by girls have risen disproportionately and this must give cause for concern. Where the greatest difference has been is not in the commission of offences but in what happens to the sentenced offender. During the past twenty years, the proportion of convicted adults received into custody has been more than halved. During the same period the proportion of juveniles receiving custodial sentences, and I do not include care orders, has more than tripled. In 1955 an adult was 20 times more likely than a juvenile to get a custodial sentence for an indictable offence. Now he is only twice as likely. (Brittan, 1979)

The Home Office has consistently rejected one option, namely to press for full implementation of the 1969 Act, which would have the effect of removing borstal training and detention centres as a sentencing option for under 17-year-olds (see above). The official explanation is always that public opinion (unspecified) would not tolerate such a move.

Consequently, the Home Office finds itself trying to cobble together a package of reforms which may reduce the proportion of 14–17-year-olds being incarcerated and yet publicly looks as though a 'hard-line' on juvenile offending is being pursued. Thus the number of attendance centres has been expanded rapidly over the past 2 years and their scope enlarged to cater for girls in some areas.

The 1980 White Paper introduces a mixture of proposals for the 14–17-year-olds, including:

retention of the detention centre, but with shorter maximum and minimum periods of detention;
powers for the court to impose on offenders aged 15–16 years (who are now liable to be sentenced to borstal training) medium term sentences of youth custody;
power for the juvenile courts to impose community service orders on offenders aged 16; and *inter alia* the ending of remands for 14-year-old boys from March 1981.

The formal policy context has thus changed substantially in the past decade. The decade started with a formally expressed faith in the 'treatment model' with arrangements made for professionals to decide on the treatment of delinquent children, for treatment programmes to be indeterminate and flexible in order to respond to the changing and developing needs of the child, and for the child to be protected from the stigma of contact with adult offenders. It ended with almost a complete reversal in formal policy with a return of decision-making power to the magistracy, determinacy of sentencing, diversion away from social work agencies and less differentiation between children and adult offenders.

The informal context

Whilst the policy debate has been pursued over the past decade children and young people have continued to pass through the juvenile justice system. The way in which that system has operated has at times been in direct contradiction to the professed aims of the current policy. Therefore it is essential to examine what has actually been happening to children. A number of the issues dealt with in this section will be examined before and after the 1969 Act to demonstrate the marginal impact formal policy may have on actual practice.

Officially recorded offending. The reservations about the use of officially recorded statistics as an index of actual offending behaviour are well documented (Radzinowicz and King, 1977). However, official statistics are unfortunately the only statistics available on a wide basis which can provide any indication of the growth or diminution of criminal behaviour. If the official statistics for the past 20 years are examined two consistent features are obvious: that there appears to be an overall increase in offences recorded, and that the proportion of offences

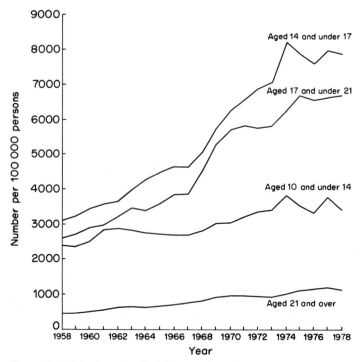

Figure 1   Males found guilty of, or cautioned for, indictable offences per 100 000 population in the age group by age (England and Wales). (Taken from Home Office 1980b)

recorded as being committed by juveniles has remained constant at about one-third of the total offences recorded.

Figure 1 shows the number of persons found guilty of, or cautioned for, indictable offences per 100 000 population covering the 20-year period up to and including 1978 (Home Office, 1980b). Although these figures have been adjusted to take account of the major changes in legislation which affect the statistics, i.e. the raising of the age of criminal responsibility in 1964 from 8 to 10, and changes in the classification of some offences from non-indictable to indictable following the Theft Act of 1968, and the Criminal Damage Act of 1971, it is not possible to adjust for the indirect effects of recent legislation, e.g. the possible changes in attitude of the police and public towards the treatment of juvenile offenders following the introduction of the 1969 Act. As the graph shows, over this period there has been a significant increase in the numbers found guilty or cautioned for indictable offences.

Growth of cautioning

There has been a marked increase since 1967 in the use of cautioning by the police. In recent years, of those persons between 10 and 17 years found guilty of, or cautioned for, indictable offences, about half have been cautioned.

Figure 2 provides an illustration of the growth of cautioning of juvenile offenders between 10 and 17 years of age over the past twenty years (Home Office 1980b) and shows cautioning by the police is the most common disposal. By 1979

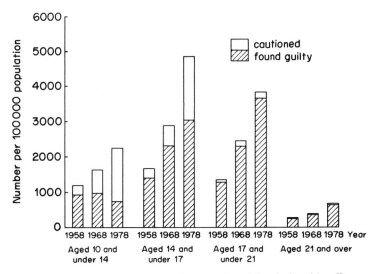

Figure 2   Persons found guilty of, or cautioned for, indictable offences per 100 000 population in the age group by age (England and Wales)

Table 1 Males 10–14 years. Sentence for indictable offences (percentages of total disposals for the age group and absolute numbers)

	1968	1969	1970	1971	1972	1973	1974	1975	1976	1977	1978
Conditional discharge	29 (6939)	28 (6404)	28 (6266)	25 (4857)	27 (5181)	26 (5242)	29 (6548)	30 (6439)	31 (6223)	32 (6797)	32 (6561)
Attendence centre	11 (2753)	11 (2668)	12 (2813)	12 (2278)	13 (2451)	12 (2434)	12 (2753)	13 (2680)	14 (2786)	13 (2760)	14 (2818)
Fines	19 (4533)	19 (4364)	19 (4353)	20 (3816)	20 (3962)	22 (4403)	22 (5012)	21 (4491)	21 (4305)	22 (4653)	23 (4681)
Treatment disposals											
Supervision or probation	28 (6824)	29 (6800)	28 (6235)	28 (5314)	26 (4957)	25 (4992)	24 (5474)	23 (4865)	21 (4295)	21 (4418)	20 (4117)
Care order or Equivalent	9 (2118)	9 (2127)	10 (2242)	12 (2324)	12 (2235)	12 (2348)	12 (2750)	12 (2519)	11 (2188)	9 (1981)	9 (1836)

Table 2 Males 14–17 years. Sentenced for indictable offences (percentages of total disposals for the age group and absolute numbers)

	1968	1969	1970	1971	1972	1973	1974	1975	1976	1977	1978
Conditional discharge	19 (7859)	18 (8107)	17 (8056)	17 (7928)	17 (8532)	17 (8981)	18 (10970)	19 (11120)	20 (11765)	20 (12566)	19 (12149)
Attendance centre	7 (3029)	7 (2924)	7 (3316)	7 (3310)	7 (3709)	8 (4026)	9 (5204)	9 (5218)	9 (5721)	10 (6390)	11 (7209)
Fines	35 (14714)	37 (16405)	38 (18015)	40 (18714)	42 (20773)	40 (20973)	40 (24241)	39 (23379)	38 (22869)	39 (24642)	40 (25558)
Detention centre	4 (1657)	4 (1827)	4 (2043)	4 (2061)	5 (2536)	6 (2999)	6 (3677)	7 (4296)	8 (4296)	8 (5151)	9 (5528)
Borstal	2 (751)	2 (799)	2 (1026)	2 (1116)	3 (1255)	3 (1378)	3 (1572)	3 (1607)	3 (1727)	3 (1656)	3 (1769)
Treatment disposals											
Supervision or probation	24 (10153)	23 (10482)	22 (10341)	19 (8893)	17 (8564)	17 (9075)	17 (10586)	16 (9724)	15 (9337)	15 (9635)	14 (8905)
Care order or equivalent	7 (3106)	7 (3211)	8 (3765)	8 (3689)	7 (3419)	7 (3608)	6 (3781)	6 (3594)	5 (2967)	4 (2738)	4 (2659)

44 per cent of young people under the age of 17 years who committed indictable crimes were dealt with in this way, proportionately more girls being cautioned than boys.

Shift to custody

What is clear from Table 1 and 2 is that those disposals which allow long-term contact between the young person and the social service agency and therefore offer an opportunity for 'treatment' are in a minority. These disposals are: the supervision or probation order which involves a social worker or probation officer having a statutory involvement in the life of the juvenile offender and possibly his family; the care order in which the parental rights are given to the social services department by the court. Under such an order the social services department will determine where the child should reside, the range of options is wide from remaining at home to retention in a secure unit. Moreover, all the indications are that such disposals are diminishing and more short-term or punitive disposals are being applied.

These shifts in disposal are even more significant than the figures suggest since they occurred at a time when the official policy was in fact the reverse. Borstal and detention centres were initially to be phased out and yet over the decade showed an astonishing increase in use of over 200 per cent. Similarly, junior attendance centres were to be phased out; instead the number of attendance centres has been expanded from seventy-one to ninety-nine, a figure which now includes six for girls and three for both boys and girls under 17 years of age. Not only has the provision for attendance centres expanded, but the proportion of juveniles sent to this short term disposal has increased from 11 per cent to 14 per cent for under 14 year olds and from 7 per cent to 11 per cent for those under 17 years. At the same time use of the supervision order and care order, both of which would involve close contact with social work agencies and were seen as the major disposal available to the courts, has not only declined in proportion to other disposals but is now showing a decline in real terms.

Decline of welfare

The decline in the use of care orders is now radically affecting the residential provision of local authorities. In 1971, when the 1969 Act was implemented, there were approximately 7500 young people, boys and girls, in open community homes with education (the former approved schools). However, at that time there were less than one hundred long-term secure places for young people. By 1980 the picture looked quite different. There are currently less than 5500 young people in Community Homes with Education (CHEs). This drop reflects a consistent downward trend since 1971 and it is continuing, if not accelerating, and leading to the closure of a number of CHEs. But at the same time the number of long-term secure places is increasing rapidly and in proportional terms dramatically; in 1980 some 300 long-term places in security are provided for children and young people. These figures exclude the growing numbers of young people in security in prison department establishments (Borstal and Junior Detention Centre). It appears, however, that the decline in Care Orders despite increases in the number of young people convicted is explained by young people being sentenced by courts to junior detention centres in preference to CHEs via a Care Order.

Some of the reduction in the use of CHEs would be accounted for by the considerable expansion of Intermediate Treatment facilities. Intermediate Treatment refers to a range of community-based activities designed to provide alternative facilities for young offenders who would otherwise be in institutional settings, or for young people at risk of entering institutional care. Such facilities have been given priority for expansion by many local authorities and represent a major plank in their policy for dealing with young offenders. In addition, the last 5 years have seen an expansion in the provision of special family placements (foster parents) for difficult and disturbed adolescents, with some apparent success (Hazel, 1978).

The Informal Context over the past decade has, then, shown a number of significant trends. The response to an apparently increasing problem of juvenile crime has been an expansion of social control and a reduction in social work intervention. This has led to an expansion of police cautioning, a much greater use of custodial disposals by juvenile courts, and expansion of the police role *after* a finding of guilt by the development of attendance centres. There has been less social work intervention, and when social workers do intervene there is a greater likelihood that they will use community based facilities, or (ironically) secure accommodation, with a consequent 'squeezing-out' of the traditional open institution.

Research and models of practice

Research in the field of juvenile offending has tended to fall into three categories: research into the causes and prevention of juvenile crime, research into the operation of the juvenile justice system, and work on the monitoring and evaluation of models of practice.

Prevention of juvenile crime. Obviously, for the benefit of both the child and the community, prevention is the best strategy to adopt. However, research findings have shifted the emphasis of preventive work with juvenile offenders away from what could be termed 'social education', e.g. provision of youth facilities, counselling services, activity leisure groups, etc., towards 'mechanical' forms of prevention, e.g. the use of physical security of buildings, greater surveillance in shops and public transport, the introduction of 'vandal proof' building materials. The problem with the early identification of children 'at risk of delinquency' and the consequent taking of preventive action from state agencies is that any such process of identification would in fact identify more children at risk than would become delinquent. The insights of labelling theory are important here.

For example, it is known that a disproportionate number of delinquents come from broken homes, but also many children from broken homes do not become delinquent. Consequently, if children were identified as 'at risk' on the basis of whether or not they came from broken homes too many children would be identified. This remains true even if complicated correlations and collations of numbers of factors are made. For example, West and Farrington, using data on five family background characteristics collected before the boys in their sample were aged 10, correctly identified thirty-one boys who were convicted before the age of 17; but thirty-two were incorrectly labelled, and fifty-three delinquents were missed, out of a sample of more than four hundred boys (West and Farrington, 1973). Even if it were possible to identify accurately the children and put them into delinquency prevention programmes, little would be gained, since first it is not known what action *is* preventive and secondly such an identification may actually help create delinquent behaviour by labelling the child and giving him a self-identity as a 'problem' to which he then responds. A good example of the way in which research into the prevention of juvenile delinquency has ultimately redirected research away from the delinquent and towards mechanical forms of prevention is the article by Jasinski in which he argues that: problems of definition of the term juvenile delinquency, problems over identification of young people involved in such behaviour and the problems of what the preventive programmes should actually contain, all add up to seriously questioning both the appropriateness and effectiveness of preventive measures based on early identification and intervention of cases at risk (Jasinski, 1977).

Instead, what is now advocated is a series of strategies aimed at reducing crime and not at preventing future delinquent behaviour. A Home Office Research Study (Mayhew *et al.*, 1976) gives a number of examples where the opportunity for delinquency appears to promote delinquent behaviour and where removal of the opportunity reduces the behaviour. For example, the wide-scale introduction of steering locks on cars reduces the opportunity for car theft and therefore the amount of illegal driving and taking away. The use of lighting and vandal-proof materials reduces the number of thefts from telephone kiosks. To take another example, the work of the housing planner Oscar Newman on 'defensible space' may mean that housing schemes can be designed in such a way as to reduce vandalism and theft.

Changes in operational services may also have an impact beyond that expected; for example, the truancy sweeps operated by the juvenile bureau in various divisions of the Metropolitan Police, in which truants were picked up by patrolling officers and returned to school or home. In one division this action coincided with a 26 per cent drop in reported auto-crimes and a 36 per cent reduction in petty crimes, mainly theft (Metropolitan Police, personal communication, 1978).

The operation of the juvenile justice system. Much of this research was promoted with the intention of trying to discover what exactly was happening within the system in order that the formal policy context would be better informed. Zander (1975) was one of the first to examine what was actually happening to those children made subject to Care Orders. Taking a sample of juveniles drawn from London Boroughs and appearing before the London juvenile courts he discovered that the majority of children (48 per cent) made subject to a care order were actually admitted to residential care. The remaining children he divided into two groups—those who were returned home or to live with a relative as the result of a considered decision by social workers (18 per cent), and those who were returned home by default because no suitable institution could be found (29 per cent). Three per cent were categorized as miscellaneous—(rounding down in the original means the figures do not add up to 100 per cent). Following these children through their placement he discovered that those sent home as deliberate policy were less likely to reoffend than those sent to institutions, despite the fact that the opportunity to reoffend theoretically ought to have been greatly reduced for the latter group since the follow up period commenced on the making of the Care Order. The group returned to the community by 'default' had the greatest likelihood of reoffending.

Cawson (1979) mounted a large-scale study to examine what happened to children on Care Orders. Using a postal questionnaire, Cawson followed up a sample of 497 children committed to the care of local authorities in England and Wales in the month of July 1975. Home Office records for the same period show 664 juveniles committed to care, whereas figures in the DHSS annual returns for the same period are only about 550. From the official statistics it is impossible to determine the completeness of Cawson's sample. Although there were some regional variations in response rates Cawson's work proved invaluable in laying some of the myths about the current workings of the juvenile justice system. First, she showed that the level of delinquency of many children committed to care is not high; 30 per cent of her sample were committed to care on their first court appearance and almost 60 per cent were committed by their second. This effect was even more marked amongst girls, three-quarters of whom were committed after their first and second appearance compared to 56 per cent of boys. Thorpe *et al.* (1980) attempted to allow for cautioning prior to court proceedings as an explanation of the early use of care orders, and still found figures compatible with those of Cawson. In both studies the vast majority of juveniles committed to care were committed following offences against property (82 per cent).

Cawson found that 32 per cent of her sample were not placed in assessment centres at any time in the study period. There was considerable variation between regions in the proportion not assessed, and girls were less likely to be assessed than boys. Children who had spent periods on remand in assessment centres were more likely to receive post-committal assessment than those who had been at home or in other residential placements prior to committal.

Less than a quarter of the sample progressed from assessment at committal to care to a permanent long-term placement. Of the potentially long-term placements made after assessment, 74 per cent survived till the end of the research period (usually between 4 and 6 months). Of the children placed directly into a long-term placement, only just over a quarter (27 per cent) survived the 9 months until the end of the research period. The most common placements were still the Community Homes with Educations (CHEs) and more children went to CHEs than to any other kind of establishment: at the same time a minority of children were in CHEs at any one point in the research period.

Reoffending was most likely to occur fairly soon after the Care Order (177 reoffenders 36 per cent of the sample) and few reoffended for the first time after 6 months. Consequently, most reoffending occurred during the first placement, suggesting that the period immediately after the Care Order is the very worst time to settle for makeshift placement arrangements.

It appeared that the children with the worst records of offending prior to committal were the most likely to reoffend, but that when this 'higher risk' factor was taken into account, children removed from home did better than might be expected while children at home did worse. This general finding masks considerable differences among both 'at home' and 'removed from home' groups, however: children placed at home by choice (the decision having been taken by social workers employed by the local authority in whose care the child had been placed) did better than those so placed due to lack of a vacancy or other problems: while children in care did better if they were in an assessment centre, or childrens home or a foster home, than if they were in a CHE. These findings were in general support of those of Zander (1975).

Thorpe et al. (1980) in a series of local studies of the working of the juvenile justice system have not only supported Cawson's findings but have highlighted the large variations between local systems due to the discretion allowed agencies within those systems. They have shown variations in cautioning, prosecutions and disposals, and between social workers and probation officers in their recommendations to courts.

The general view that emerges from these systems studies is that the system is, if anything, now 'tighter' rather than more flexible, with an inflation of cautioning rates, an increase in incarceration recommendations, use of custody earlier in a child's delinquent career and an increasing failure of residential institutions to arrest reoffending.

Monitoring and evaluation of models of practice

Inevitably much research into practice has focussed on residential institutions dealing with juvenile offenders: 'inevitably', since agreed outcome objectives could be used (reconviction rates) and also institutions made it easier to target research than community programmes since some variables could be controlled at least. Tutt (1974) outlined a model describing the various objectives expected of Community Homes with Education. The framework of this model was based on the 1969 Act and the underlying philosophy of care, control and treatment of delinquency. More recent research allowed an evaluation of how, if at all, establishments meet these objectives, and indeed questioned whether the objectives could ever be realized within a system of institutional based treatment.

Most studies of the effectiveness of treatment programmes adopted research designs involving the comparison of a single, often experimental, institution or regime with one or more established ones. Intakes to the regimes were made comparable by the use of various techniques such as the employment of predictive categories, matching or random allocation. Those who had been 'treated' were followed up for two or three years after their release to determine reconvinction rates. Typical of such experimental studies was a 'controlled trial' carried out within one English approved school (Cornish and Clarke, 1975). One house in the school introduced a 'modified' therapeutic community regime. Boys deemed eligible on pre-determined criteria for this form of treatment were then randomly allocated between the experimental house and control house which operated a more traditional programme. No difference was found between the houses in terms of their long-term effectiveness in reducing delinquent behaviour, despite evidence of many other differences between the regimes in respect of aims, staff attitudes and policies, and the boys' behaviour while at the school. As the authors pointed out, these results are in agreement with most other evaluative work in the field. Indeed, not only has such research characteristically failed to produce evidence of the differential effectiveness of different programmes, but it has also indicated that the overall levels of success which institutional programmes for delinquents achieve are usually low (about 70 per cent those admitted to approved schools were reconvicted within two years of their release).

The more sensitive an experimental design, of course, the more likely it will be to pick up any small differences in effectiveness which might exist between institutional regimes. In consequence, work by Sinclair and Clarke (1973), Dunlop (1975) and—to some extent—Millham *et al.* (1975) using 'cross institutional' designs and involving larger numbers of institutions was able to provide evidence of small variations in long-term effectiveness amongst approved schools. The fact that only in these designs does it appear possible to find differences, however, attests to the marginal importance of the latter finding. Moreover, such results have failed to provide convincing evidence that some programmes were more effective than others at *reducing* post-institutional delinquency; it may be merely that those described as 'better' were neutral in their effects.

In contrast to the apparently marginal effect institutions have been shown to have on subsequent delinquent behaviour, cross-institutional studies have found them to have had a very powerful influence upon the behaviour of inmates while they were in residence. In his study of twenty-three probation hostels, Sinclair (1971) found that the proportion of boys who left prematurely because they had absconded or re-offended during their stay varied from 14 per cent to 78 per cent. Similar variations in 'drop-out' rates, ranging from 15 per cent to 66 per cent, amongst fifteen community homes with education were found by Tutt (1976). To some extent these findings explained and supported the high rate of reoffending of children shortly after the making of the care order when the child was in residential care reported above by Cawson. In Sinclair's study this variation could not be accounted for by differences amongst intakes to each hostel nor by the more obvious differences of hostel size, age-range admitted, or location. A large amount of the variation in rates of premature leaving could, however, be accounted for by the different ways in which wardens ran their hostels. It was concluded that the hostel environment was the most important factor in determining its success while the boys were in the hostels, but had no effect upon post-release reconviction rates of the boys.

The importance of the institutional environment in determining current behaviour patterns was stressed by Clarke and Martin (1971) in their study of absconding from approved schools. Most of the considerable variation in absconding rates between schools (those in senior schools, for example, ranged from 10 per cent to 75 per cent) and much of the variability among individuals seemed to be due to the influence of the schools' environments; personal factors were largely unrelated to absconding behaviour. They also found that persistent absconding appeared to be a learned behaviour. Just as results from evaluative research have shown both the lack of evidence for differential effects and poor overall levels of effectiveness in reducing delinquent behaviour in the post-institutional environment, so evidence from Clarke and Martin's and Sinclair's work demonstrated the importance of the immediate environment in determining current behaviour.

As the decade progressed the focus of research shifted from the effectiveness of open institutions to the development and population of secure units and the effectiveness of community-based programmes, thereby reflecting the policy split described above. Tutt (1979) provided a classification of types of secure units developed over the decade, and both Cawson and Martell (1979) and Millham et al. (1978) provided evidence on the children accommodated in security. Both stressed the children's massive welfare needs, regardless of offending behaviour.

As Millham showed

The boys in secure accommodation are likely to have: run away from home at an early age (26 per cent), been brought up by relatives (15 per cent), had step-parents (34 per cent), experienced cruelty and neglect (38 per cent), been separated from mother (31 per cent), been rejected by father (29 per cent), and rejected by mother (21 per cent). They have parents who are mentally unstable (38 per cent), violent (28 per cent), heavy drinkers (28 per cent), frequently absent from home (43 per cent). (Millham et al., 1978; p. 40)

Both Millham *et al.* and Cawson and Martell found evidence to show that the children referred to security were more likely to be the 'failures' of existing institutions, i.e. those children who were persistently disruptive or persistently absconded from open local authority establishments, than children who posed a serious threat to the community through serious acts of violence. Millham *et al.* (1978) showed that the reconviction rates of children leaving security were extremely high; of their sample of 593 children only 74 per cent were released to the community, the remaining 26 per cent were transferred directly to other institutions. Of those released 24 per cent committed no further offence, 14 per cent offended but did not receive a custodial sentence and 62 per cent of offended and received a custodial sentence.

These reconviction rates are not radically different from the 81 per cent of 15–17 year olds discharged from Borstal who reoffend or the 73 per cent of 14–17 year olds who reoffend after discharge from junior detention centre.

Research into community based projects has been carried out on a small local scale and often fails to achieve reasonable standards of evaluation. However, two important attempts at monitoring community based programmes are worthy of comment. Hazel (1978) carried out an action research project to assess the viability of establishing foster care as an alternative to institutional placement of difficult and disturbed adolescents. Hazel's work led her to conclude that the placement in foster care of 14–15-year-old boys straight from the juvenile court could be an effective strategy. This research has had a far-reaching impact on the operation of social services departments, a substantial number of whom have set up specialist family placement schemes following the success of Hazel's work.

The other community programme of a quite different nature is that organized by Community Service Volunteers who in their Child in Care programme place adolescents, many of them with serious histories of offending and in the care of the local authority, as volunteer workers in local authority or voluntary placements. Placements have included work in playgroups, with the mentally handicapped, hospitals, homes for the physically handicapped and elderly. Millham *et al.* (1980) monitored the performance of the project and of the 432 young people referred to the scheme. Their results suggested 'The CSV rates [of reconviction] compare well with the Borstal figures although the numbers of young people involved are insufficiently large to make the comparison conclusive.' They continue

While we cannot be conclusive about the effectiveness of the CSV scheme for young offenders, it is clear from this evidence that this approach has helped some very serious offenders just as effectively, and perhaps more successfully, than institutional remedies. It has not only kept these young people in the community but seems to have also markedly reduced their delinquent tendencies. Indeed the fact that only 6% of the cohort were in penal establishments at the time of our follow-up study adds weight to this supposition. (Millham *et al.*, 1980; p. 41)

International trends

So far this chapter has dealt with juvenile offending and its treatment in England and Wales. Scotland has operated a different system of juvenile justice since the passing of the Social Work (Scotland) Act (1968). This act established the children's hearings system in Scotland (for a fuller description see Social Work Services Group 1970, Curran 1977) and yet despite a fundamentally different 'judicial' system a number of similar effects have been recorded. For example Scotland is currently experiencing a decline in the number of juveniles sent by the Children's Panels to List D schools (the equivalent to Community Homes with Education in England). Scotland has twenty-six List D schools and to date one (Thornley Park) has been closed but others are showing an increasing number of vacancies. Research carried out by Petrie (1980) involving a comparative study of open and closed (secure) residential placements echoed the findings of Millham *et al.* (1978) and Cawson (1979), in England. For example: 'The level of reconviction in both groups (i.e. boys in open and closed provision) was not significantly different nor did it differ significantly from the results found in the English system' (Petrie 1980; p. 151).

Meanwhile Northern Ireland which despite a decade of social unrest had not altered its system of juvenile justice in the reforming period of the late 1960s which saw changes in both England and Wales (1969 Act) and Scotland (Social Work (Scotland) Act (1968)), looked to the United States for a lead. The Northern Ireland Office published the Black Committee Report in 1979 and incorporated in it a number of features which had been developed in the United States throughout the seventies, the two most important trends being the development of justice and decarceration.

The development of justice

Proposals from the American Bar Association (1977) and the Canadian Solicitor Generals Office (1977) are mirrored in the Black Committee Report (1979) and in the growing pressure in the United Kingdom (Morris and Giller, 1980) for a more justice-oriented policy on juvenile offending as opposed to a system based on enforced-treatment and social welfare. The American Bar Associations — Juvenile Justice Standards Project outlines a number of standards which it believes would incorporate both justice and fairness. These proposals are proving very persuasive in both North America and the United Kingdom and therefore bear repetition:

I. Sanctions for juveniles should be proportional to the seriousness of the offence which they have committed. The Justice Standards project in fact proposes a specific schedule of sanctions or tariffs. The detail of this proposal is not directly relevant here. Of more importance is the impact acceptance of this proposal would have on theory and practice within the juvenile justice system. Such a proposal is opposed to the widely held view that each case should be dealt with by the courts on its own merits, pleas of mitigation would presumably carry less weight. The staff of institutions would have little or no control of the length of stay of individuals since the sentence would depend on pre-institutional behaviour, the offence, rather than behaviour presented during institutional treatment. This would reduce the opportunity for individual variations in treatment programmes and levels of staff control as exercized through the use of remission for good behaviour.

II. Sentences or dispositions should be determinate. This would have a profound impact on current theories and practice of treatment which is based on indeterminacy with length of stay according to the treatment response of the juvenile offender. Such a proposal removes the power of decision making from the professionals involved in the juvenile justice system – probation officers, social workers, psychologists – and replaces it with the judiciary.

III. Courts should choose the least restrictive category and duration of disposition that is appropriate to the seriousness of the offence. This proposal arises in part from the wealth of research which indicates that neither non-custodial or custodial treatment is effective in reducing offending behaviour (Martinson, 1974; Romig, 1978). This being so, the American Bar Association chose to see both welfare and penal intervention as a loss of civil liberties and therefore to be kept to the minimum commensurate with ensuring the protection of the public.

IV. Non-criminal behaviour (status offences) such as running away from home, truancy, consensual sexual behaviour and alcohol use should be removed from the jurisdiction of the juvenile court. In the U.K. in the past ten years, there has been little deliberate differentiation between the 'deprived' and the 'depraved'. The American Bar Association would argue that this has discriminated against the deprived and has been contrary to natural justice. The rediscovery of the delinquent has been predicted by Tutt (1978).

V. Limitations of the discretion in processing juveniles are to be established by producing formal criteria for the processing of referrals at each stage of proceedings. Currently there are wide variations in practice and outcome between police forces undertaking cautioning of juveniles and between court disposals of juveniles. These variations are seen as injustices rather than as positive variations according to local conditions or the individual circumstances of juveniles (Parker *et al.*, 1981).

VI. Legal representation should be provided as a right to all parties (juveniles and parents) at all critical stages in the proceedings. Currently legal representation in criminal proceedings in the U.K. is available to the juvenile but not the parent. This proposal strengthens the belief that the adversarial court system is a satisfactory way of establishing guilt and disposing of offenders.

VII. Once the category and duration of the disposition are established by the judge, the choice of programme should be determined by the needs and desires of the individual. The American Bar Association proposal to involve the individual more fully in the choice of programme can be seen as an attack on the professions currently making such decisions, i. e. social workers, psychologists. However, it can also be argued that they are reiterating some of the concerns of those professions about current theories and practices in assessment and allocation of children (Tutt, 1981).

VIII. Limitations should be made on state intervention prior to adjudication and disposition. Currently substantial numbers of young people both in the U.S.A. and U.K. spend time in institutions whilst still technically innocent and awaiting trial. As mentioned earlier in this chapter such a system has allowed substantial numbers of young people not eligible for prison sentences to be held in prison on 'unruly certificates' awaiting court appearances.

The American Bar Associations' proposals and their interpretation in the Black Committee Report seem to be based on three basic principles: proportionality, determinacy, and objectivity. As Morris (1978) has argued these principles appear to give a greater emphasis to punishment than treatment.

Decarceration

Decarceration is the term given to a policy or strategy aimed at the systematic removal of offenders from institutions. It may or may not be preceded, coincidental with, or followed by the development of, community-based alternatives. As a policy in the juvenile offenders field it originates from Massachussetts State in the early 1970s when Jerome Miller, Director of Youth Services in the State deliberately and systematically set about closing down the training schools or institutions for all juvenile offenders under the age of 17 years. Hitherto all previous attempts at reform had been based on improving methods in or resources available to institutions in attempts to establish and maintain humane, effective, treatment regimes. Miller originally started with that intention but changed to believing that institutions were incapable of such change and therefore must be closed. The history of this period in Massachussetts and its outcome is well documented (Rutherford, 1978; Miller *et al.*, 1977).

The policy established in Massachussetts has had widespread repercussions across the United States.

There are other states [however] where the movement is strong in the direction of decarceration; states such as Washington and Ontario, a major industrial state, or Vermont, a rural state which in fact has closed its training schools already and moved completely into community-based programmes with a couple of small secure units to back it up. So there is movement in this direction, but all the time backed by a substantial input of new federal dollars. The Federal policy announced in the 1974 Federal Delinquency Act and confirmed and enlarged in the amendments of 1977 have endorsed the policy of decarceration for all children. [However] In many of the states, as in this country (U.K.) there is a strange ambivalence. Firstly, there is the rather conservative mood on law and order issues especially in the area of adult crime, but also in the area of juvenile violence. So that we witness two trends, one moving in the direction of deinstitutionalisation and the growth of community based alternatives, and the other is to strengthen juvenile court authority and sentencing patterns especially in case of juvenile violence. So it seems that we have on the one hand the movement towards taking people out of the institutions which is aided, of course, at this time by the enormous costs of residential care and the attempt on the part of all states to reduce their human service budgets. This leads to a sharper focus on isolating those youth who appear to be most dangerous or threatening to others and the conditions necessary for community protection. (Professor Lloyd Ohlin, Harvard Law School in Tutt, 1979; p. 19).

The policy of decarceration is beginning to gain ground in the UK (Tutt, 1981) and as argued earlier in this chapter is, as in the USA, appearing simultaneously with the growth of secure accommodation.

Conclusion

Any current overview of intervention must conclude that the present system of juvenile justice lacks a coherent underlying philosophy. Consequently, because there is no clear underpinning for policy it has become a pragmatic response to pressures from within the system such as overcrowding and public expenditure cuts and, from outside the system, such as partisan pressure and public myth. The lack of any clear philosophy or system of practice has led to a very clear split between non-social work intervention (cautions, fines, attendance centre orders), and social work intervention (supervision and care orders). This split is widening with less and less use being made of social work intervention. Moreover, where social work intervention is accepted, a further split occurs between community based and secure programmes. These splits and divisions are reflected in the priorities set for current research. Much of this book attempts to heal these divisions by offering a practical philosophy for dealing with juvenile offenders which can be adapted to both community and secure settings.

References

Black Committee (1979). *Report of the Children and Young Persons Review Group*, HMSO, Belfast.

Brittan, L. (1979a). In *Getting on with Intermediate Treatment. A report of the Sheffield Conference*, DHSS, London.

Brittan, L. (1979b). *Young Offenders: The Way Forward. Evolution or Radical Change.* An address given in Derby on 15 November 1979.

Cawson, P. (1979). *Children in Care—some Preliminary Findings*, DHSS, London.

Cawson, P. and Martell, M. (1979). *Children Referred to Secure Units*, Research Report No. 5, DHSS Research Division, London.

Clarke, R. V. G. and Martin, D. N. (1971). *Absconding from Approved Schools*, HMSO, London.

Cornish, D. B. and Clarke, R. V. G. (1975). *Residential Treatment and its Effects on Delinquency*, Home Office Research Study, 32, HMSO, London.

Curran, J. H. (1977). *The Children's Hearing System. A Review of Research*, HMSO, Edinburgh.

Department of Health and Social Security (1979). *Social Services for Children in England and Wales, 1976–78*, HMSO, London.

Dunlop, A. B. (1975). *The Approved School Experience*, Home Office Research Unit Report, HMSO, London.

Eleventh Report from the Expenditure Committee (1975). *The Children and Young Persons Act (1969)*, HMSO, London.

Hazel, N. (1978). The use of family placements, in *Alternative Strategies for Coping with Crime* (Ed. N. Tutt), Basil Blackwell, Oxford.

Home Office (1965). *The Child, the Family and the Young Offender* (Cmnd. 2742), HMSO, London.

Home Office (1968). *Children in Trouble* (Cmnd. 3601), HMSO, London.

Home Office (1969). *Children and Young Persons Act, 1969*, HMSO, London.

Home Office, Department of Health and Social Security, Department of Education and Science, and Welsh Office (1976). *Observations on the Eleventh Report of the Expenditure Committee* (Cmnd. 6494), HMSO, London.

Home Office, Department of Health and Social Security, and Welsh Office (1980a). *Young Offenders* (Cmnd. 8045), HMSO, London.

Home Office (1980b). *Criminal Statistics 1979*, HMSO, London.

Institute of Judicial Administration and American Bar Association (1977). *Juvenile Justice Standards Project*, Ballinger, Cambridge, Mass.

Jasinski, J. (1977). Preventive measures against juvenile delinquency: Identification of cases at risk, early intervention and procedure for treatment, in *New Approaches to the Treatment of Young Offenders*, United Nations, Lillehammer, Norway, pp. 27–32.

Martinson, R. (1974). What Works?, *Public Interest* (Spring).

Mayhew, P., Clarke, R. V. G., Sturman, A. and Hough, J. M. (1976). *Crime as Opportunity*, Home Office Research Study No. 34, HMSO, London.

Miller, A. D., Ohlin, L. E. and Coates, R. B. (1977). *A Theory of Social Reform: Correctional Change Processes in Two States*, Ballinger, Cambridge, Mass.

Millham, S., Bullock, R. and Cherrett, P. (1975). *After Grace-Teeth*, Human context Books, London.

Millham, S., Bullock, R., Haak, M., Hosie, K. and Mitchell, L. (1980). *Give and Take*, Community Service Volunteers, London.

Millham, S., Bullock, R. and Hosie, K. (1978). *Locking up Children—Secure Provision within the Child-Care System*, Saxon House, Farnborough.

Morris, A. M. (1978). Revolution in the Juvenile Court: The Juvenile Justice Standards Project, *Criminal Law Review*, September, 529–539.

Morris, A. M., and Giller, M. (1980) *Juvenile Justice*, Department of Social Administration, University of Lancaster.

Newman, O. (1972). *Defensible Space: People and Design in the Violent City*, Architectural Press, London.

Parker, H., Turnbull, D., and Casburn, M. (1981). *Receiving Juvenile Justice*, Basil Blackwell, Oxford.

Petrie, C. (1980). *The Nowhere Boys*, Saxon House, Farnborough.

Radzinowicz, L. and King, J. (1977). *The Growth of Crime*, Penguin Books, Hammondsworth.

Romig, D. A. (1978). *Justice for our Children* Lexington Books, Lexington.

Rutherford, A. (1978). Decarceration of young offenders in Massachussetts, in *Alternative Strategies for coping with Crime* (Ed. N. Tutt), Blackwell, Oxford.

Sinclair, I. A. C. (1971). *Hostels for Probationers*, HMSO, London.

Sinclair, I. A. C. and Clarke, R. V. G. (1973). Acting out and its significance for the residential treatment of delinquents, *Journal of Child Psychology and Psychiatry*, **14**, 283–291.

Social Work Services Group (1970). *Childrens Hearings*, HMSO, Edinburgh.

Solicitor General of Canada (1977). *Proposed New Legislation for Young Offenders*, Solicitor General's Office, Ottawa.

Thorpe, D., Green, C., and Smith, D. (1980). *Punishment and Welfare*, Department of Social Administration, University of Lancaster.

Tutt, N. (1974). *Care or Custody*, Darton, Longman and Todd, London.

Tutt, N. (1976). Recommittals of juvenile offenders, *British Journal of Criminology*, **16**, 385–388.

Tutt, N. (1978). Working with children in trouble. Delinquency—social work's changing role, *Social Work Today*, **4**, 30, 13–18.

Tutt, N. (1979). Children in trouble: an American view, *Community Care*, 2 August, 18–21.

Tutt, N. (1981). *Report of the Observation & Assessment Working Party*, DHSS, London.

West, D. J., and Farrington, D. (1973) *Who Becomes Delinquent*, Heinemann, London.

Zander, M. (1975). What happens to young offenders in care? *New Society*, 24 July, 185–187.

Developments in the Study of Criminal Behaviour
Volume 1: The Prevention and Control of Offendering
Edited by P. Feldman
Crown Copyright, 1982

2

Police Strategies of Crime Control

Mike Hough and Kevin Heal

Introduction

Law-breaking is the province of the young. Certainly adults commit crime; but more than half of all offenders known to the police are under 21, and for some offences the proportion is far higher—72 per cent for burglary for example. The mid-teens are the peak years for offending, with around one in fifteen males between the ages of 14 and 18 coming to police attention annually. As people grow out of their teens and into their mid-twenties, they rapidly disappear from police statistics. Official figures may slightly distort the real picture—if, for example, older offenders are more successful in avoiding police attention—but there is no evidence to suggest a large hidden army of adult offenders.

This chapter looks at the effectiveness of the police response to crime. In view of the age structure of offending it is inevitably concerned with the police response to crimes committed by the young. Most of the strategies which are examined here are not aimed exclusively at young people, but this group is, by sheer weight of numbers, their primary target. The first section of the chapter offers a brief sketch of police organization and police work. The second section reviews research on the effectiveness of conventional policing methods—preventive patrol and detective work. This research has questioned conventional wisdom, suggesting that the impact of police crime-fighting strategies is somewhat limited. The third section examines some of the reasons for this; and the final section considers some alternative approaches to policing.

Police organization and police work

There are forty-three police forces in England and Wales, with an average strength of around 2000 officers. They are independent of one another and enjoy a considerable autonomy of control. Each force is divided into a number of geographical divisions—around six per force—which on average serve populations in the region of 200 000, although there are wide variations. Each division will usually comprise between two and four sub-divisions. A thumb-nail sketch is offered below of a 'typical' sub-division in a large city.

Such a sub-division might cover a population of 70 000 and have a police strength of around 140. The uniformed branch would be made up of 120 or so of these—a superintendent, a chief inspector, five inspectors, fifteen sergeants and the rest constables; the majority of these would be allocated to general patrol duties. Whilst patrol organization varies considerably both within and between forces, the sub-division might field between three and six panda-cars (small, conspicuously marked vehicles which usually provide 24-hour coverage of a panda beat). There will also be a smaller number of foot patrols providing coverage for at least some part of the day in some areas. In addition there may be between six and twelve area constables, who are permanently assigned to cover half a panda beat, provide 8-hour coverage in this area and function within it as a 'local bobby'. There may also be a general-purpose van on patrol and a double-manned, fast-response vehicle or incident car which patrols the whole sub-division, and of course the sub-divisional station has also to be manned. Depending on the time of day, therefore, there may be between eight and fifteen units on patrol duties. Around half their time will actually be spent on preventive patrol; the remainder will be spent attending a variety of incidents, doing paperwork, taking refreshment breaks and so on (cf Hough, 1980). Given the number of personnel assigned to these sub-divisions, this coverage may appear sparse; but most of the posts have to be manned for 24 hours a day, absorbing a large amount of manpower. The sub-division may also have a few uniformed officers on specialist duties—a community liaison officer, or schools liaison officer, and a crime prevention officer, for example. In addition to the uniformed branch there might be ten CID officers and four CID aids (trainees) allocated to the sub-division. There would also be a limited number of officers from other branches of the force operating in the area—traffic patrols and CID officers from headquarters, for example. These, however, would not be attached to the sub-divisional station.

Being in a large city, this would probably be a busy sub-division in terms of crime. Around eighty indictable offences would come to the attention of the police each week. A typical week might yield around nineteen shopliftings, twenty burglaries, twenty thefts of or from motor vehicles, one robbery, three assaults, three meter thefts, one sexual offence, and a number of other miscellaneous offences. Of these offences, around 40 per cent would be cleared up, meaning, in the vast majority of cases, that a person is prosecuted or cautioned (formally warned) for the offence or has it taken into consideration by a court sentencing him on another charge. Thus twelve to fifteen indictable offenders would come to light each week, these collectively being responsible on average for thirty offences. Most of these would be aged under 25, between half and two-thirds under 21—though the proportion would be higher for some offences such as burglary. In addition to these indictable offenders, there might be half-a-dozen arrests for non-indictable drunkenness offences, and a dozen arrests or summonses for other non-indictable offences each week. This excludes motoring offences which for the most part are handled by the organizationally separate traffic department. In other words, arrests are rare and usually unspectacular events. If arrests for indictable offences were shared evenly between the constables and sergeants in the sub-division (which of course they are not), each could expect to make an arrest once every 2 months.

It should be said, however, that these figures do not indicate the full extent of crime in such a sub-division. It is now widely recognized that only a proportion of crimes are reported by the public to the police, and that only a proportion are recorded by the police as crimes (Bottomley and Coleman, 1980). There are problems both of definition and of measurement in assessing the 'dark figure' of crime, and estimates vary widely, both between offence category and between studies. One such estimate, from the (British) General Household Survey, is that around half the number of events perceived by people as burglaries find their way into police records (HMSO, 1980a). Another, by Sparks et al. (1977) is that one in eight crimes in London are recorded in official statistics.

In the main, adult offenders dealt with by the police are charged or summoned and appear in court. The same was broadly true for juveniles until the late sixties when many forces introduced juvenile bureaux, which place heavy emphasis on the need to divert young offenders from the criminal justice process. In place of prosecution young offenders now frequently receive cautions, or formal warnings, from senior police officers. In fact, around half of offenders aged under 17 who come to the attention of the police are now cautioned (see Ditchfield, 1976, for a fuller discussion).

Of course, by no means all police work is concerned with crime. Calls for police assistance, over the 999 telephone system, by phone to local police stations and in person, cover a wide variety of incidents. These range from occurrences which are usually unequivocally criminal, such as burglaries, and those such as fights and arguments where the law might be invoked, to those which have nothing to do with law-breaking—incidents involving the physically or mentally frail, reports of lost and missing persons, accidents, and of course the apocryphal cat stuck up a tree. And just as levels of reported crime have increased, these day-to-day demands on police time have very probably seen a marked increase over the post-war period. Until recently the maintenance of public order at demonstrations and pickets and at public events such as football matches, did not absorb an enormous proportion of police time. For example, in London, where such events are most frequent, no more than 2 per cent of police time was absorbed in 1979 in handling large public-order events (estimated from Appendix 11, HMSO, 1980b); and the figure for all public-order events in London in 1979 is unlikely to be much in excess of 5 per cent. At the time of writing it is not possible to estimate the demands on police resources of wide-spread civil disorder as seen in the summer of 1981.

Police resources as well as police workloads have increased substantially over the post-war period. Manpower has more than doubled, and technology—cars, telephones, radios and computers—have greatly increased the police capacity to respond to demands made on them. It would be wrong, however, to assume that police resources have simply increased to keep pace with workloads. The relationship between police resources and the volume of work performed by the police is highly complex. Any organization which provides free services is likely to find that demands for these services increase with its capacity to provide them. Certainly, some of the increases in calls for police assistance can be understood as a function of the increasing ease with which people can summon a patrol to their door. An increased preparedness to make use of the police would account for at least some of the increase in recorded crime. It has also been argued (for example by Manning, 1977) that in so far as they are indicators of police workload, criminal statistics are subject to manipulation by the police; in particular, high levels of recorded crime may be useful in bartering for additional resources.

This said, one would be hard put to argue that the five-fold increase in recorded crime since the war is a complete artefact of public reporting of crime and police recording of it. For this to be true, an implausibly small proportion of crimes must have found their way into police records in the fifties. At least some types of crime have become more frequent; it is hard to say to what extent, but that there have been increases seems undeniable. It is this increase in crime which is a cause for concern as much as the absolute volume. The weekly crime count provided above in a busy urban sub-division does not conjure up the image of a sea of crime. Nevertheless, the fact remains that 25 years ago these would have been monthly and not weekly crime figures.

The impact of conventional police strategies on crime

The solutions to rising crime which enjoy most popular support—and a good measure of support amongst the police, the magistracy and the judiciary, involve adjustments to the criminal justice system. If crime rates rise, the argument goes, then the deterrent threat offered by the criminal justice system is either insufficiently heavy or insufficiently plausible; and to reduce crime the severity or likelihood of punishment must be increased. Thus people suggest severer sentencing policies, changes in court procedure to increase the chances of guilty verdicts and, of course, strengthening the police force. Chief constables have throughout the post-war period argued for, and secured, successive increase in their authorized establishments. Their arguments—as articulated in their public pronouncements—have stressed that rising crime is a result of insufficient police strength. The media have echoed the assumption that more police will result in less crime; and it is well accepted amongst the general public. For example, in one survey as many as 86 per cent of respondents thought that crime could be reduced if police numbers were increased (Durant et al., 1972). And although there is no firm evidence, the tenor of public debate about 'law and order' suggests that people are unaware of the rate at which police resources have been increasing, with many actually attributing rising crime rates to an absolute fall in police numbers.

Calls for additional police resources presuppose that the conventional police strategies of deterrence have a potential for curbing crime—or at least slowing the increase in crime—which would be realized if they were pursued with greater intensity: more patrols and more detectives would achieve the desired impact. This presupposition tends to be shielded from critical scrutiny by its common-sensical plausibility. However, the evidence to support it is thin (cf Morris and Heal, 1981).

Econometric studies

One way of assessing the impact of conventional policing methods is to look for very general relationships between police manpower and crime rates. A number of studies have employed econometric methods to do this. They have examined variations in levels of police provision and police activity which can be observed over time and area and have tried to relate these to levels of reported crime. Unfortunately, such research has done little more than demonstrate the complexity of the issues. At the simplest level, studies have found a positive correlation between levels of police manpower and levels of reported crime. This apparently counter-intuitive relationship is readily explained: high levels of policing are a response to high levels of crime, and high levels of policing facilitate both the discovery and recording of crime. More sophisticated studies have related measures of police activity such as clearance rates, as well as measures of resources, to crime rates. They have also attempted to control statistically for (to make allowances for) other factors besides policing which are known or believed to affect crime. These studies have yielded no consistent results about the relationship between police manpower and crime. The most recent and most sophisticated in this country, by Carr Hill and Stern (1979), found:

(i) areas with high levels of policing have high rates of crime;
(ii) the higher the clearance rate in an area, the lower the crime rate;
(iii) the more police there are allocated to an area, the lower the clear-up rate.

Carr Hill and Stern attribute these results to the 'recording phenomenon' whereby more police lead to more crimes being recorded, because they discover more crime, or because more crime is reported to them by the public, or because they record more of the crimes reported to them. They argue that no conclusions can be drawn from their research about the effectiveness of the police. At their present state of development, therefore, econometric techniques are not sensitive enough to unravel the relationships between policing and crime. But in itself, this can tell us something: it should alert us to the absence of any close and direct relationship between policing levels and crime. Questions about the impact of the police on crime become more manageable if one focuses more sharply on specific strategies for dealing with crime.

Conventional patrol

A considerable body of research on conventional preventive patrol has now accumulated. Much of this work has been conducted in the United States, and of course one cannot say for certain just how generalizable these findings are to the British context.

One of the first studies to assess the impact of routine foot patrol on crime was carried out in 1954 by the New York Police Department (NYPD, 1955). Unfortunately it tells us more about the pitfalls of police research than about policing. The study assessed the impact of increases in foot patrols and 'proved' that additional manpower reduced crime; however, it is now accepted that the police rigged the data (Farmer, 1980). A more rigorous study of foot patrolling was carried out in four British cities by Bright (1969). The findings suggest that crime rises on the beat which has no patrol allocated to it; however, provided that there is some police presence, the precise number of patrols on a beat makes little difference to crime.

These findings are echoed by Heller (1977) in St Louis and by Schnelle *et al.* (1975) in Nashville, Tennessee, who both found that increases in foot patrol were unaccompanied by decreases in crime. In fact, the latter study found *increases* in crime, which it attributed to increased reporting of crime by the public, and thus exemplifies the limitations of research which relies solely on statistics gathered by the police.

The most recent and most thorough study of foot patrols has been conducted by the Police Foundation in New Jersey (Police Foundation, 1981). The study had an experimental design in which patrols in Newark were removed from some beats and introduced into others. These changes had no impact on crime, whether measured by recorded crime rates or by victim surveys. However, foot patrols contributed to people's feelings of security and lessened their fear of crime.

A number of studies have looked at the impact of mobile patrols. Press (1971) found that a 40 per cent increase in the number of mobile patrols in the 20th Precinct of New York resulted in reductions in those reported crimes which are visible from the street. A displacement effect was also observed, whereby crime rose in an adjacent precinct. The study, however, has been criticized for its reliance on police statistics and more specifically for the fact that the police recording system itself changed during the project (Wilson, 1975). Fisk (1970) analysed the effects of an increase in *perceived* police presence, when the Indianapolis Police Department bought additional patrol vehicles which patrols were expected to retain for their personal, off-duty use. This had no clear effect; the levels of some crimes increased, whilst others fell.

The Kansas City Preventive Patrol Experiment is probably the most exhaustive assessment of mobile patrol (Kelling *et al.*, 1974). Different levels of routine patrol were monitored for a little more than a year in three sets of beats, which together covered a population of some 150 000. One set of beats received no preventive patrol, uniformed police only entering them in response to people's calls for assistance. In the second set, patrol levels were increased by two to three times their normal level, whilst normal levels of patrol were maintained in the third. Variations in patrol level had no effect on crime (whether measured by police statistics or victim surveys), on people's feelings of security or on their satisfaction with the police. The study aroused a great deal of controversy; its findings have often been misrepresented as showing that *no* level of mobile patrol will affect crime, and, not surprisingly, it has also attracted more than its fair share of criticism (see, e.g. Larson, 1976; Fienberg *et al.*, 1976). Certainly, like any research, the study has its limitations, but it provides strong evidence that within quite broad limits levels of mobile patrol can be varied with no effects on crime. Its findings open up the possibility that patrol officers can profitably do something other than routine preventive patrol, provided that some level of visible police presence is maintained.

Other studies have assessed the value of fast response by mobile patrols to calls for assistance. The rationale for this practice is that fast response increases the likelihood of arrests, and also creates a sense of police omni-presence. The validity of fast response as a deterrent strategy has been at least in part undermined by studies such as Bieck's (1977) in Kansas. This showed that any improvement in response time is unlikely to produce more arrests, as in the vast majority of cases the first recourse of people who have been victimized is to seek reassurance and advice from friends and neighbours; only after a considerable period—between 20 and 40 minutes on average—do they call the police; calls where the speed of response can affect the probability of arrest were shown to be very rare. Whether or not a particular speed of response results in a sense of 'omni-presence' is difficult to assess. Certainly, responding to *all* calls quickly seems an uneconomical way of signalling to the public that the police have a capability for fast response in cases where it matters.

Specialized patrols

The use of specialized patrols is now quite widespread. These have been called, variously, 'aggressive patrol', 'crime attack control', 'split force patrols', 'tactical squads', 'high-impact anti-crime programmes' and so on (Kelling *et al.*, 1980). Typically, these consist in a specialization of function whereby officers are assigned to specific areas to handle specific forms of crime. They may involve highly visible police presence or, alternatively, the use of covert surveillance, disguises, unmarked cars and so on. Anecdotal evidence within the police service suggests that these forms of patrol are effective in reducing crime, at least in the immediate area in which they operate; and there is also some research evidence to this effect. Thus Chaiken *et al.* (1974) assessed the impact of increasing the number of uniformed patrols in the New York subway system. Like the study of foot patrols in New York, this was also beset by problems of data corruption by the police (Chaiken, 1978), but it seems that subway crime was reduced by the extra manpower. There was, however, evidence of displacement of crime, as robberies on buses increased. Dahmann (1975) reported that 'targeted' patrols in high crime areas in three American cities reduced crime in these areas; he found no evidence of displacement to adjacent areas. Schnelle et al. (1977) also found that a short period of saturation patrolling (by mobile patrols) in Nashville reduced burglaries at night but not in daylight hours. It was argued, however, that the number of night-time burglaries prevented did not justify the very high cost of this level of patrol. Boystun (1975) in San Diego evaluated one component of 'aggressive patrolling strategy'—stopping and searching people in the streets. Suspension of this practice apparently led to rises in crime while its reintroduction led to reductions. An evaluation of the New York Police Department's Street Crime Unit, which relied on decoy strategies, suggests that this was successful in reducing street crime (Halper and Ku, 1975). Assessing a 'special operations programme' in Kansas, Pate et al. (1976) reported that arrest rates can be increased both by 'targeting' criminals and by patrolling well-defined high-crime areas. In Britain Howard Parker's (1974) ethnographic study *View from the Boys*, set in Liverpool, describes how a group of boys who were heavily engaged in theft from cars eventually gave this up quite largely as a result of intensive police activity aimed specifically at them. However, not all evaluations report such positive findings; for example, an anti-burglary squad in Nashville, evaluated by Schnelle et al. (1975) apparently had no crime preventive effect at all.

If specialized patrolling strategies seem to achieve some impact on crime, they nevertheless encounter a number of problems. They are often very expensive. They may lead to displacement, so that offenders operate elsewhere, or at different times, or engage in different forms of crime. They tend to attract a reputation for heavy-handedness, whether or not this is deserved. For example, one of the patrol strategies evaluated by Pate, mentioned above, resulted in increased complaints against the police. Nichols and Bannon (1972) describe the disruption of community relations which stemmed from an otherwise successful 'decoy' patrol unit's operation in Detroit. Hall et al. (1978) in Britain, have described some of the tensions, especially amongst ethnic minorities, surrounding the operation of specialized patrol strategies. James (1979) questioned the extent to which specialized units discriminate against minority groups; but he nevertheless argues that specialization provides an organizational structure which enhances the autonomy of staff and facilitates an 'action-oriented hedonistic style of policing' and extra-legal tactics which may not always be appreciated by the policed. A further problem is that the process of specialization tends to rob non-specialist personnel of the interesting and the rewarding parts of their work, so that their morale and eventually their performance decline (cf Tien et al., 1978; Jones, 1980).

Criminal investigation

Little experimental research analogous to the patrol studies has been carried out on criminal investigation. What research there is suggests that once a certain level of investigative manpower has been reached, there are few returns to be gained from further investments in manpower. Studies have consistently emphasized the routine nature of detective work and the dependence of detectives both on information readily available at the scene of the crime, and on admissions by offenders already charged with other offences. Greenwood's (1977) well-known study of American police departments found that only 3 per cent of all index arrests (broadly equivalent to arrests for indictable offences in this country) appeared to result from special investigative efforts where organization, training or skill could make any conceivable difference. A broadly similar picture emerges from research in Britain (Woodley, 1976; Mawby, 1979; Bottomley and Coleman, 1980; Steer, 1980). These studies suggest that a large proportion of crime is cleared up either as a result of unequivocal identification of the offender at or near the scene of the crime, or because offenders charged with other offences admit to them as 'offences taken into consideration'. All these studies show that a small proportion of crime is detected by those procedures typically thought to comprise 'real detective work'—that is, the sifting of forensic evidence, the methodical elimination of suspects and the use of informants.

It seems therefore—at the risk of some simplification—that crimes fall into two main categories: those which are very difficult to detect and those which are easy. The proportion falling into the grey area in between is rather limited. Thus, even if investigative resources were greatly increased, the overall detection rate would in all probability be only marginally affected—provided, that is, that investigative manpower has already reached a level which permits the detection of all straightforward offences (cf Greenwood *et al.*, 1977). But one should take care not to overstate the case. Crimes of spectacular outrage—to which a great many personnel are often allocated—are in most cases eventually cleared up (even if good luck plays an important part in their detection). And some American researchers (e.g. Bloch and Bell, 1976; Elliott, 1978) have found that clearance rates improved when investigative departments are reorganized along team policing lines—findings which contradict those of Greenwood. No research to date can be regarded as a definitive assessment of the scope (or lack of scope) for improving clearance rates.

Police strikes

Finally, some evidence about the general impact of police activities on crime can be drawn tentatively from the experience of police strikes. There have only been a handful of police strikes in industrialized countries this century. It emerges from these that chaos sometimes, but by no means always, ensues upon a strike; more specifically, riots may be triggered off by a police strike, but if they are not, life continues without perceptible surges of crime. In 1918, when almost all of London's constables struck for a period of 36 hours, disturbances were restricted to the demonstrating policemen themselves. The 1971 strike in New York lasted for 6 days and extended to 85 per cent of the patrol force; again, there was no loss of order. However, widespread rioting occurred during the 1919 Liverpool strike which lasted 3 days and involved little more than half the constables in the force. The 1919 Boston strike and the 1969 Montreal strike similarly resulted in looting and widespread disorder. Contemporary newspaper reports described drunken all-night street parties in Boston, and a carnival atmosphere—a sort of pre-Christmas festivity—in Montreal. It is hard to say why one police strike should spark off mayhem and another should not. A number of factors are probably implicated: the degree of general discontent in a city's population; or their attitudes to the police (the Liverpool Police were particularly unpopular in 1919); and even the weather (the New York Police chose to strike in an exceptionally cold January). On the scant evidence available, the proportion of police on strike appears not to affect the outcome. Whatever the case, the experience of police strikes demonstrates the existence of strong informal modes of social control which in some circumstances can survive the breakdown of formal social control for several days.

Summary of section

A number of conclusions can be drawn from research on the effectiveness of police deterrent strategies. The preventive effects of routine patrolling are unproven, and the weight of evidence suggests that within broad limits patrol strength can be varied without any detectable effects on crime. But routine patrolling, especially on foot, may contribute to people's feelings of security. More specialized patrolling strategies can sometimes achieve an impact on crime, though they may have a number of drawbacks—they can be very expensive, they may lead to displacement and they may disrupt community relations. Research on criminal investigation suggests that there is only limited scope for improving detection rates. All told, therefore, research findings have provided little support for solutions to rising crime which propose 'more of the same'.

Limits on deterrent policing

The research outlined above suggests that the pay-offs in more intensive deterrent policing would at best be marginal. However, it only hints at the reasons for this. This section discusses in greater detail some of the factors which may limit the effectiveness of deterrent policing.

First, the very nature of law-breaking often makes it impracticable to achieve significant increases in the chances of apprehending or detecting offenders. Crimes are very rare events. A very small proportion of offenders in this country are apprehended by uniformed patrols, and in the United States it has been estimated that a patrol officer in a large American city can expect to intercept a street robbery in progress once every 14 years (President's Commission, 1967). Each household in Britain will be burgled on average once every 35 years— assuming, that is, that around twice as many burglaries occur as are reported to the police. And these relatively few incidents are distributed over an extensive geographical area; to take the 'typical' sub-division described earlier, between eight and fifteen patrol units will be covering an area of 3000 acres with 75 miles of public roadway. Of the dozen or so indictable offences which come to the attention of the police in this sub-division each day, little more than half can possibly be intercepted by patrols, as the remainder are not committed in public places. Law-breakers may perceive the risks of apprehension by conventional patrols to be so low that even if the risk were doubled or tripled it would still be negligible. And as discussed above, research on criminal investigation has shown that it is very difficult to detect offenders unless a large amount of information is available at the start of the investigation; any improvements which can be achieved in detection rates may be insufficient to affect people's decisions to break the law.

Alternatively, potential law-breakers may simply fail to notice any but the grossest changes in the risks they run of apprehension or detection. For example, in the Kansas City Preventive Patrol Experiment, informal soundings of the local criminal networks revealed that 'street people' knew nothing about the experiment at all (Kelling *et al.*, 1974). Offenders in this country may be similarly imperceptive—especially the younger and less experienced. Offenders are even less likely to be aware of any improvement in detection rates; their assessments of the risks of detection at any particular time can only be based on their own limited experience and on fragmentary information from friends and acquaintances.

Implicit in these arguments is the idea that in principle at least, deterrent policing strategies can achieve a 'critical mass' beyond which crime will be reduced. The arguments render the research findings compatible with the commonsense belief that at some point deterrent strategies are bound to work. But this commonsense belief, grounded in people's own experience, may be blind to the relative immunity of others to deterrent threat. A threat has the logic: 'unless you do what I want, I shall dispossess you of something you value'. Those who possess least, or who place least value on what they do possess, will be least responsive to threats. Arguably, this is a category into which, more than any other age group, young people fall. Little surprise, therefore, that offending is most heavily concentrated amongst the young.

Leaving this aside, intensive deterrent policing may have unintended consequences which limit its long-term viability. Experience of criminal justice as an offender may—especially for young people—precipitate rather than discourage further law-breaking in a number of ways. At the simplest level, someone who has acquired a criminal record may find that legitimate avenues to money and status become closed to him—his employment opportunities, for example, are restricted. He may also find fresh illegitimate avenues open to him, if he finds himself in a community home, borstal, or prison—the idea is well-established that custodial institutions can be 'schools for criminals'.

Theories of 'deviancy amplification' and 'labelling' draw attention to more subtle ironies of law enforcement. Wilkins (1964) argued that official action against law-breakers may increase their sense of alienation and lead to further law-breaking; this in turn will lead to less tolerance of law-breaking and more official action; and so the vicious circle of 'deviancy amplification' continues. The labelling approach is not so much a theory or a limited number of propositions as a perspective which embraces several diverse theoretical positions (cf Plummer, 1979). Like Wilkins, labelling theorists (e.g. Becker, 1963, 1964; Lemert, 1967, 1970; Kitsuse, 1972) use cybernetic principles of mutual causality to describe the process of becoming involved in crime. But they are more centrally concerned with the way in which people's conceptions of themselves as law-breakers, delinquents, deviants, etc., can be reinforced when they are labelled as such. They argue that people tend to conform to definitions of themselves which they receive from officials, friends, family, workmates and so on. Thus, law-breaking may provoke reactions from the police, but equally police actions which identify someone as a 'criminal type' may provoke further offending.

Labelling theories are intuitively very plausible, but can only be tested empirically at the risk of over-simplification. Despite this, there is some research evidence to suggest that criminal convictions lead to further offending amongst adolescents. In Britain Farrington (1977) for example, compared a group of 18-year-old boys convicted since the age of 14 with a control group of unconvicted boys who had been equally delinquent at the age of 14 and who were, presumably, equally at risk of conviction thereafter. (Delinquency was measured by self-report questionnaires.) The convicted group were more heavily involved in delinquent behaviour than the control group, suggesting that their being convicted may have confirmed their delinquent behaviour. In America, Wolfgang et al. (1972) as part of a larger study, looked at the consequences of different forms of treatment by the police of first-time juvenile offenders. They found that two factors were associated with subsequent offending—the seriousness of the first offence and the severity of official action; those who were arrested and prosecuted were more likely to re-offend than those who were dealt with informally.

Both Wolfgang's research and a number of other studies on both sides of the Atlantic have found that juveniles' race, class, dress and demeanour can affect the treatment they receive at the hands of the police (Piliavin and Briar, 1964; Terry, 1967; Black and Reiss, 1970; Bennett, 1979; Stevens and Willis, 1979;

Landau, 1981.) Some of these studies suggest that more severe treatment of, for example, working-class and black juveniles stems not from straightforward prejudice on the part of the police but from the greater severity of their offences, or from their antagonistic manner. Whatever the case, the possibility remains that police officers' decisions to question or to stop-and-search or to arrest or to charge juveniles are sometimes based on criteria of demeanour, class or race which turn out to be self-confirming.

If unintended consequences of law-breakers' contact with criminal justice sets one sort of limit to the effectiveness of deterrent policing, the impact of intensive policing on those who have not broken the law may form another. From its start, the police service has fostered the confidence and support of the general population; policing requires consent from the majority of the policed. However, the consent which many people offer is fragile, tentative rather than absolute, and can easily be jeopardized by intensive policing. As noted above, researchers have found that some of the specialized patrolling strategies disrupt relations between police and public. The policing of racially mixed inner city areas provides another example; the slightest suspicion that the police are acting heavy-handedly or discriminate against particular groups, such as blacks, can precipitate a downward spiral of antagonism between the police and increasingly larger sections of the population. And it is all too clear that intensive policing provides a breeding ground for such suspicions, whether these are justified or not. Finally, it is worth mentioning one further variant of the argument that there are self-defeating or self-limiting elements in systems of formal criminal justice. It is that formal and informal modes of social control are antipathetical rather than complementary (see e.g. Pepinski, 1976, 1980). Strengthening the formal criminal justice system may simply displace perceived responsibilities for crime control from individuals and communities to criminal justice bureaucracies: and the formalization and bureaucratization of social control may actually erode people's sense of community or common interest on which effective self-policing is dependent. Such ideas are very speculative, but to the extent that they are true, any expansion of formal criminal justice, including the deterrent function of the police, may prove a double-edged sword.

Summary of section

There are a number of factors which may limit the effectiveness of deterrent policing strategies. These include: the practical difficulties in achieving significant increases in the risks facing law-breakers of apprehension or detection; the likelihood that law-breakers' contact with the criminal justice system may compound rather than decrease their subsequent criminal behaviour; and the possibility that intensifying deterrent strategies may alienate the quite law-abiding majority of people from the police and erode the communities' capability for self-policing.

Alternatives

The response of the police to rising crime over the last 25 years has been to demand (and secure) more resources. These resources have bought additional manpower and new technology, much of which have been devoted to deterrent policing. Crime has risen over this period, and in all probability will continue to do so. Given that 'more of the same'—further increases in deterrent policing—are unlikely to achieve the desired reduction in crime, what alternatives are open to the police?

One might of course take the view that crime is the product of social conditions beyond the control of the police, such as structural inequalities of wealth, and that the sort of intervention needed to achieve any significant impact on crime lies outside the remit of police administration. This implies a retrenchment of police objectives rather than the pursuit of new policing methods: police and public alike should simply come to terms with the limited capability of the police to affect crime.

Such a minimal approach to policing is likely to be unpalatable to many people, and may well be over-pessimistic. Whilst research suggests that more intensive deterrent policing is a poor investment, this is not to say that the police are without effect. Rather, the research shows that whatever effects the police have, these are not achieved in the straightforward way posited by deterrence theory. One source of police effectiveness is seen, for example, by Manning (1977), to stem from 'the dramatic management of the appearance of effectiveness'; if the police can sustain public confidence in their ability to control crime, this confidence can prove self-confirming—if people believe that the police are effective, then they will be effective.

To some, this might open up the possibility of rather more aggressive news management and other devices to consolidate popular belief in police effectiveness. There may be arguments in favour of 'the noble lie' but there are obvious political dilemmas in policing by legerdemain. Besides, the practical risks would be high; if the police were seen to be disingenuous in accounting for themselves, the costs in terms of loss of public confidence would be excessive. Nevertheless, the possibility that people consistently over-estimate police effectiveness poses an uncomfortable question for administrators and researchers alike; should anyone attempt to correct such misconceptions if these are functional to the maintenance of law and order? Its resolution turns on preferences between democratic and paternalistic forms of social control—an issue which falls outside of the scope of this chapter.

Community policing

If the police achieve a degree of effectiveness by appearing to be effective, much of their impact must also derive from the way in which they are seen to symbolize and affirm aspects of the moral and social order. Recognition of this lies at the heart of policing methods which fall under the umbrella of 'community policing'. The core assumption of community policing is that the police can and should support and strengthen informal mechanisms of social control. In some ways the community policing movement is a backward-looking one, in that its model of ideal relations between policed and police is to be found in a real or mythical past, where communities were at one with themselves and their 'bobbies'. If anything, the attractiveness of this potent imagery tends to obstruct critical assessment both of the various objectives of community policing and of the means to achieve these objectives.

The emergence (or re-emergence) of community policing can be located in the late sixties. Increased use of mobile patrols had provoked fears that relations between police and public were becoming attenuated. To offset this, the 'unit beat policing' schemes adopted at that time supplemented conventional mobile patrols with area constables or home-beat officers. Most British police forces now operate some such system of community constables. The officers are assigned long-term to one beat which they patrol on foot. They are expected to develop close links with the people living and working on their beat, and, in the case of the home-beat officer, they also live on their beat. The general rationale for community constables—the maintenance of good relations with the public-—spans several more specific functions: close contact with the public should enable them to function as moral exemplars and educators—this aspect of their work focusing on young people; they are expected to promote a sense of community and a spirit of self-help in their area; they should be able to provide crime prevention advice to those who want it and to those who need it; and they should exploit their close contact with the community to collate and disseminate criminal intelligence within their force.

A number of forces have set up specialized community involvement departments, typically with a headquarters staff and one to three officers allocated to each division. These may co-ordinate and supplement the work of community constables, or they may function as an alternative. As with community constables, their work involves liaison with community groups—particularly minority groups—contact with schools, counselling of young offenders and other youth work, and provision of crime prevention advice. In addition they may have a catalytic function in stimulating other parts of the force to perform these tasks. They are also likely to play a liaison role with other local authority departments—housing, social services and planning, for example—and with voluntary organizations (see, e.g., Schaffer, 1979; Shanks, 1980 provides a helpful summary of community involvement schemes in Scotland; these differ little from schemes elsewhere in Britain).

The work both of community constables and of community involvement officers has been criticized for its marginality—its isolation from the mainstream of policing. It has been argued, by John Alderson (1979, 1981) for example, that the impact of a few such officers will be swamped by the working ethos of the majority of the force. Alderson, whose name is now most closely associated with community policing in this country, advocates a style of community policing to be pursued throughout a police force rather than in a specialist department. This form of broad-based community policing embraces the objective of community involvement schemes; if anything, there is a more explicit emphasis on 'activating the good' in the community.

Little attention has been paid to date in Britain to discovering the best organizational structure for such broad-based community policing, though in the United States team policing schemes have been tried out quite extensively. In these, small teams of uniformed officers (and sometimes detectives) are assigned long-term to one area and are given primary responsibility for policing it. Teams are usually given extensive autonomy; decision-making is more decentralized than in conventional police organization and the style of management more participatory. These changes are intended to result in improved performance, increased contact with people in the team's area and a greater responsiveness to community needs and wishes. Some schemes have been successful, whilst others have encountered resistance from various sectors of the police. In particular, middle management tends to see its function threatened by team policing and obstructs effective implementation—sometimes even positively sabotaging the scheme (Sherman et al., 1973; Gay et al., 1977).

What are the prospects for community policing? As yet, there has been little formal or rigorous assessment, though research is beginning to address the issues. For the present, therefore, one can do little more than speculate about its impact on crime. There is a considerable amount of anecdotal evidence that various community policing schemes can achieve improved relations between the police and some sectors of the public. This is what one would expect if police officers establish personal relations with people in their area and make a point of responding to their needs and wishes. Whether this effect percolates through to all sectors of the community, and especially to young delinquents, is a more open question. It seems likely that in the fragmented communities typical of large towns and cities, young offenders and potential offenders may remain insulated from the effects of any general improvement in the relationship between the police and the public. The scope for community policing may be greatest in more tightly-knit communities. Ironically, such communities tend to be in places where crime is no real problem, such as rural areas. However, some inner city areas with high proportions of ethnic minorities often display both a strong sense of community and a relatively high level of antagonism towards the police. Such areas may turn out to be well suited to community policing methods, and successes are claimed where these have been introduced. However, it should be recognized that even in such areas there may well be a variety of dissimilar cultures whose needs and wishes cannot all be simultaneously met by the police.

The educational objectives of community policing are aimed explicitly at the young. Some variants involve formal instruction in schools, to provide pupils with an understanding of police work and a respect for the law. Others rely on more informal contact, whereby officers organize youth clubs, sports activities and so on. The impact of these sorts of 'school liaison' activity can be assessed no more easily than other attempts at 'moral education'. There are grounds for some pessimism. Faced with the blandishments of authority—whether from headmasters, teachers, priests or policemen—children and especially adolescents can be thorough-going sceptics: they can easily recognize and discount exhortations to good behaviour. And any effect which is achieved may be small; when one considers all the competing influences on children's behaviour a police officer has a pitifully limited time in which to make a lasting impression. Against this, it should be said that some people have a particular gift for establishing contact with the young; those who have these skills may achieve a great deal in other directions. Manolias (1980) has suggested, for example, that where effectively organized school liaison work can foster, at least in the short term, improved relationships between children (particularly young children) and the police, and that they serve to counter the hostility of some ethnic minorities to police officers. Others (e.g. Pollard, 1979; Schaffer, 1980) have suggested, perhaps optimistically, that reductions in crime can be anticipated from such schemes, but only in the long term.

Though it has drawbacks and limitations, community policing has a healthy prognosis. It would be naive to expect a panacea; one should expect of an innovation not that it will solve every problem to which it is addressed, but simply that it does better than existing alternatives. The principle of community policing—strengthening communities' informal mechanisms of social control—may seem over-ambitious. However, this principle can be reformulated more modestly; community policing can be seen as an attempt to slow down the erosion of informal mechanisms of social control. A pessimist might see the machinery of justice as a necessary evil and the task of police administration as the minimization of harm rather than the maximization of benefit. Viewed from this perspective, community policing has much to recommend itself.

Opportunity reduction

Suggestions for dealing with juvenile crime are very varied: punish young offenders more severely; punish them less severely; provide them with therapy or treatment; offer them better recreational facilities; improve their educational and employment opportunities; and change the whole basis of social structure. Suggestions for modifying criminogenic environments have been heard rather rarely. Quite recently, however, as the limitations of 'people-changing' strategies have come to be recognized more clearly, interest has grown in strategies aimed at the *situations* in which crimes are committed rather than the *offenders* who commit them (cf Clarke and Mayhew, 1980; Engstad and Evans, 1980; Argyle *et al.*, 1981).

This 'situational' or 'crime-specific' approach is based on the assumption that some sorts of crime can be reduced through the skilful management, design or manipulation of the immediate environment in which crime occurs; it involves a systematic attempt to reduce the opportunities for crime.

Some situational measures consist of straightforward 'target hardening'— physical obstruction. For example, in West Germany during 1963, steering-column locks were made compulsory on all cars (old and new), with a resultant and enduring reduction of more than 60 per cent in the rate of car theft. In this country the Post Office has succeeded in virtually eliminating theft from telephone kiosks by replacing vulnerable aluminium coin boxes with stronger steel ones (Mayhew *et al.*, 1976). Other measures involve rather more complex manipulation of criminogenic environments. The 'defensible space' measures associated with Newman (1972) have centred on housing design which gives residents a better view of vulnerable areas around their homes and a greater sense of responsibility for these areas. Other measures exploit the potential of certain sorts of employee, such as caretakers, doormen and shop assistants (Mayhew *et al.*, 1979). And at public events such as football matches it is sometimes possible to reduce opportunities for vandalism and violence: arrival and departure of supporters can be managed so as to avoid long periods of delay; rival supporters can be separated from one another within the ground; and the sale of alcohol can be controlled within and around the grounds. Truancy patrols—police return truanting children to their schools—are yet another form of opportunity reduction, based on the assumption that children commit a lot of crimes whilst truanting. (However, Ekblom (1979) has questioned the accuracy of this assumption; he found that truanting school children in one British city could only have been responsible for a tiny proportion of crimes known to the police.)

Many situational measures are not in themselves new and are often little more than commonsense precautions. Individuals as well as organizations in both public and private sectors have consistently made use of them. Police crime prevention officers have for a long time promoted the use of a variety of target-hardening measures. Few people doubt that some situational measures can provide those who use them with a measure of protection against crime. But the situational approach has been neglected as a means of bringing about *overall* reductions in crime. It is often assumed that situational measures will simply displace crime to unprotected targets. However, the likelihood of displacement may well have been over-estimated. The more that crime is opportunistic the less likely it is to be displaced by situational measures. Even the less opportunistic forms of crime may be prevented without displacement provided that a measure is implemented on a sufficiently large scale.

If strategies of opportunity reduction hold out promise for achieving even limited reductions in specific forms of crime, there is scope for the police to pursue them more vigorously. As mentioned above, most police effort in this direction is channelled through the work of crime prevention officers. Arguably their impact is limited both by insufficient analytic capability—inability to identify the most effective strategies—and insufficient negotiating strength to persuade people to adopt opportunity-reducing measures. Crime prevention officers usually offer advice on a restricted range of target-hardening measures to victims of crime who may or may not choose to act on this advice. Establishing more effective specialist units may be one solution to these problems. For example, under the aegis of community policing, the Devon and Cornwall Constabulary have set up a Crime Prevention Support Unit (Alderson, 1977; Blaber, 1979). One of its functions is the detailed analysis of crime problems, and it has generated a number of crime prevention initiatives, including various forms of opportunity-reduction. The unit has also sought to ensure that its proposals are actively taken up—by developing improved avenues of negotiation (through a consultative group) with other local agencies and organizations, and by improving channels of communication with the general public. To provide one example of the Unit's work, it discovered that public transport services in one city shut down before the pubs closed, leaving some customers stranded and in high spirits—with resultant vandalism, theft of cars and bicycles and so on. The transport authority was persuaded to eliminate the precipitating conditions by scheduling bus services to coincide with pub closing.

A more broadly-based approach to the implementation of opportunity-reducing strategies may also be possible. At present both uniformed patrols and detectives in most forces act reactively to problems; crimes tend to be dealt with one by one as they come to light, thereafter to be forgotten, and no-one has any clear responsibility to look for patterns and trends and thus identify preventive measures. There is rarely any effective organizational or technological provision at local (sub-divisional) level for crime analysis. As computerized information technology develops such analysis should become easier to undertake; but the technology's potential will only be exploited if patrol officers and detectives are encouraged to look for preventive as well as reactive solutions to crime problems (cf Hough, 1980). Some promising experiments are under way, for example in Skelmersdale (Heaton, 1980).

Summary and conclusions

Policing has traditionally relied on deterrence, and preventive patrolling and detection are the main crime-fighting strategies of the police. In their rationale, these strategies are not aimed at any specific age group; but in practice their primary targets are young people, as offending is predominantly a youthful phenomenon. Crime—as reflected by official statistics at least—has consistently risen, the increase being most marked in the post-war period. The police response has been to invest more resources (of manpower and technology) in deterrent policing.

Over the last decade or so, research has called into question the effectiveness of conventional policing methods. This research does *not* indicate that patrolling and detective work are without impact, though it is sometimes construed to do so, both by critics and defenders of conventional policing. However, it suggests strongly that the marginal gains from additional deterrent policing will be negligible. There are a number of possible reasons for this. In the nature of crime it is difficult to achieve significant increases in the risks which offenders run of being caught red-handed or detected. Small increases may simply not be noticed by offenders; large increases may be achieved only at considerable cost—in terms both of finance and of disrupted community relations. Deterrent policing may have the unintended consequence of amplifying criminal behaviour—by reducing the opportunities of convicted offenders for 'going straight', by fuelling resentment against authority or by confirming people's conceptions of themselves as law-breakers. It is also possible that extension of formal systems of social control may erode rather than supplement communities' informal self-policing mechanisms.

Some alternatives have been discussed. Those under the heading of community policing emphasize the centrality of informal systems of social control and the need to nurture these. Community policing schemes may be aimed at the general public (improving relations between police and public) or at young people (moral/civil education, youth work, counselling of young offenders). One may be sceptical about the larger claims for community policing; mechanisms of informal control are complex, a combination of a great range of pressures on people to conform to socially acceptable standards. Whether or not the police can do much to *increase* the impact of such mechanisms is an open question. However, the priority which community policing schemes attach to the maintenance of informal control mechanisms makes it unlikely that they will actually damage or erode these mechanisms. This is perhaps the main strength of community policing, one not to be under-estimated.

Most strategies for reducing crime are offender-based, and this is especially the case when solutions are sought to offending by a particular age-group. Little attention is paid to offence-based measures intended to modify criminogenic environments. The scope for such situational or opportunity-reducing prevention may have been considerably underestimated. Detailed and systematic analysis of the situations in which crimes are committed can suggest ways in which environmental design or management can eliminate the precipitating factors. Critics would argue that the situational approach is vitiated by displacement of crime—that is, when one opportunity for crime is closed up, offenders simply discover others. Whilst this may be true for some sorts of measure and some sorts of crime, it seems most unlikely that all opportunity-reducing strategies will result in total displacement. Situational prevention is by no means the province solely of the police. There may be a role for more co-ordination and negotiation at central governmental level; and at local level, the central planning departments of local authorities may sometimes be more appropriate bodies for co-ordinating local agencies than the police. However, if the situational approach proves to be a viable strategy, the police can play an important part in its advocacy and in its implementation.

Community policing and the situational approach have several things in common. (Indeed, opportunity-reducing prevention may often comprise an important element of community policing schemes.) They have both been proposed as a response to the perceived limitations of conventional policing methods—to the limited capability of the police for crime control. Both involve a reallocation of responsibility for crime control from the police to the community; community policing views the main resource for social control as residing within the community, and the preventive measures likely to be identified by the situational approach often have to be implemented by others apart from the police. In both, the police tend to have a catalytic function, initiating rather than carrying through action. These common elements mark an important shift in approach to crime control, which amounts to an inversion of the conventional proposition that the police need the co-operation of the public in fighting crime. People need the help of the police in protecting themselves against crime.

Crown Copyright, 1982

References

Alderson, J. (1977). *Communal Policing*, Devon and Cornwall Constabulary, Exeter.

Alderson, J. (1979). *Policing Freedom*, McDonald and Evans, Plymouth, England.

Alderson, J. (1981). Letter published in *New Society*, 29 January.

Argyle, M., Furnham, A. and Graham, J. A. (1981). *Social Situations*, Cambridge University Press, Cambridge.

Becker, H. S. (1963). *Outsiders: Studies in the Sociology of Deviance*, Free Press, New York.

Becker. H. S. (1964). *The Other Side: Perspectives on Deviance*, Free Press, New York.

Bennett, T. (1979). The social distribution of criminal labels, *British Journal of Criminology*, **19**, 134–145.

Bieck, W. (1977). *Response Time Analysis*, Kansas City Police Department, Kansas City.

Block, D. J. and Reiss, A. J. (1970). Police control of juveniles, *American Sociological Review*, **35**, 63–77.

Blaber, A.(1979). *The Exeter Community Policing Consultative Group*, NACRO, London.

Black, P. B. and Bell, J. (1976). *Managing Investigations: the Rochester System*, Police Foundation, Washington, D. C.

Bottomley, A. K. and Coleman, C. A. (1980). Understanding crime rates, in *The Effectiveness of Policing* (Eds R. V. G. Clarke and J. M. Hough), Gower, Farnborough, England.

Boystun, J. (1975). *San Diego Field Interrogation*, Police Foundation, Washington D. C.

Bright, J. A. (1969). *The Beat Patrol Experiment*, Home Office Police Research and Development Branch. (Unpublished).

Carr Hill, R. A. and Stern, N. H. (1979). *Crime, the Police and Criminal Statistics*, Academic Press, London.

Chaiken, J. M. (1978). What is known about deterrent effects of police activities? in *Preventing Crime* (Ed. J. A. Cramer), Sage Publications, Beverly Hills.

Chaiken, J. M., Lawless, M. W. and Stevenson, K. A. (1974). *The Impact of Police Activities on Crime: Robberies in New York City Subway System*, The Rand Corporation, Santa Monica.

Clarke, R. V. G. and Mayhew, P. (Eds). (1980). *Designing Out Crime*, HMSO, London.

Dahmann, J. S. (1975). *Examination of Police Patrol Effectiveness*, Mitre, McClean.

Ditchfield, J. A. (1976). *Police Cautioning in England and Wales*, Home Office Research Study No. 37, HMSO, London.

Durant, M., Thomas, M. and Willcock, H. D. (1972). *Crime, Criminals and the Law*, HMSO, London.

Engstad, P. and Evans, J. (1980). Responsibility, competence and police effectiveness in crime control, in *The Effectiveness of Policing* (Eds R. V. G. Clarke and J. M. Hough), Gower, Farnborough.

Ekblom, P. (1979). Police truancy patrols, in *Crime Prevention and the Police* (Eds J. Burrows, P. Ekblom, and K. Heal). Home Office Research Study No. 55, HMSO, London.

Elliott, J. F. (1978). Crime control teams: an alternative to the conventional operational procedure of investigating crimes, *Journal of Criminal Justice*, **6**, 11–23.

Farmer, D. J. (1980). Out of hugger-mugger: the case of police field services, in *The Effectiveness of Policing* (Eds R. V. G. Clarke and J. M. Hough), Gower, Farnborough.

Farrington, D. P. (1977). The effects of public labelling, *British Journal of Criminology*, **17**, 2, April, 112–125.

Fienberg, S., Kinley, L. and Reiss, A. S. (1976). Redesigning the Kansas City preventive-patrol experiment, *Evaluation*, **3**, 124–131.

Fisk, D. (1970). *The Indianapolis Police Fleet Plan*, Urban Institute, Washington, D. C.

Gay, W. G. Day, H. T. and Woodward, J. P. (1977). *Neighbourhood Team Policing*, Law Enforcement Assistance Administration, Washington, DC.

Greenwood, P. W., Chaiken, J. M., Petersilia, J. and Prusoff, L. (1977). *The Criminal Investigation Process*, D. C. Heath, Lexington.

Hall, S., Critcher, C., Jefferson, T., Clarke, J. and Roberts, B. (1978). *Policing the Crisis: Mugging, the State, and Law and Order*, Macmillan, London.

Halper, A. and Ku, R. (1975). *New York City Police Department Street Crime Unit: An Exemplary Project*. Law Enforcement Assistance Administration, Washington, DC.

Heaton, M. (1980). Skelmersdale co-ordinated policing experiment, *Police Research Bulletin*, No. 34, 29–31.

Heller, N. B. (1977). *A Review of Police Research in the United States*, The Institute of Public Program Analysis, St Louis, USA (unpublished).

HMSO (1980a). *Criminal Statistics England and Wales 1979*, HMSO, London.

HMSO (1980b). *Report of the Commissioner of the Metropolis for the Year 1979*, (Cmnd. 7932), HMSO, London.

Hough, J. M. (1980). *Uniformed Police Work and Management Technology*, Research Paper 1, Home Office, London.

James, D. (1979). Police – black relations: the professional solution, in *The British Police* (Ed. S. Holdaway), Edward Arnold, London.

Jones, M. (1980). *Organisational Aspects of Police Behaviour*, Gower, Farnborough.

Kelling, G., Pate, T., Dieckman, D. and Brown, C. (1974). *The Kansas City Preventive Patrol Experiment*, Police Foundation, Washington, DC.

Kelling, G., Wycoff, M. A. and Pate, T. (1980). Policing: A research agenda for rational policy making, in *The Effectiveness of Policing* (Eds R. V. G. Clarke and J. M. Hough), Gower, Farnborough.

Kitsuse, J. (1972). Deviance, deviant behaviour and deviants, in *An Introduction to Deviance* (Ed. W. J. Filstead), Markham Books, Chicago.
Landau, S. F. (1981). Juveniles and the police, *British Journal of Criminology*, **21**, 1, January, 27–46.
Larson, R. C. (1976). What happened to patrol operations in Kansas City? A review of the Kansas City preventive patrol experiment, *Journal of Criminal Justice*, **3**, 267–297.
Lemert, E. (1967). *Human Deviance, Social Problems and Social Control*, Prentice-Hall, Englewood Cliffs.
Lemert, E. (1970). *Social Action and Legal Change*, Aldine, Chicago.
Manning, P. (1977). *Police Work: The Social Organisation of Policing*, MIT Press, London.
Manolias, M. (1980). *The Gainsborough Experiment in Community Policing*, Home Office Police Scientific Development Branch (unpublished).
Mayhew, P., Clarke, R. V. G., Burrows, J. N., Hough, J. M., and Winchester, S. W. C. (1979). *Crime in Public View*, Home Office Research Study No. 49, HMSO, London.
Mayhew, P., Clarke, R. V. G., Hough, J. M. and Sturman, A. (1976). *Crime as Opportunity*, Home Office Research Study No. 34, HMSO, London.
Mawby, R. (1979). *Policing the City*, Saxon House, Farnborough.
Morris, P. and Heal, K. H. (1981). *Crime Control and the Police*. Home Office Research Study No. 67, HMSO, London.
Newman, O. (1972). *Defensible Space: Crime Prevention through Urban Design*, MacMillan, New York.
New York Police Department (1955). *Operation 25.*
Nichols, J. F. and Bannon, J. D. (1972). S.T.R.E.S.S. zero visibility policing, *Police Chief*, **39**, 33–36.
Parker, H. (1974). *View from the Boys*, David and Charles, Newton Abbot.
Pate, T., Bowers, B. A. and Parks, R. (1976). *Three Approaches to Criminal Apprehension in Kansas City: An Evaluation Report.* Police Foundation, Washington, DC.
Pepinski, H. E. (1976). *Crime and Conflict*, Martin Robertson, London.
Pepinski, H. E. (1980). *Crime Control Strategies: An Introduction to the Study of Crime*, Oxford University Press, New York.
Piliavin, I, and Briar, S. (1964). Police encounters with juveniles, *American Journal of Sociology*, **70**, 206–214.
Plummer, K. (1979). Misunderstanding labelling perspectives, in *Deviant Interpretations* (Eds D. Downes and P. Rock), Martin Robertson, Oxford.
Police Foundation (1981). *The Newark Foot Patrol Experiment*, Police Foundation, Washington, DC.
Pollard, B. (1979). *A Study of Leicestershire Constabulary Highfields Community Policing Scheme*, Cranfield Institute of Technology, Bedford (unpublished).
President's Commission on Law Enforcement and Administration of Justice (1967). *Task Force Report: the Police*, Government Printing Office, Washington, DC.
Press, S. I. (1971). *Some Effects of an Increase in Police Manpower in the 20th Precinct of New York City*, Rand Institute, New York.
Schaffer, E. B. (1980). *Community Policing*, Croom Helm, London.
Schnelle, J. F., Kirchner, R. E., McNees, M. P. and Lawler, J. M. (1975). Social evaluation research: the evaluation of two police patrolling strategies, *Journal of Applied Behaviour Analysis*, **4**, 353–365.
Schnelle, J. F., Kirchner, R. E., Casey, J. D., Useltor, P. H. and McNees, M. P. (1977). Patrol evaluation research: a multiple-baseline analysis of saturation police patrolling during day and night hours, *Journal of Applied Behaviour Analysis*, **10**, 33–40.
Shanks, M. J. (1980). *Police Community Involvement in Scotland*, Central Research Unit, Scottish Office, Edinburgh.

Sherman, L. W., Milton, C. H. and Kelly, T. V. (1973). *Team Policing: Seven Case Studies*, Police Foundation, Washington, DC.

Sparks, R. F., Genn, H. G. and Dodd, D. J. (1977). *Surveying Victims*, Wiley, London.

Steer, D. (1980). *Uncovering Crime: The Role of the Police*, Royal Commission on Criminal Procedure, Research Study No. 7, HMSO, London.

Stevens, P. and Willis, C. F. (1979). *Race, Crime and Arrests*, Home Office Research Study No. 58, HMSO, London.

Terry, R. M. (1967). Discrimination in the handling of juvenile offenders by social control agencies, *Journal of Research on Crime and Delinquency*, **4**, 218–230.

Tien, J., Simon, J. and Larson, R. (1978). *An Alternative Approach in Police Patrols: the Wilmington Split Force Experiment*, Public Systems Evaluation, Cambridge, Mass.

Wilkins, L. T. (1964). *Social Deviance*, Tavistock, London.

Wilson, J. Q. (1975). *Thinking About Crime*, Basic Books, New York.

Wolfgang, M. E., Figlio, R. M. and Sellin, T. (1972). *Delinquency in a Birth Cohort*, Chicago University Press, Chicago.

Woodley, A. C. (1976). *Thames Valley Collator Project*, Home Office Police Scientific Development Branch, (unpublished).

Development in the Study of Criminal Behaviour
Volume 1: The Prevention and Control of Offending
Edited by P. Feldman

3

Predicting, Treating, and Explaining Delinquency: The Lessons from Research on Institutions

IAN SINCLAIR AND RON CLARKE

Introduction

During the 1950s and 1960s Home Office researchers carried out a number of major projects concerned with the treatment of delinquency. It was hoped to identify effective forms of treatment for specific groups of offenders as well as ways of reducing problems of institutional management such as absconding. The main focus was on institutional treatments—approved schools, probation hostels and borstals—and on probation, though there was also some coverage of fines and other court disposals. The earlier studies sought to identify the characteristics of offenders who were likely to be reconvicted after treatment and paid rather little attention to the treatment process itself. Later work sought to relate particular aspects of treatment both to the chances of reconviction and to institutional misbehaviour.

The main findings of the research can be briefly summarized as follows:

(i) Though it is difficult to predict reconviction, the best predictors are pretreatment delinquency, current family environment and, to a lesser extent, delinquency during treatment.
(ii) There is little to choose between the differing forms of treatment in their long-term effectiveness in preventing reconviction.
(iii) In contrast to the lack of differences in long-term effectiveness, the great variety of organization and methods exhibited between the different forms of treatment is matched by large differences in misbehaviour (as measured by offending or absconding) during treatment.

These findings have helped to bring about a general awareness of the limitations of penal treatment. As this chapter hopes to show, they also provide the basis for a theoretical understanding of delinquent behaviour. The discussion will be located within a general framework of social learning theory and will attempt to draw out some of the practical implications for the treatment of delinquency and the prevention of crime. There will be little analysis of specifically behavioural forms of treatment (most of which have been developed in America) as these are discussed in detail in other chapters in this book. Instead, the chapter will aim to provide a common explanation for the findings on the predictors of reconviction and the effects of treatment which we have summarized above.

In brief, it will be argued that delinquency is mainly a response to a current living situation (for example the family or an institution) which provides the stimuli and opportunities for offending as well as the reinforcements. In so far as the situation remains unchanged, delinquency itself is likely to persist. Some transfer of learning is possible from one environment to another, but the general unpredictability of delinquency is a function of changing environmental pressures which make a delinquent response more or less likely. The influence of the environment also helps to account for the ineffectiveness of treatment: though willing conformity or compliance may be found among those under treatment, the contemporary environment re-asserts its power on release.

In developing this argument we will describe the Home Office research under three headings: prediction studies, experimental studies and cross-institutional designs. These latter studies are particularly important to our argument for two reasons. They provide a means of examining the features of institutional environment which produce large differences in behaviour and, secondly, they provide a convenient way of studying the persistence of behaviour across different situations and the part played in this by constitutional factors and early experience.

Prediction studies

The early focus of the Home Office research upon the prediction of reconviction had two main rationales. First, for reasons described below, it was hoped to predict future criminal careers and secondly, some though not all, researchers hoped that by predicting reconviction they would gain an understanding of its causes.

As exemplified by Mannheim and Wilkins (1955), the prediction study had little to do with understanding delinquency. Its main aim was to divide delinquents (in this case borstal boys) into risk groups according to the probability of reconviction after treatment. Two purposes can be served by such risk groups. First, they can be used to examine whether boys receiving certain kinds of treatment are more or less likely to be reconvicted than the distribution of risk groups would lead one to expect, and secondly, administrators can be assisted in choosing the most appropriate form of treatment or in deciding how long the offender should be kept in custody.

Mannheim and Wilkins' study is now a classic and only a brief resumé of some of its main points will be given here. The authors took a representative sample of

Table 1   Mannheim and Wilkins' (1955) borstal prediction table: validation sample

Score	Success	Failure	Total	Successful (%)
0– 9.9	52	12	64	81
10.0–14.9	38	18	56	68
15.0–23.9	50	76	126	40
24.0–39.9	27	56	83	33
40.0 and over	0	9	9	0
	167	171	338	49

$r\phi = 0.50$.

720 youths entering borstals during 1946–47 and extracted about 60 variables from their files, of which only a small number were found to be significantly correlated with reconviction. The best predictor was obtained by combining the following variables: evidence of drunkenness; prior offences resulting in a fine, probation, or committal to prison or approved schools; whether living with parents; whether home was in industrial area; and longest period in any one job. A five-class table of risks of reconviction was derived and this was validated on a second and representative sample of 338 youths who were followed up for exactly 3 years after release (Table 1).

Wilkins (unpublished) subsequently attempted to undertake a prediction study on an approved school sample of 618 senior boys entering schools in the North of England in 1950. He extracted ninety-three items of information from their files covering home background, delinquent history, school and employment records, medical record, personality and intelligence. Because he was unable to produce a satisfactory prediction equation he regarded this work as a failure not worth publishing, but an important finding was that the prediction of reconviction was greatly improved by the inclusion of information about absconding during the period of training. Absconding itself, however, could not be successfully predicted from any of the ninety-three pre-training items.

After these two studies, further important work on prediction was carried out by Hammond (1964), who analysed data on some 2000 offenders aged 8–21 who had been given a variety of different sentences and by Davies (1969) and Simon (1971), who both studied probationers aged 17–21. In general, the main factors found to be related to reconviction in all these studies were much the same and corresponded to those identified by Mannheim and Wilkins.

The first of these factors was age. In general, it was found that the younger the offender, the more likely he was to be reconvicted. Hammond (1964), for example, found that over 50 per cent of offenders aged under 14 at their first conviction were reconvicted within 5 years compared with 30 per cent of first offenders aged 21–29, and only 9 per cent of first offenders aged 40 or over. It was only where offenders came from a relatively narrow age band, for example 17–21 in Davies' study, that age was not found to be related to reconviction.

The second group of factors identified in almost all studies concerned previous convictions. A large number of previous convictions, a first court appearance at an early age and a concentration on burglary, larceny and taking motor vehicles were all found to be positively associated with future conviction.

The idea that there might be a pattern of delinquent conduct conforming to the common stereotype was further suggested by the fact that various measures of 'poor' work record were also associated with further offences as indeed, in the study by Mannheim and Wilkins, was heavy drinking. As in other branches of social science it was sometimes assumed that behaviour (in this case poor work record and criminal behaviour) might be explained by underlying personality characteristics, and some of the studies included an attempt to measure these. The main measures used were ratings of behaviour made by practitioners or based on records which they kept and scores on the Jesness Inventory (1963). Both kinds of measure were found to be associated with reconviction (Davies, 1967, 1969) although not always with great efficiency or indeed consistency (cf Mott, 1973). Mannheim and Wilkins found that behavioural assessments gathered from housemasters' records were less useful in predicting offences than 'hard' data concerning previous convictions and so forth. Simon and Davies, however, both found that ratings made by probation officers, including such assessments as 'lack of conscience' or 'unstable personality' did predict further convictions.

Two groups of factors found to be consistently associated with reconviction concerned the environmental variables of family circumstances and peer group associates. Davies (1969) concentrated on these factors in his sample of probationers. Family cohesiveness, firm consistent discipline, and good relationships between the probationer and his parents (particularly his father) were associated with low reconviction rates (Table 2). These findings are largely consistent with those obtained on unselected samples of delinquents (e.g. Glueck and Glueck, 1934; West and Farrington, 1973). Davies also found that probationers who were said to mix mainly with non-delinquents were half as likely to be reconvicted as those who were said to mix mainly with delinquents. Similarly, Simon (1971) found that a probation officer's opinion that his client was a member of a delinquent group predicted reconviction.

Lastly, there was evidence that the social class of the individual and social characteristics of his area of residence were both predictors of continued criminality. Probationers in the lower socio-economic groups (Davies, 1969) and those from areas with few people eligible for jury service (a measure at that time of lower social class, cf Simon 1971) were more likely to be reconvicted, as apparently were borstal boys living in highly industrialized areas (Mannheim and Wilkins, 1955).

Although a number of factors associated with reconviction rates were

Table 2 Failure-rate of probationers (p) according to their relationships with parents

	F-R	N	Significance level	df
(a) Factors significantly associated with failure-rate:				
Father–son relationship is 'the best possible'	0.12	65	0.001	3
Father's control over P is firm but kindly	0.13	85	0.001	3
P is attached to his father	0.19	142	0.001	2
Father's affection for P is warm	0.20	158	0.001	3
There is a marked degree of family cohesiveness	0.22	100	0.001	2
Father–son relationship is 'probably good'	0.22	63	0.001	3
P's parents are basically compatible (i.e. the relationship is 'good')	0.25	217	0.001	2
P is attached to his mother	0.28	254	0.01	2
Father's affection for P is over-protective	0.30	30	0.001	3
Father's control over P is over-strict	0.33	24	0.001	3
There is 'some' degree of family cohesiveness	0.35	214	0.001	2
Father–son relationship is probably 'poor'	0.39	44	0.001	3
P is emotionally indifferent towards his father	0.40	109	0.001	2
Father's control over P is lax	0.41	83	0.001	3
Father's control over P is erratic	0.41	107	0.001	3
Father's affection for P is indifferent	0.42	71	0.001	3
Father–son relationship is 'the worst possible'	0.45	113	0.001	3
P is hostile towards his mother	0.46	24	0.01	2
P's parents are basically incompatible (i.e. the relationship is 'fair')	0.47	75	0.001	2
P is hostile towards his father	0.48	50	0.001	2
P is emotionally indifferent towards his mother	0.50	58	0.01	2
Father is hostile towards P	0.54	41	0.001	3
There is no family cohesiveness	0.61	33	0.001	2
P's parents are living permanently apart	0.72	18	0.001	2

(b) Factors not significantly associated with failure-rate:
The type of affection (warmth, indifference, hostility, over-protection) shown by the mother for P ($df = 3$)
The type of control (firm but kindly, lax, erratic, over-strict) exercised by the mother over P ($df = 3$)
The overall measure of the relationship between P and his mother ($df = 3$)
The extent to which either or both parents exerted an over-protective influence over P ($df = 3$)

Source: Davies, 1969.

successfully isolated in the prediction studies, their combined predictive power was not great. Small groups with either high or low chances of reconviction could be identified, but for most offenders it remained difficult to say whether or not they would re-offend. It was also difficult to know whether the factors associated with reconviction were causes, consequences or merely correlates of further offending. As a result it remained uncertain whether the difficulties of making precise predictions arise from a lack of knowledge about the offender and his living situation or from the fact that other variables, such as opportunities for crime, need to be taken into account by the social scientist as they are by the offender. As it happens, studies of institutional treatment provided further evidence about the importance of opportunities and the offender's environment and this issue will be examined afresh in the light of the further research discussed below.

Prediction studies and treatment effectiveness

Prediction scores were used by Mannheim and Wilkins and by Hammond as a basis for evaluating treatments. Using their prediction table, Mannheim and Wilkins provided evidence that, even allowing for the better intake, open borstals were more successful. This conclusion has been questioned by Cockett (1967) who suggested that allocation to open and closed borstals may take into account factors other than those reflected in the prediction table.

The range of variables that Hammond (1964) included in his study for *The Sentence of the Court* was much narrower than in either of Wilkins' studies and his results are therefore that much less reliable. For juvenile first offenders, fines seemed to be the most effective disposal, approved schools the least with probation in between (see Table 3). It may be, of course, that lenient sentences are indeed more effective, but it is more likely that the better risks were given the lighter penalties and that, in the same way as the Mannheim and Wilkins' prediction scores were not sufficiently sensitive to take account of all the factors involved in borstal allocation, Hammond was unable to consider all the factors influencing the courts' choice of particular sentences.

The evidence from prediction studies about treatment effectiveness was therefore equivocal. It suggested some rather weak effects of treatment though there was doubt about how real these were. An individual's chances of reconviction seemed more powerfully related to his previous history of

Table 3   Chances of reconviction following sentence for some 2000 juvenile offenders with or without previous convictions (Base expectancy = 100; greater scores indicate relative failure, lesser scores relative success)

	First offenders	Offenders with previous convictions
Discharge	87	100
Fine	75	83
Probation	118	101
Approved school	138	102

Source: Hammond, 1964.

delinquency, the nature of his home background, and also perhaps, to his behaviour during sentence than they were to the sentence he actually received.

As any treatment effects were likely to be small, it became even more important to ensure that differences in intake were properly controlled in future evaluations and, as there would always be some doubt about the adequacy of 'matching' designs, whether or not based on prediction scores, the case for random allocation of subjects between treatments became stronger. There was also growing recognition of the need to undertake more detailed studies of treatment process in an attempt to isolate the more effective components.

Experimental designs

An example of this second wave of research is provided by Cornish and Clarke's (1975) random allocation study comparing a 'therapeutic community' with a traditional approved-school regime. The study was undertaken in a West Country approved school catering for boys aged 13–15 years on admission. A therapeutic community based on the four principles of democratization, communalism, permissiveness and reality confrontation enunciated by Rapoport (1960) had been introduced by the schools' psychologist in one of the houses. Because of the controversy surrounding what was then a new form of treatment for approved schools, the school managers decided that an evaluation of the regime should be attempted.

The research design ensured that those judged 'suitable' for the therapeutic community (an estimated two-thirds of the boys admitted to the school) would be randomly allocated on admission between the therapeutic community and a 'control' house which had a well-established regime run on traditional, paternalistic lines. Boys judged 'unsuitable' were allocated to the school's third house. Over 4 years, 280 boys were assigned between the three houses of the school. A detailed study of the regimes showed the therapeutic community house staff to be more treatment-oriented (in overall ideology, in attitudes and in policy) than those in the control house. Differences in behaviour between boys in the houses being compared were also in the expected direction: those in the therapeutic community, for instance, were more likely to act out by absconding or by damaging the furniture and fabric of the house.

No differences were found between the therapeutic community and the control house in the number of boys reconvicted within a 2-year period after release (see Table 4) or between the two comparison houses and the third house receiving the 'unsuitable' boys. Nor were the reconviction rates any different from those of two neighbouring schools which also began to operate as therapeutic communities during the latter part of the research.

Cornish and Clarke's results are in line with the generality of research into the institutional treatment of delinquent youths (cf Brody, 1976; Martinson, 1974). As far as British studies are concerned, McMichael (1974) found no significant

Table 4   Reconvictions of boys taking part in Cornish and
Clarke's (1975) controlled trial of a therapeutic community

House	Number admitted	Number reconvicted	Reconvited (%)
Therapeutic community	86	60	70
Control house	87	60	69
Third house	107	73	68
All boys	280	193	69

differences between the reconviction rates of boys from a Scottish approved
school run as a therapeutic community and a control group of boys from other
schools. Craft et al.'s (1964) study of authoritarian and permissive regimes for
adolescent psychopaths found no differences between them in numbers of boys
subsequently offending, and Craft's (1965) study of an exceptionally well-
organized 'family type' programme in one approved school for junior boys
showed that it achieved no better than average success. With older offenders,
Bottoms and McClintock (1973) found that two different borstal regimes (one
giving traditional, and the other more individualized training) produced similar
reconviction rates. The only British experimental study to show significant
differences in the reconviction rates of young offenders treated in different
regimes, was carried out by psychologists in the Prison Service. In a random
allocation experiment reported by Williams (1970) it was found that a borstal
which relied on individual casework was significantly, though only slightly, more
effective than two other regimes with comparable intakes.

A pattern of predominantly negative findings also exists in relevant American
research: differential outcomes have not emerged from studies which have
utilized methods of satisfactorily matching inputs to the programmes being
compared (e.g. Jesness, 1971; Empey and Lubeck, 1971; Jesness et al., 1972). In
those cases (e.g. the original Highfields research, Weeks, 1958, and Jesness's
Fricot Ranch study, 1965) where differences in outcome were found, there is
almost always doubt about the validity of the results because of failures in, or
lack of, adequate input matching. As with the findings on prediction, this
conclusion could reflect factors associated with the individual offender (in
particular, the difficulty of modifying the effect of early training or heredity or a
settled determination to offend) or alternatively; the power of the environment
over the offender after his release from an institution.

Cross-institutional studies

Until recently, it seemed that the controversy over treatment effectiveness had
been conclusively settled. In 1979, however, Murray and Cox published some

research suggesting that, as judged from the number of police contacts before and after treatment, two groups of youths subjected either to a community-based regime (UDIS) or an institutional placement were less likely to be further involved in crime, as a result—so it is implied (cf Wilson, 1980)—of the shock of that experience.

Unfortunately, Murray and Cox (1979) failed to present the basic descriptive statistics necessary for their conclusions to be evaluated, and their case is in part unproven and in part fallacious. There was a logical necessity for those included in their study to have at least one pre-treatment contact with the police, but no such necessity for a post-treatment contact. Even among the most hardened criminal *some* do not offend again after a conviction, however they are treated, and of those that do, some are not convicted after that. It was thus almost inevitable that the average number of offences in a limited period after treatment would be less than those before it.

Whatever the conclusion to be drawn from Murry and Cox's work, there was in any case already some evidence of a weak and variable treatment effect in the results of a set of studies which we will call 'cross-institutional'. In experimental designs, the treatments being compared have to be regarded as perhaps unique constellations of individual variables—staff ratios, size of living groups, regime style, staff training and personality, and so forth. This leaves open the possibility that even though it has not been possible to identify successful *treatments*, there may be individual *treatment variables* which are important in relation to outcome but whose effects are being swamped by those of other factors. For example in Cornish and Clarke's (1975) study, any beneficial effects of the therapy provided might have been cancelled out by a higher incidence of absconding or, indeed, by some other combination of factors. Equally if a positive effect had been found it would not have been possible to identify the precise factors responsible.

The methodological advantage of the 'cross-institutional' studies described here is that in principle they afford a solution to the problem of isolating the effect of particular variables. They also afford a useful methodology for studying absconding and other institutional misbehaviour. Essentially, the method proceeds by comparing a large number of institutions of a particular type within a single research design. The research will usually involve comparing different prisons, for example, rather than prisons with borstals or with any other kind of institution. Allowances are made for differences in intake through appropriate statistical techniques, and measures of aspects of treatment process are correlated with measures of outcome. Since the method depends on correlating scores which have been assigned to each institution for the various dimensions under study, it probably cannot be used with a sample of fewer than eight or ten institutions. Given this number, the method is particularly suitable for relating specific aspects of treatment to specific effects (cf Tizard *et al.*, 1975).

Sinclair's (1976) study of the probation hostel system in England and Wales, an early example of this kind of study, was carried out in the mid-1960s. He began

Table 5   Distribution of 'failure rate' in forty-six
probation hostel regimes

Failure rate (%)	Number of regimes	Number of boys
10–14	1	37
15–19	4	200
20–24	4	432
25–29	9	972
30–34	8	738
35–39	5	951
40–44	8	797
45–49	2	59
50 +	5	157
Total	46	4343

Source: Sinclair, 1971.

by studying records on over 4000 boys and found that depending on the warden
in charge of the hostel the proportion who left prematurely as a result of
absconding or further offences (the 'failure rate') varied greatly with a range of 14
per cent to 78 per cent (see Table 5). This variation could not be accounted for by
differences in the boys entering each hostel: careful study of 429 boys who
entered the hostels in a particular year showed that those who had left home or
had an above average number of previous convictions were more likely to leave
the hostel prematurely, and that those who had been removed from bad homes
were less likely to do so—but that the regimes with high rates of premature
leaving had not taken abnormal proportions of either category. Nor was the
variation explicable by the more obvious differences among hostels such as size,
location, age range, or the policies of the local police and courts. In fact, the
differences between 'success rates' of wardens who succeeded each other in the
same hostel were as great as the differences between those of wardens in different
hostels.

Further evidence of the importance of the warden and matron was provided by
the facts that absconding doubled in the months when wardens or matrons were
away (Table 6), and that wardens differed significantly in terms of the ages of the
boys most likely to 'fail' in their hostels. (Some did better with younger boys,
others with older boys). Although there was evidence that hostels were liable to
epidemics of absconding or offending, it could also be shown that these were
more prolonged or more frequent with some wardens than with others.

In attempting to understand these variations Sinclair carried out case studies
of sixteen regimes which had particularly high or low 'failure rates' and then
tested his conclusions statistically on a year's intake to a further sixteen hostels.
To do this he used a measure of permissiveness, various measures of staff

Table 6 Absconding and offences related to months in which probation hostel wardens or matrons were on leave or away sick

	Months in which hostels open	Abscondings		Offences		Abscondings and offences	
		No.	Average per month	No.	Average per month	No.	Average per month
Warden/matron absent	87	78	0.9	55	0.63	133	1.53
Warden/matron present	258	113	0.44	120	0.47	233	0.90
		$t = 2.78$; $df = 14$ $p \leq 0.01$		ns		$t = 2.92$; $df = 14$ $p \leq 0.01$	

Source: Sinclair, 1971.
Note *t*-tests calculated as for correlated means.

Table 7 Partial correlations on failure rate of attitude difference, emotional distance and premissiveness for staff of sixteen hostels

	Permissiveness	Variable held constant attitude difference	Emotional distance
Permissiveness	—	0.03	0.64*
Attitude difference	0.50	—	0.65
Emotional distance	0.67**	0.55	—

Source: Sinclair, 1971.
*$p < 0.05$; **$p < 0.01$.

attitudes taken from a staff attitude questionnaire developed by Jesness (1965), and a measure of 'attitude difference' derived by comparing the answers of different staff to the same questionnaire. He found that wardens with the lowest rates of premature leaving were those who ran a strictly-disciplined hostel but who also expressed warmth towards the boys and were in agreement with their wives about how the hostels should be run (Table 7). Other combinations of attitude and practice, such as kindness and permissiveness or strictness and harshness, were relatively unsuccessful in terms of the proportion of boys who left as a result of absconding or of a further offence.

A very important finding was that, with the exception of one warden, the reconviction rates of boys who did not leave prematurely were unaffected by the hostels in which they had been resident. The evidence for the impact of the environment on immediate rather than long-term criminal behaviour was paralleled by findings on families. As can be seen from Table 8, boys who were sent to the hostel in order to be removed from a poor home were significantly less likely than other boys to be reconvicted while in the hostel, but were more likely to be reconvicted on return home.

Table 8   Reconviction and removal from home for boys in probation hostels

	Year of Reconviction						Not reconvicted		Total	
	Year 1		Year 2		Year 3					
		(%)		(%)		(%)		(%)		(%)
Removal emphasized	63	32	51	26	20	10	61	31	195	100
Removal not emphasized	99	45	44	20	13	6	63	29	219	100
Total	162	39	95	23	33	8	124	30	414	100

Source: Sinclair, 1971.
Considering those reconvicted: χ^2 for trend = 8.06; $df = 1$; $p < 0.005$

Table 9   Absconding rates for senior boys' training schools in 1964 and 1966

	Absconding rate	
School	1964	1966
1	10	10
2	13	38
3	14	14
4	21	18
5	21	23
6	22	14
7	22	21
8	24	29
9	25	33
10	26	37
11	27	25
12	28	47
13	29	45
14	32	43
15	34	26
16	46	27
17	75	59
Average	27.6	29.9

Source: Clark and Martin, 1971.
Correlation   (Spearman's coefficient) = 0.65; $p < 0.01$

Sinclair's findings about the importance of regime in influencing behaviour during training were supported by Clarke and Martin's (1971) independent research into absconding from what were then known as approved schools (since called Community Homes with Education on the Premises or CHEs). Clarke and Martin found very marked and persisting differences in the absconding rates of different approved schools (ranging, for example, from 10–75 per cent of the populations in individual senior approved schools, see Table 9) and showed that these could not be accounted for by differences in boys admitted and must have been the result of exposure to differing school environments. They went on to consider particular environmental factors and from studies undertaken in one or two schools (Clarke and Martin (1975) found that the chance of absconding was related to the nearness of a boy's admission or return from leave, and to whether or not he was admitted in busy periods (see Table 10), into house units which were unusually full, or in the company of others with a previous record of absconding (Table 11). Absconding was also more common when it had not recently been dealt with by corporal punishment (Table 12) and when the staff in charge demanded less in terms of respect and obedience from the children (Martin, 1977).

Clarke and Martin used these findings to argue that any event that produces even temporary unhappiness or insecurity could lead a boy to abscond and that the more opportunities to abscond provided by the regime, the more absconding there would be. The main evidence concerning the role of opportunity was provided by a study of the seasonal variation in absconding at one classifying school during 1960 to 1964. This variation was consistent and very marked,

Table 10   Time span of admission in relation to absconding by each admission group of ten boys (300 consecutive admissions to one training school)

No. of weeks during which group admitted	No. of admission groups	Mean of groups' abscondings
3	1	21.00
4	6	13.17
5	5	12.20
6	5	7.20
7	5	7.00
8	2	3.00
9	3	8.33
10	3	7.67
All	30	9.53

Source: Clarke and Martin, 1975.
$\chi^2 = 42.30; p < 0.10$

Table 11 Previous absconders in each admission group of ten boys in relation to absconding by other members of the group (300 consecutive admissions to one training school)

No. of previous absconders in group	No. of admission groups	Mean abscondings by boys with no previous record
0	10	0.58
1	7	0.77
2	9	1.10
3	4	1.00
	30	0.82

Source: Clarke and Martin, 1975.
$\chi^2 = 15.02; p < 0.01$.

Table 12 Use of the cane and interval between absconder's return and next absconding by any boy (for all 'senior' boys absconding from one classifying school during 1960–64)

		Mean days between absconder's return and next absconding by any boy	Standard deviation
Caned	237	10.42	10.22
Not caned	131	7.86	7.84

Source: Clarke and Martin, 1975.
Standard error or difference between means = 0.95; $p < 0.01$.

rising to a peak in the autumn and dropping to a low in the summer and seemed to be accounted for by the additional abscondings taking place between the hours of 6–9 pm during the months of October to March (see Table 13). This suggested that it was the opportunity afforded by the cover of darkness in the winter evenings that provided the explanation. If so, opportunity is indeed a powerful determinant of absconding behaviour: there were about two-and-a-half times as many abscondings on winter evenings as in the summer.

As psychologists, Clarke and Martin were interested in the question of whether an act of absconding, encouraged perhaps by the presence of opportunity, could lead to a more or less stable pattern of behaviour. On the grounds that learning will increase the probability of absconding in a given situation and that through stimulus generalization it will increase the range of situations in which abscondings might occur, they predicted that the more often a boy or girl had absconded, the shorter would be the interval between recovery and the next absconding. As absconding is generally at a peak soon after admission, this

Table 13 Number of abscondings from one classifying school taking place 6.00–9.00 p.m. during the summer and winter months 1960–64

Time of abscondings	April to September	October to March
6.00 to 9.00 p.m.	64	150
All other times	207	189
Total	271	339

Source: Clarke and Martin, 1975.
χ^2 (with Yates' correction) 27.25; $p < 0.01$.

prediction might have seemed to go against existing knowledge, but it was confirmed in a study of very persistent absconders. The decline in intervals for both boys and girls studied was statistically significant and, moreover, analysis of variance showed that it fitted a typical exponential learning curve, with most 'learning' taking place as a result of earlier rather than later abscondings. This pattern was not evident in all schools and it was argued in the report that the environment in some schools brought absconding and the reinforcements for absconding under control, whereas in other schools, it allowed a habit of absconding to develop quite rapidly.

The suggestion that absconding could be learned raised the question of whether this learning could be generalized to other delinquent behaviour. This could occur because both acts are commonly regarded as delinquent or, more simply, because an absconder is more likely to commit a delinquent act while absconding (for example, by breaking into a house to get food or money). As already mentioned, Wilkins had found that the success of approved-school training could only be predicted if information about a boy's absconding was included in the equations. Clarke and Martin argued that if absconding was mainly determined by the school environment but was nevertheless associated with reoffending, this was probably because it was in some way confirming the boy in delinquency.

Following Clarke and Martin's work, two further studies (Sinclair and Clarke, 1973; Dunlop, 1974) examined the possibility that approved schools with high absconding rates or, more generally, with a high incidence of 'misbehaviour' would have higher reconviction rates than would be expected from their intakes. Sinclair and Clarke studied sixty-six approved schools and correlated school reconviction rates for boys released in 1965 with school absconding rates in 1964 (when most boys released in 1965 would have been in residence), holding constant the mean IQ and the mean number of previous court appearances for boys released from each school in 1965. The results (which were similar for all three groups of schools studied) confirmed that schools with disproportionately high absconding rates had the worst reconviction rates (see results for senior

Table 14   Senior schools' absconding rates in 1964, together with the success rates, mean intelligence, and mean previous court appearances of those discharged to after-care from each school in 1965 (correlations at foot of table)

School	Absconding rate	Success rate	Mean I Q	Mean previous court appearances
1	6.5	42.5	89.4	2.43
2	14.0	31.3	87.1	2.53
3	14.0	39.4	94.6	2.81
4	16.0	42.6	94.2	2.65
5	19.0	32.8	92.4	2.62
6	20.5	43.8	96.9	2.21
7	21.0	40.0	97.3	2.31
8	23.0	45.7	99.8	2.33
9	23.0	46.3	101.6	2.25
10	24.5	31.1	98.5	2.75
11	25.5	32.0	92.4	2.70
12	26.5	45.6	118.0	2.18
13	28.0	36.8	100.9	2.40
14	28.5	51.0	102.0	1.82
15	30.5	37.8	97.4	2.63
16	31.0	28.8	97.3	2.56
17	32.5	35.4	94.4	2.88
18	34.5	33.3	85.8	2.75
19	35.0	29.6	88.1	2.33
20	35.5	46.4	92.2	2.37
21	39.0	27.8	84.2	2.15
22	44.0	22.7	88.8	2.47

Absconding vs success rate	− 0.41
Absconding vs IQ	− 0.13
Absconding vs previous court appearances	− 0.13
Success rate vs IQ	0.58**
Success rate vs previous court appearances	− 0.46*
IQ vs previous court appearances	− 0.32
Partial correlation of absconding and success rate	− 0.51*

Source: Sinclair and Clarke, 1973.
* $p < 0.05$;   ** $p < 0.01$.

schools in Table 14). For obvious reasons this does not prove that absconding leads to failure. Nevertheless the findings lent weight to Clarke and Martin's suggestions that absconding could lead to reconviction and the implications will be discussed in more detail below.

Rather similar results were obtained in the much more detailed study of intermediate approved schools (those catering for boys aged 13–15 on admission) carried out by Dunlop. She interviewed some 400 boys who were in 8 schools during the mid-1960s about their experience of training. On the basis of their replies, scales were constructed to measure the emphasis given by each school, in the eyes of the boys, to the following aspects of training: trade training; education; relationships with adults; relationships with peers; responsibility and maturity; punishment and deterrence; leisure activities; and religion.

The main findings were that, after controlling for differences in intakes, the schools which were seen as emphasizing trade training were significantly more successful in terms of their reconviction rates, were more likely to stress mature and responsible behaviour, and had lower rates of absconding and misbehaviour. The study was, therefore, in keeping with the others summarized in this section. Firmness, consistency, and an emphasis on responsible behaviour and work can affect subsequent delinquency, but only to a very limited extent. Thus in Sinclair and Clarke's study absconding accounted for only about 10 per cent of the variation in reconviction rates, while in Dunlop's study a boy's chances of being reconvicted was only marginally related to the school he attended. Difficult behaviour, it seems, is strongly influenced by the pressures of particular environments (for example, by badly run probation hostels) and by the opportunities and models provided for particular forms of delinquency (for example, absconding). Having arisen in this way a delinquent response can generalize from one environment to another, but the ability to use behaviour in one setting as a predictor of similar behaviour in another is limited. As argued below, this conclusion has important implications for the understanding and treatment of delinquency.

Explanations

In summarizing these studies we have raised a number of key questions. Why do certain factors predict future delinquency? Why is prediction so difficult in individual cases? Why are penal treatments so ineffective? What are the theoretical implications of the variations in behaviour found in different institutions? Taken together the findings go some way to providing answers to these questions, with cross-institutional studies clarifying the implications of earlier work on prediction and the evaluation of treatment.

By way of recapitulation, the factors found to be associated with reconviction in the prediction studies were; youth, long criminal record, poor work record, absconding/misbehaviour during treatment, 'delinquent/unstable personality', 'stress/lack of support at home', 'delinquent friends', deprived urban environment. While each of these factors has a place in criminological explanation, there is no single theory that encompasses them all. Criminologists usually prefer to concentrate on one group of explanatory variables rather than attempting a more global theory. Thus some stress explanations in terms of personality traits, holding, for example, that an extraverted person is difficult to socialize and is hence resistant to discipline and the norms of respectable life. Some emphasize delinquent associates, on the premise that birds of a feather flock together thus providing models for each other's behaviour, or the contacts and knowledge required for successful criminal action. Others regard criminality and poor work record as evidence of maladaptive learning, for which the remedy should be retraining, whereas yet others see them as evidence of unhappiness or family stress for which the remedy might be casework, psychiatry or psychotherapy. More radically, some regard the association of reconviction with low social class or deprived family circumstances as evidence of a labelling process whereby the police pay more attention to the deviant activities of deprived, inner-city youth than they do to those living in middle-class suburbs.

From a practical point of view, there is an important distinction between those explanations which emphasize the delinquent's current environment (e.g. family stress or lack of supervision) and those which emphasize his behavioural and emotional inheritance. If it is personal rather than environmental factors which are important, treatment may well need to be aimed at the delinquent himself. It may therefore be reasonable to remove him from his home and family in order to provide an intensive and comprehensive period of treatment. If on the other hand it is the current environment that counts, this strategy may only be temporarily effective. Removal from home should indeed provide an effective antidote for delinquency—always providing that the new environment is less likely to induce delinquency than the last—but on return to his former home, the delinquent may be expected to return to his former ways. He is only likely to be reformed if he is removed from home for good or leaves of his own accord.

A second rather similar point relates to the degree to which the possible causal factors are seen as actually determining criminal behaviour, or simply increasing the chances that a delinquent will encounter a series of circumstances which are the true determinants of offending. For example, it could be that offending is determined by a combination of heredity and current family stress. In principle, if one then knew enough about the delinquent and his family, further offending could be predicted with certainty. Alternatively, it may be that offending and even more conviction, cannot, in principle be predicted by the kind of factors so far discussed. Criminal convictions on this view would result from a chain of circumstances: a row with a girl-friend in a pub, too much to drink, a poorly lit street, the open window of a warehouse, an alert passer-by, and a swift police response. In these circumstances prediction must necessarily remain a very approximate business.

The evidence of the prediction studies is somewhat equivocal in relation to these theoretical quandaries. The association between past offences and reconviction might be explained on the basis of personality factors, learning or, indeed, continuity of environmental stress. However, it does seem that among delinquents, future criminality is very difficult to predict with any certainty. No more than about 20–25 per cent of the variance in reconviction can be accounted for in even the most successful studies. On the face of it, this suggests that the determining effect of personality factors is not as great as some would argue. On the other hand, the general unpredictability of reconviction is consistent both with explanations which rely on individual learning (he may have acquired new responses) and with those which emphasize the role of circumstantial or temporary factors of the post-treatment environment.

The studies of treatment effectiveness, or more properly, ineffectiveness allow a similar variety of explanations. It may be that the power of the immediate environment is so great that treatments which have traditionally been aimed at the individual delinquent have little chance of success. Equally it could be that heredity or the early learning of typical delinquents is of a kind which makes them peculiarly difficult to reform.

On these issues the evidence from the cross-institutional studies is more conclusive, particularly in regard to the importance of the immediate environment in determining delinquency. In the probation-hostel study, a youth's chances of getting into further trouble with the courts varied by a factor of five depending on the hostel in which he found himself. Similar variations were found in the studies of approved schools. Moreover, the kinds of hostel regime (warm, consistent but strict) associated with low offending rates were similar to the nature of the family support found to be associated with a probationer's reduced chances of re-offending (Davies and Sinclair, 1971).

As far as this argument is concerned, the important point raised by the probation hostel study is methodological. In the case of hostels, as against families, the association between delinquency and difficult behaviour could not be explained in terms of heredity or early deprivation, or as it happens, by variations in the practices of local police or welfare workers. Thus the hostel data together with that from approved schools and the studies of probationers in the community suggested that, at least among children who had been judged delinquent, it is the immediate living situation which has a paramount effect on their chances of reoffending.

This conclusion carries with it a less-welcome corollary. If the immediate environment is so important, the influence of residential institutions may be expected to be powerful but short-term. Thus it was not surprising that, with one exception, the influence of the hostel regime though potent, was transitory, and that on return home it was the family rather than the regime that predicted the youth's chances of reoffending.

A qualification to these conclusions is provided by the approved school data which suggested that some schools were having a long-term effect, although this was almost certainly not strong. Thus in Sinclair and Clarke's (1973) study, absconding accounted for only about 10 per cent of the variation in reconviction rates, and in Dunlop's (1974) study, a boy's chance of being reconvicted was only weakly related to the school he attended. Clarke and Martin (1975) explained these effects by invoking 'social learning theory' concepts:

We believe that the main reason why boys (and girls) feel impelled to run away from the school is that they have met or been placed in a situation that makes them unhappy or anxious, and absconding is a way of dealing with these feelings. There are a great many situations in which a boy could be made anxious; it may be because he has been bullied, because he is in trouble with the staff, because a friend has left the school. . . . Even in the best-run schools all boys will from time to time encounter situations that make them unhappy. But not all boys run away and this is because absconding is only one of a number of competing responses to feelings of misery and anxiety. For example, a boy who is miserable may deal with his feelings by picking a fight with another boy . . . he may share his feelings with another boy or a member of staff. . . Which of these competing responses he makes will depend on the variety of internal and environmental cues he experiences at the time. . . If he has not experienced directly comparable situations, the most influential cues may be. . . the opportunities open to him to abscond (or perform a competing response). . . The experiences consequent upon absconding, if it occurs, will help to determine whether or not the boy will abscond again when placed in a similar position. . . The simple relief of getting away from an anxiety-provoking situation in the school might be a sufficiently powerful reinforcement in some cases, but there are other ways in which a boy could find absconding rewarding. He may initially be welcomed at home, he may enjoy himself while away from school, and on his return he might have some brief prestige among the other boys. The probability of repeating the behaviour could be lowered through being caught quickly, having a miserable time on the run, or even, perhaps, through being caned on return to school.

Clarke and Martin further argued, for reasons given above, that absconding increases the probability of future delinquent responses and the theoretical links between school environment, absconding and reconviction are illustrated in Figure 1.

Clarke and Martin's theory explains the initial unpredictability of misbehaviour by individual boys and also the fact that absconding or difficult behaviour tends to predict similar behaviour in other situations. The theory therefore knits together the results we have presented and provides answers to the questions raised at the beginning of this section. There is some persistence of behaviour from one situation to another and to this extent effective treatment is possible. However, what is probably learned is a repertoire of responses which can be drawn on in particular situations and the power of the immediate environment is clearly much greater than usually thought. This basic premise provides a plausible explanation for what are at best the weak effects of treatment.

More ambitiously this argument could form part of a general theory of the process of acquiring and persisting in a delinquent way of life. Such a theory needs to show how broad social factors (social class, urban residence etc.) affects the distribution of opportunities to offend, the availability of delinquent models,

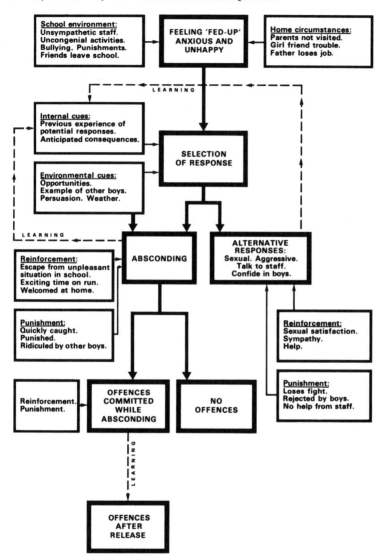

Figure 1 The development of absconding and its relationship with offending after release

and the nature of the response from police or other agencies, as well as the way in which heredity and early learning can make an initial delinquent response more probable. The range of factors needing to be accommodated in such a general explanation have been summarized by Clarke (1977).

Practical implications

Most of the research described above had been completed and reported by the mid-1970s. At the time, the focus upon reconviction attracted considerable criticism, on grounds that the offences involved were often trivial, follow-up periods were too short, and other indices of adjustment such as employment and personal relationships were neglected. However, even if offending had not provided the main reason for being placed in treatment in the first place, it has been found to be associated with poor adjustment in many other areas of a person's life (Glueck and Glueck, 1934; Scott, 1964; Hood, 1966). In practice, the use of longer periods of follow-up than the standard 2- or 3-year period provides an even more depressing picture, as shown in a Home Office study undertaken by Hammond (1968): he found that about 60 per cent of 254 senior approved school boys followed up till their twenty-fifth birthdays had become continuous and persistent offenders, and 40 per cent had received sentences of imprisonment as adults. Most researchers, including ourselves, have therefore considered reconviction an essential measure of the effectiveness of treatments aimed at delinquents (cf Tutt, 1978).

The ineffectiveness of institutional treatments in terms of reducing reconviction is now widely accepted, and some local authorities have made use of the findings in closing down CHEs or reducing their size. There are now some fifteen fewer CHEs than there were approved schools, and, because many have been reduced in size, between them they provide only about two-thirds of the places formerly available. Some of the children who would otherwise have been cared for in CHEs are now fostered (Hazel, 1978), supervized at home, or placed in some other form of care. It is likely, however, that the authorities have been influenced as much by a distaste for institutions and a need to save money as by their demonstrated ineffectiveness in terms of reconviction. Magistrates seem to have been either less impressed by the findings or to have greater regard for the need to put delinquents where they can do no harm. The other side of the coin is that some boys who would formerly have been in approved schools are now in borstals, where the numbers of offenders aged 15 and 16 sentenced to borstal training increased from 260 in 1971 (when the community homes system came into being) to 1666 in 1979.

It is not altogether surprising that the net effect of the research on institutional provision has been no greater. Apart from treatment, institutions fulfil a number of other functions—deterrence, containment, provision of shelter and education—which are difficult to serve in alternative ways. For many deprived children an institution may provide their only experience of concerned and sustained care. On the other side, there is the wish to demonstrate by means of firm punishment that certain delinquent acts are unacceptable. Many people also believe that the best way to deal with delinquents is a spell of custody, and that where this has not worked in the past it is because the regimes have been too soft.

Reconviction essential measure of effectiveness of Treatment

Faced with these conflicting requirements, a court may decide that, irrespective of any remedial effects, committal to an institution is the most appropriate response to the persistent criminality of a homeless and deprived youth.

A more radical response to the research findings requires a new analysis of the role of institutions, which places less emphasis on treatment and more on the other goals that institutions can actually achieve. In the light of such analysis, it would be possible to examine, for example, how far institutions are in fact being used for children who are either dangerous or deprived (cf Cawson and Martell, 1979), and whether the public demand for punishment could be satisfied by other forms of disposal.

On the arguments presented in this paper, changes in institutional regime are unlikely to improve long-term effectiveness. Thus the guiding principle for those in charge of institutions should be to provide the kind of environment in which children might be expected to live (cf Tizard, 1975). Such institutions should still be concerned to reduce absconding—it makes very little sense to remove boys and girls from homes where they are receiving inadequate care if they are subsequently exposed to the even greater dangers of being 'on the run'. They might also attempt to provide those skills required on release as well as the combination of firmness, consistency and kindness which appears to evoke the best behaviour from residents.

In fact, we know of few attempts to apply the lessons of the research reported in this paper to the way in which institutions are actually run. Instead, the changes which have been reported in the literature seem to be more in response to political pressures (additional places in secure accommodation, cf Millham et al., 1978), or to have been the result of very broad trends in child care and clinical psychology. In particular, there have been some conscious attempts to establish therapeutic regimes in order to bring about behavioural change (e.g. Mayers, 1980), despite the unfavourable verdict of previous evaluations, and some experimentation with behaviour modification (e.g. Hoghughi, 1979). While these latter experiments may ease problems of institutional management, it is very unlikely that improvements in behaviour will generalize to the post-treatment environment.

The hopes placed in such innovations may reflect the fact that the reasons for the ineffectiveness of institutional treatment are not widely understood. Put at their simplest, these are that institutional treatments necessarily operate on a 'medical model' which assumes that it is the child himself who needs to be changed, rather than, as has been suggested by the research, his current living circumstances, especially those relating to his home and family. Institutions certainly induce short-term change in children, but neither they nor fieldworkers find it easy to change families, who are therefore likely to undermine the effects of institutional placement. The only real alternative may therefore be to remove the child entirely, by adoption, fostering, or as was sometimes the case in the past, by following institutional placement by a life at sea or in the services. Generally, more attention should be paid to plans for children after they leave care, and particularly to the possibility that not all may need to return to their families and that some may wish to maintain links with institutional staff or foster parents to whom they have become attached.

In the final analysis, the most appropriate role for institutions might be the task of caring for the small minority of offenders who are very deprived or likely to become a long-term danger to the community. Other measures will be needed to cope with the very different problem of the volume of crime. In this connection it is important not to invest community treatments with the mantle that institutional ones divest. In particular, there is no reason to expect that schemes of 'intermediate treatment' (Thorpe, 1978), which concentrate upon the provision of leisure opportunities or casework for delinquent children, and which do not attempt to alter the quality of the relationships between child and parents, the nature of the supervision afforded, or the influence of peers, will be any more effective than the treatment provided in CHEs or other institutions.

Apart from being generally cheaper than institutional treatment, however, community treatments have the major advantage of involving minimal intervention, which the evidence suggests may be the most rational response to most delinquency. The overwhelming majority of delinquent acts consists rather trivial property offences of theft or damage. Nearly all children commit such acts at one time or another (cf Belson, 1975) and the great majority of offenders—even a substantial proportion of the more persistent ones—grow out of the behaviour (Knight and West, 1975). This seems to be because their lives change in ways incompatible with continuing delinquency (they get a job they want to keep, they form a relationship with a girl who disapproves of delinquency, the peer group breaks up, they lose their emotional or physical dependence on their parents). In keeping with this situation, most disposals take the form of cautions, conditional discharges or fines. Even so, the incidence of institutionalization in this country seems to be high compared to that in others. The danger with more extreme intervention, however well intentioned, is that it may impede a natural process of 'desistance' (cf Trasler, 1979), and that a delinquent identity may be reinforced as a result of 'labelling' (cf Farrington et al., 1978).

These arguments suggest that the social services have little to offer in respect of delinquency per se. This may be a difficult conclusion for them to accept. Given the pressures upon them to 'do something' about delinquent children, there is the temptation to argue that all would be well if only they had the resources to do the job properly, or if the service could be truly preventive with intervention being at a much earlier stage. Such hopes are vain. The number of children who behave in a delinquent way is so great and their future delinquency is so unpredictable that no treatment programmes could reach all those likely to become confirmed offenders. Moreover, the track records of all acceptable treatments are so poor that to use them to try to reduce reconviction among persistent offenders is to waste resources that could be better directed elsewhere. For example, more than 70 per cent of children who have been in secure units—the most intensive (and expensive) residential provision for delinquents currently available—go on to some other form of custody either on leaving the unit or within two years from release (Millham *et al.*, 1978).

These points have to be put strongly, because attempts to prevent or cure delinquency can divert social service departments from tasks such as the provision of home helps for the elderly and the disabled, or day nurseries for the children of families under stress, which are equally important and which they can successfully perform. In addition, their attempts to deal with delinquents can divert resources and public support away from other more promising approaches to the management of crime such as the court referral procedures for truants pioneered in Leeds (Berg *et al.*, 1978), the development of community policing (Alderson, 1979), or the possibilities of school reform (Rutter *et al.*, 1979).

One other general approach to prevention has derived from the lesson of the institutional research that opportunity can be a powerful determinant of crime. This idea has been subjected to test in an extensive programme of Home Office research, and the conclusion reached is that certain troublesome forms of offending can be significantly reduced by 'situational' measures aimed at reducing opportunities for crime through environmental management and design (Clarke, 1980; Clarke and Mayhew, 1980).

What began as a rather narrow focus of research into institutional treatment has therefore provided the basis for a more generalized understanding of delinquent conduct, and has opened up a number of other possibilities for crime prevention which in turn need to be systematically evaluated. What is needed is a fresh look at the various objectives of the measures we have been discussing, and a fresh attempt to define the minimum acceptable response to a delinquent act. A new approach to criminal policy cannot be achieved, however, by research alone, or even by policy-makers and practitioners attempting to apply the lessons from research. It is also dependent on what enough of the public will accept. In our view the ideology of treatment has for too long obscured the key issues of criminal policy, and hindered the public debate which must precede long-term change.

References

Alderson, J. (1979). *Policing Freedom*, Macdonald and Evans, Plymouth.
Belson, W. A. (1975). *Juvenile Theft: The Causal Factors*, Harper and Row London.
Berg, I., Consterdine, M., Hullin, R., McGuire, R., and Tyrer, S. (1978). A randomly controlled trial of two court procedures in truancy, *British Journal of Criminology*, **18**, 232–244.
Bottoms, A. E. and McClintock, F. H. (1973). *Criminals Coming of Age*, Heinemann, London.

Brody, S. R. (1976). *The Effectiveness of Sentencing—A Review of the Literature*, Home Office Research Study No. 35, HMSO, London.

Campbell, J. and Davies, G. (1965). Success rates, *Approved Schools Gazette*, October, 299.

Cawson, P. and Martell, M. (1979). *Children Referred to Closed Units*, DHSS Statistics and Research Division, Report No. 5, HMSO, London.

Clarke, R. V. G. (1977). Psychology and crime, *Bulletin of the British Psychological Society*, **30**, 280–3.

Clarke, R. V. G. (1980). 'Situational' crime prevention: theory and practice. *British Journal of Criminology*, **20**, 136–147.

Clarke, R. V. G. and Martin, D. N. (1971). *Absconding from Approved Schools*, Home Office Research Study No. 12, HMSO, London.

Clarke, R. V. G. and Martin, D. N. (1975). A study of absconding and its implications for the residential treatment of delinquents, Tizard, J., Sinclair, I. A. C., and Clarke, R. V. G. (Eds) in *Varieties of Residential Experience* (Eds J. Tizard, I. A. C. Sinclair and R. V. G. Clarke) Routledge and Kegan Paul, London.

Clarke, R. V. G. and Mayhew, P. (Eds) (1980). *Designing Out Crime*, HMSO, London.

Cockett, R. (1967). Borstal training: a follow-up study, *British Journal of Criminology*, **20**, 150–183.

Cornish, D. B. and Clarke, R. V. G. (1975). *Residential Treatment and its Effects on Delinquency*, Home Office Research Study No. 32, HMSO, London.

Craft, M. (1965). A follow up study of disturbed juvenile delinquents, *British Journal of Criminology*, **5**, 55–62.

Craft, M., Stephenson, G., and Granger, C. (1964). A controlled trial of authoritarian and self-governing regimes with adolescent psychopaths, *American Journal of Orthopsychiatry*, **34**, 543–554.

Davies, M. (1967). *The Use of the Jesness Inventory on a Sample of British Probationers*, Studies in the Causes of Delinquency and the Treatment of Offenders No. 12, HMSO, London.

Davies, M. (1969). *Probationers in their Social Environment* Home Office Research Study No. 2, HMSO, London.

Davies, M. and Sinclair, I. A. C. (1971). Families, hostels, and delinquents: an attempt to assess cause and effect, *British Journal of Criminology*, **11**, 213–29.

Dunlop, A. (1974). *The Approved School Experience*, Home Office Research Study No. 25, HMSO, London.

Empey, L. T. and Lubeck, S. G. (1971). *The Silverlake Experiment: Testing Delinquency Theory and Community Intervention*, Aldine Publishing Co., Chicago.

Farrington, D. P., Osborn, S. G., and West, D. J. (1978). The persistence of labelling effects, *British Journal of Criminology*, **18**, 277–284.

Glueck, S. and Glueck, E. T. (1934). *One thousand Delinquents: Their Treatment by Court and Clinic*, (Reprinted 1965). Kraus Reprint Corporation, New York.

Hammond, W. H. (1964). Research reported in the *Sentence of the Court*, HMSO, London.

Hazel, N. (1978). The use of family placements in the treatment of delinquency, in *Alternative Strategies for Coping with Crime*. (Ed. N. Tutt) Basil Blackwell and Martin Robertson, Oxford and London.

Hoghughi, M. (1979). The Aycliffe token economy, *British Journal of Criminology*, **19**, 384–399.

Hood, R. G., (1966). *Homeless Borstal Boys: A Study of their After-Care and After Conduct*, Occasional Papers on Social Administration, No. 18, Bell and Sons, London.

Jesness, C. F. (1963). *Redevelopment and Revalidation of the Jesness Inventory*, California Youth Authority Research Report No. 35, Sacramento.
Jesness, C. F. (1965). *The Fricot Ranch Study*, California Department of the Youth Authority, Sacramento.
Jesness, C. F. (1971). The Preston Typology Study: an experiment with differential treatment in an institution, *Journal of Research in Crime and Delinquency*, **8**, 38–52.
Jesness, C. F., DeRisi, W. J., McCormick, P. M., and Wedge, R. F. (1972). *The Youth Centre Research Project*, American Justice Institute in co-operation with California Youth Authority, Sacramento.
Knight, B. J. and West, D. J. (1975). Temporary and continuing delinquency, *British Journal of Criminology*, **15**, 43–50.
Mannheim, H. and Wilkins, L. T. (1955). *Prediction Methods in Relation to Borstal Training*, HMSO, London.
Martin, D. N. (1977). Disruptive behaviour and staff attitudes at the St. Charles Youth Treatment Centre, *Journal of Child Psychology and Psychiatry*, **18**, 221–228.
Martinson, R. (1974). What works?—questions and answers about prison reform. *The Public Interest*, Spring, 22–34.
Mayers, M. O. (1980). *The Hard-Core Delinquent*, Saxon House, Farnborough.
McMichael, P. (1974). After-care, family relationships, and re-conviction in a Scottish approved school, *British Journal Of Criminology*, **14**, 236–347.
Millham, S., Bullock, R., and Hosie, K. (1978). *Locking up Children: Secure Provision within the Child-Care System*, Saxon House, Farnborough.
Mott, J. (1973). Relationship between scores on the Jesness Inventory and reconviction for approved school boys, *Community Schools Gazette*, **67**, 212–214 and 220–221.
Murray, C. A. and Cox, L. A. (1979). *Beyond Probation: Juvenile Corrections and the Chronic Delinquent.*, Sage Publications, Beverly Hills.
Rapoport, R. (1960). *The Community as Doctor*, Tavistock Publications, London.
Rutter, M., Maughan, B., Mortimore, P., Ouston, J., and Smith, A. (1979). *Fifteen Thousand Hours: Secondary Schools and their Effects on Children*, Open Books, London.
Scott, P. D. (1964). Approved School success rates, *British Journal of Criminology*, **4**, 525–556.
Simon, F. H. (1971). *Prediction Methods in Criminology*, Home Office Research Study No. 7, HMSO, London.
Sinclair, I. A. C. (1971). *Hostels for Probationers*, Home Office Research Study No. 6, HMSO, London.
Sinclair, I. A. C. and Clarke, R. V. G. (1973). Acting-out behaviour and its significance for the residential treatment of delinquents, *Journal of Child Psychology and Psychiatry*, **14**, 283–291.
Thorpe, D. (1978). Intermediate Treatment, in *Alternative Strategies for Coping with Crime* (Ed. N. Tutt), Basil Blackwell and Martin Robertson, Oxford and London.
Tizard, J. (1975). Quality of residential care for retarded children, in *Varieties of Residential Experience* (Eds J. Tizard, I. A. C. Sinclair, and R. V. G. Clarke), Routledge and Kegan Paul, London.
Tizard, J., Sinclair, I. A. C., and Clarke, R. V. G. (1975). *Varieties of Residential Experience*, Routledge and Kegan Paul, London.
Trasler, G. B. (1979). Delinquency, recidivism, and desistance, *British Journal of Criminology*, **19**, 314–322.
Tutt, N. (Ed.) (1978). *Alternative Strategies for Coping with Crime*, Basil Blackwell and Martin Robertson, Oxford and London.

Weeks, S. Ashley (1958). *Youthful Offenders at Highfields* University of Michigan Press, Ann Arbor.

West, D. J. and Farrington, D. P. (1973). *Who Becomes Delinquent*, Heinemann, London.

Wilkins, L. T. (unpublished) Prediction methods in relation to approved school training. Home Office Research Unit Report (unpublished).

Williams, M. (1970). *A Study of Some Aspects of Borstal Allocation*, Report No. 33. Office of the Chief Psychologist, Prison Department, Home Office, HMSO, London.

Wilson, J. Q. (1980). 'What works?' revisited: new findings on criminal rehabilitation, *The Public Interest*, No 61, 3–17.

Developments in the Study of Criminal Behaviour
Volume 1: The Prevention and Control of Offending
Edited by P. Feldman
© 1982 John Wiley & Sons, Ltd.

4

The Development and Maintenance of a Behavioural Regime in a Secure Youth Treatment Centre

IAN REID

Glenthorne Youth Treatment Centre (GYTC) is situated in a suburb of Birmingham. It is a purpose-built secure unit with three living units, a studies block and recreational facilities within a secure perimeter. In addition, there is an open unit outside security and a hostel sited in the grounds of the Centre. The Centre is designed to take up to Sixty children.

Introduction

In the United Kingdom, local authorities carry the major responsibility for the residential care of young offenders as well as children in need of care and protection. Under the Children and Young Person's Act (1969), Approved Schools in their existing forms were abolished and an integrated system of Community Homes for all children in need of care was established. Many approved schools, which had been under the overall responsibility of the Home Office were made the direct responsibility of local authorities and renamed Community Homes with Education. Regional planning committees were also introduced to ensure the most effective use and development of resources in a given geographical area. Perhaps the most significant result of the 1969 legislation was, that at central government level the responsibility for the overall development of the services passed from the Home Office to the Department of Health and Social Security (DHSS).

There are a variety of other residential provisions for maladjusted and emotionally disturbed children, particularly those with learning difficulties and problems of school adjustment provided by local authorities. In addition, a number of independent residential schools provide places for maladjusted pupils and for those children displaying signs of mental illness, there are units and hostels attached to psychiatric hospitals and child guidance clinics.

It was felt, however, that there was a minority of children for whom any of the foregoing facilities had proved inadequate. To meet the needs of this relatively small group of children, additional specialized treatment provision was made by the DHSS in the form of the Youth Treatment Centres. The first was opened in 1971 and the second, Glenthorne, received its first child in February, 1978.

Youth Treatment Centres were not intended to serve an homogeneous population of disturbed children of just one type of problem, but have developed as a response to various problems arising in different parts of the child care world. The needs YTCs are intended to meet are clearly summarized by Barlow (1978).

1. There was originally a small group of both boys and girls who could not be coped with by the existing Approved School system. Special Units offering secure accommodation had been set up to take boys out of the Schools who were seen as a disruptive 'hard core' but amongst these were a few more who were regarded as 'highly disturbed' and thought to need more specialised, long term care than these Units could offer. (Martell and Cawson, 1975).
2. At that time there was a lack of any secure provision whatever (except prisons and remand centres) for the care of difficult girls. There was no equivalent to the boys' secure units which could take the disruptive or habitual absconders out of girls' Approved Schools.
3. Finally, a number of cases began to appear before the courts involving children who had committed very serious offences (an eleven year-old girl's conviction for murder among them; Sereny, 1972), and which attracted considerable publicity and political interest. The lack of any suitable place for these children which was both secure in the interests of public safety and also more appropriate for the child than adult offender establishments, caused some embarrassment to the authorities.

Youth Treatment Centres were designed to meet these differing needs. It is only when attempts are made to reconcile these aims in practice that the considerable difficulty of the task becomes clear. While legislation and professional advice might appear to make it clear which types of young people were 'in need of security' and the type of provision they required, the practice which continued and 'developed' was manifestly lacking in clarity.

The early admissions policy for YTCs provides one such example. All applications were and still are, considered by an admissions panel under the chairmanship of an administrator and consisting of professional advisers at the DHSS, together with the Directors of the two Youth Treatment Centres. Selection is basically a paper exercise—files are read and a decision is made whether or not a child is suitable for YTC placement. It is only some time after this panel that Centre staff will actually meet the child.

Youth Treatment Centres are a scarce national resource and despite an early attempt to produce a typology covering different groups from which admissions would be made it was of limited usefulness. The lack of clear criteria for admission involves far more than consideration of a child's reported behaviours. Many reports received show clear evidence of the labelling processes which often invade assessment (Cawson and Martell, 1979; Gibbons, 1975) yet provide little data on the frequency problem behaviours, their antecedents and maintaining consequences.

If investigation extends beyond the child's pathology a variety of other problems come to light. Authorities differ widely in the provision they make for difficult adolescents. To what extent, therefore, should some authorities be rescued from, and perhaps reinforced for, their failure or inability to make adequate provision? Similarly, individual institutions vary considerably in their ability to cope with absconding and violent or disruptive young people (Cawson and Martell, 1979; Millham et al., 1978). How far should they be provided with an option which may perpetuate their bad practice or lack of skills? Emotive labelling, e.g. highly disturbed, political pressure and public anxiety, all play their part but having raised the problems of admissions criteria, it is important to note that certain factors are relatively clear.

As a rule the centres admit boys and girls between the ages of 12 and 18. Although they may prefer younger children of 13–14 so as to maximize potential treatment gains, they frequently admit older children. Secondly, children should have been committed to the care of the local authority, or the local authority have assumed parental rights, or a child may have been sentenced by a court to a period of detention under Section 53 of the Children and Young Person's Act (1933). Thirdly, authorities are expected to demonstrate that other resources have been tried first and proven inadequate. A professional would only seek to use the secure condition of a YTC if no other suitable alternative could be found. However, it can also be strongly argued that an early placement in a YTC with its relatively high level of treatment resources may be in the long-term interests of the child. An early concerted treatment intervention may well have a better chance of success than a succession of placements based on expediency.

Barlow (1979), argues that probably the most influential single factor deciding an admission is the existence of an element of danger either to others or the child himself. With improvement in assessment methods, it is hoped that later discussion may be able to indicate some groups of behaviour which might be effectively modified in conditions of graded security.

While the stated aim of YTCs 'to provide long term care and treatment first within conditions of total security, and then in increasingly open conditions' appears to make it clear what types of treatment provision is necessary, investigation of the Child Care field gave little clear idea as to how effective treatment methods could be tailored to the needs of the client group in secure conditions. Even now, many of the 'innovations' in the Child Care field represent shifts in ideology, e.g. Intermediate Treatment is good, with scant attention being paid to the technology needed to underpin an approach. For example; what is the *treatment* ingredient of IT? As Mayers (1980) notes, 'the words "treatment" and "therapy" have been so bandied about for the past decade that they have become meaningless purely because they have been given so many different meanings'.

Clearly many treatment programmes within the Child Care system fail to meet their stated therapeutic goals. Often failure reflects practical difficulties, e.g.

staffing, finance, etc., but frequently it is a result of a deeper deficiency within the Child Care system itself. While the commitment of most care workers is beyond question, their therapeutic value may be suspect. Indeed, many workers in the field readily question their own efficacy as 'agents of change'. The fault is not theirs. In addition to the practical problems they face, at least two other factors play a part:

1. The translation of theoretical concepts, behavioural of otherwise, into practical, replicable therapeutic techniques is frequently inadequate.
2. The training that many residential staff receive (if any) to equip them to become competent therapists is frequently directed towards nebulous or inappropriate goals, e.g. a disproportionate amount of time appears to be devoted to self-analysis and the importance of relationships (often ill-defined) and significantly less attention to what could be done about problem behaviours and the means of doing so.

Glenthorne

In the light of the conflicting and unresolved debates on theories of behaviour and their translations into practice, senior management at Glenthorne decided that a clear lead needed to be given. The decision was based on two grounds:

1. Stoll (1968) points to the sources of strain in any social control network which may derive from the wide ideological perspectives held by staff. Therefore, it was felt crucially important to provide a framework which would achieve an initial level of staff consistency, and
2. following several fact-finding visits to Achievement Place, Boys Town in the USA and Chelfham Mill School in the UK, the progress in care and treatment seen in these programmes encouraged senior management to opt for a specific treatment approach. The decision was made to commit the centre to a global approach based on the principles of Social Learning Theory.

The overall philosophy was that no one should be allowed to hide behind professional roles or lobby for the dominance of his profession. All involved were expected to assess and treat the problem behaviours faced as and when required. Equally the aim was to design a system that is as clearly defined (for both staff and children), and is as positive and flexible as possible.

As any practitioner knows, to implement such as aim depends on far more than a decision to follow a particular theoretical orientation. Any programme is dependent for its success on the complex interaction between a number of important factors.

1. The planning of a sufficiently clear basic treatment programme which would serve as a workable therapeutic model but also serve as the basis for future developments.
2. An understanding on the part of local and national resource allocators as to the therapeutic requirements of the system, e.g. the provision of reinforcers, staff training, etc.
3. The mechanisms by which 'specialist' advice and training could be made readily available to staff at all levels.
4. The kinds of problem behaviours children have exhibited prior to admission in terms of deficits and excesses, e.g. lack of temper control, self-mutilation, etc. Perhaps of equal importance are the kinds of problem behaviours which may arise following admission as a result of living in secure conditions with other disturbed adolescents.

Staffing

Originally the centre was under the management of a Director, assisted by a Deputy Director in charge of the treatment programme and staff training. Each unit, then as now, has a Unit Leader and a team of twelve 'groupworkers'. These are men and women qualified in residential social work, teaching or nursing, all of whom share in the therapeutic and child-care elements of the programme. In addition, there was a small group of specialist teachers, accountable to the Assistant Director (Education) who worked a normal teaching day in the studies block. Their function was to provide the core of the studies programme and they were assisted on a daily basis by groupworkers in both the behavioural and academic teaching. These 'front line' therapists had access to a limited amount of specialist support: one full time and one part time clinical psychologist and a senior social worker. Staff received weekly support on a group basis from a visiting psychotherapist whose function was to discuss difficulties encountered during work. The task of the treatment staff was facilitated by administrative civil servants al local and national level.

While most of senior and middle management had experience of working with difficult adolescents and/or working in secure conditions, many of the group-workers did not. Although some had experience of therapeutic communities, community homes and work in ordinary schools, a significant minority had no practical experience at all, coming direct from training colleges or University. In addition, only two members of the original staff had any experience of working within behavioural programmes.

Staff were bonded together in teams and although paid widely differing pay scales, depending on their professional background, were expected to deal equally with the problems encountered. All were expected to cope with problem bahaviours of the young people, learn the administration of a unit, cope with security, communication problems and, for many, adapt to a shift system. In addition, staff were expected to assist in the design and implementation of a bahavioural regime consisting of an overall management system together with individual programmes for each boy and girl. It is no surprise that these demands had a marked effect on staff's behaviour and the nature and development of the programme.

Programme planning

Despite a management decision to introduce a programme based on social learning theory, the amount of support in terms of detailed planning, specialist support and staff training was far less than that needed to guarantee the development of the treatment programme.

Concerted efforts were made to provide staff with as much experience of social learning theory as possible in practice. Before the centre opened, many went on placement to units whose task approximated to that of Glenthorne. Two senior memers of staff visited the USA (Achievement Place, Kansas, the new regime at Boys' Town, Nebraska and the Centre for Community Youth Development and Achievement, Tucson) in order to gain practical advice on programme design and recording methods. Many 'specialists' within the UK contributed their advice and provided training sessions for the staff. However, although the centre quickly realized the need to appoint a permanent behavioural psychologist as overall adviser to the programme it took more than a year of Civil Service deliberation and 6 months after the centre opened before the appointment was made.

The staff made strenuous attempts to assimilate and consolidate their increasing awareness of the social learning approach and relate their knowledge to the behaviour problems anticipated. Lengthy group meetings determined policy on rights, points systems, punishment contingencies and as many other areas of the centre's proposed functioning as possible. Much of the credit for these efforts must go to the then Deputy Director (G. Barlow). Although it is possible to criticize the preparation and planning, it is difficult to identify an alternative course of action given the centre's resources at that time.

Nevertheless, while utilizing the staff group to design the system has advantages in terms of reaching general agreement on certain issues, such as children's rights, there were also problems with this approach. Aspects of the programme were based on sound behavioural principles, e.g. earning reinforcers for acceptable behaviour, others were based on previous experience of members of the group (particularly from St Charles—the original YTC), and still others were due to pressures by individuals in the group, e.g. a ban on smoking (later reversed). Finally, a number of strategies were based inevitably, on the staff's hypotheses about situations they might encounter, e.g. the punishment system. The overall result was a programme labelled as behavioural but containing elements drawn from widely different theoretical and practical models, which were later to conflict when the centre became optional.

Administrative framework

Many of the resources needed to facilitate and implement the treatment programme are not under the control of professional staff within the centre. Social Work Service and Medical divisions of the DHSS provide a valuable specialist contribution and channel communications with the Home Office on Section 53 children. Unions and local authority social work departments also, rightly, make a contribution to the nature of the therapeutic service. Programme planning apart, most important areas are controlled by a variety of administrative departments within the DHSS (see Figure 1).

Overall budget and spending, e.g. equipment, staff training, etc., are controlled by Finance Division and Children's Division. All matters relating to staff recruitment, pay and conditions are the province of Establishments and Personnel branches. Perhaps the strangest anomaly, from a professional point of view, is that all repairs and alterations to the building are controlled by the Property Services Agency of the Department of the Environment. Therefore, any changes or urgent repairs have to be negotiated with a completely separate government department. On occasions, it has been extremely difficult to convince them of urgent treatment needs, e.g. the replacement of damaged windows and locks which can seriously compromise security and endanger both staff and children.

Within the centre all budgets are controlled by Administration as are

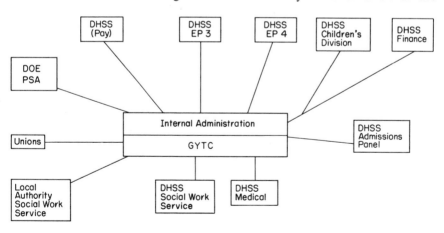

PSA; Public Services Agency
DOE; Department of the Environment

Figure 1   Official departments with direct input to GYTC

transport, food and clerical support. As in many institutions, the reinforcers of internal and external administration frequently conflict with those of professional staff. As a result continuous major efforts need to be made to ensure the maintenance of treatment principles, e.g. that reinforcers should be contingent on appropriate behaviour, be delivered as quickly as possible and should be defined as far as possible, by the recipients. The efforts needed to shape these behaviours match anything that has been needed in treatment terms.

Behavioural categories

The types, intensity, frequency and duration of problem behaviours are many and varied. Table 1 summarises many of the major problems encountered.

Clearly, any defined treatment programme needed to be sufficiently all embracing to encompass the area of concern. Given the wide variations encountered and the particular problem that some problem behaviours cannot be dealt with directly in the centre, e.g. certain offence behaviours and much of the family work, constant attempts were required to broaden the areas of therapeutic

Table 1

1. Major offence behaviours 　Murder 　Manslaughter 　Armed Robbery 　Sexual Assaults 　Arson	5. Behavioural excesses 　Physical violence 　　(persons and property) 　Self mutilation 　　(head banging, wrist slashing, 　　overdoses) 　Verbal violence
2. Minor offence behaviours 　Theft 　Take and drive away 　Burglary 　Prostitution	6. Institutional problem behaviours 　Hostages 　Sit in/barricades 　Sexual behaviour 　Violence 　Attempted escapes
3. 'Clinical' problems 　Obessional rituals e.g. 　　washing, dressing, thoughts 　Enuresis 　Faecal smearing 　Anxiety	7. Problems of generalization 　Self-help skills 　Job skills—interview behaviour, 　　work skills, etc. 　Family conflicts 　Deviant peer-group influences 　Abscondings
4. Behavioural deficits 　Limited intellectual ability 　Lack of educational attainment 　Lack of social skills 　　(verbal and non-verbal) 　Lack of survival skills 　　(e.g. self-help, budgeting, etc.)	

intervention and provide the resources necessary to do so. Considerable effort was needed from all involved in the treatment programme to even attempt to meet the stated aim of providing an individual programme for each boy and girl.

The original programme

As soon as the initial programme was put into effect, it immediately highlighted many of the theoretical and practical anomalies discussed earlier. Following a paper selection process, centre staff were able to visit each young person but the primary aim of such visits did not involve formal assessment. As Barlow (1978) notes,

the purpose of the visit is to meet the young person . . . facilitate his/her admission by removing uncertainties/worries about the kind of people and place we are. To learn more about the young person and his feelings about admission, to elicit any prospects of active participation in the treatment method and establish any goals the young person, social services or family have.

Although later assessment was by standard questionnaire (GYTC Behavioural Checklist) much of the early assessment was subjective and/or based on reports of earlier placements.

Initial intervention

The aim of the induction period was to introduce the youngsters to the programme. For the first 10 weeks in the secure units each child began on a time-based scheme. The management system concentrated on the child's performance of a daily schedule, including getting up and bed-time routines, compulsory daily meetings of the unit group, being 'on-task' during the studies programme and general behaviour on the unit. Points were earned for successful completion of each session of the schedule and not given if the required behaviour did not occur. Definition of acceptable and unacceptable bahaviours were determined as clearly as possible in advance. Each child could earn approximately 1080–1200 points per day (depending on bonus earnings) which could be 'spent' on a variety of reinforcers. These included, within units, buying TV time, extra sports facilities and additions to rooms, e.g. stools, posters, etc. In addition, the centre shop could be used to purchase consumables, e.g. coke, sweets, etc. And other longer-term reinforcers, such as LPs, toys, specific clothing, personalized items, etc. The banking system also ensured that all children could 'save' to purchase regular reinforcers, e.g. additional camping trips, pop concerts, etc. One of the most potent reinforcers was, and is, the earning of 'mobility'. Periods out of the centre were, and are, graded on both time and variety situation basis.

Initially, over a period of months and based on points earnings, any individual could earn an increasing number of trips out for recreational/social purposes.

Once a basic level of mobility had been attained, certain additional mobility trips could occur. As part of the educational programme, increasingly long periods were used to practice skills outside the centre, such as budgeting and job-finding skills. Although such trips were contingent on a period of acceptable behaviour prior to the trip they were not specifically point dependent. Similarly, children's pocket money was, and is, regarded as a right and is not within the earnings system.

Even with a largely positive programme, it was recognized that problem behaviours would occur and that some form of judicious control system was necessary. As Ross and Price (1976) rightly caution, a regime can become too punative. Punishment frequently has an immediate (if temporary) suppressing effect on behaviour which could become sufficiently reinforcing to staff such that sanctions became the technique of choice rather than the last resort. Moreover, demotion could lead to the recipient's 'losing hope' and, therefore, no longer responding positively.

Therefore, the punishment system was based on three premises:

1. It should be as limited as possible and have maximum opportunity for each child to correct his behaviour.
2. It should be as explicit as possible so as to protect both staff and children.
3. Medication would not be used unless no other means could be found to prevent a child causing serious physical harm to himself. (It has only been used once since Glenthorne opened.)

The system had graded levels of sanction. Acceptable and unacceptable behaviours were designated in advance. The latter included violence, stealing, abuse and damage to property and certain points levels were assigned to each behaviour. If prompting failed a penalty card would be given, replacing the usual earnings card. This card would carry a penalty point value which had to be 'earned off' in the usual way before access were regained to the earning (and spending) card. It is important to note that points earned previously were not deducted but 'frozen' until access was regained. Penalty points values varied from minor offences (250 points approximately) through medium (700) to a ceiling level of 1000 points, which was about a day's earnings. This could be reached either by accumulation of minor unacceptable behaviours or a very serious misdemeanour, e.g. major physical assault on staff/children. If reached, a child would then be placed in Time Out for 15 minutes and then expected to rejoin activities. (The Time Out room is an empty bedroom).

If violently out of control, the young person would be removed to a secure room for 15 minutes and then, if in control, would return to the programme. If not they might remain in the secure room for up to 3 hours (checked for return every 15 minutes) which would allow ample time for senior management to review the problem, and, if necessary, determine an individual punisher usually related to each child's previous point-spending habits. This represented the ultimate sanction and could be, for example, loss of cigarettes for a week, loss of a trip out or contribution towards repair of damage caused. The control system and the positive reinforcement system operated within studies area and the two secure units then open.

Second stage

When a child had achieved constant attainment of both management and, to an increasing degree, individual targets on the secure units, he became eligible for movement to the 'open unit'. Selection involved the additional criteria of; (a) no abscondings or attempted abscondings in the previous 3 months, (b) no major physical assaults in the same period, and (c) where it was clear that continued progress of a programme required a less secure setting.

Although the open unit has the facility to lock doors, the aim was always to fade artificial systems, e.g. points, and to begin to approximate to the contingencies operating in the real world. Knowledge of the Shape project (Reid *et al.*, 1980) and of Preston's (Personal Communication) 3 Rs concentrated attention on fading artificiality and attempting to define; (a) the relevant behaviours for an individual's natural environment, (b) their relevant reinforcers, and (c) rehearsal and practice of desired behaviours in the relevant environments. Daily points were faded out over the first 6 weeks stay on the open unit and a weekly credit system (approximating to a 'wage') was operated. While children might still attend the studies programme an increasing emphasis for the older children was placed on work skills and future placement. As a result training was geared more and more to job-seeking skills, working with families with a view to reintegration and teaching those skills necessary for independent living within the community. A control system still operated in terms of lack of access to the increased range of reinforcers, e.g. greatly extended, unsupervized mobility and Time Out as the ultimate unit sanction. There was no secure room. Should behaviour become so severely problematic, return to a secure unit was a possibility. .

Comment

It would be extremely easy, with hindsight, to criticize early developments. Undoubtedly, even a relatively unsophisticated programme was immensely difficult for largely inexperienced staff to implement. Given the limited specialist advice available in 1978 and early 1979, innovation and increasing flexibility in progress terms, were areas which generated considerable anxiety and some degree of resistance. Coupled with the overriding administrative constraints, in terms of building and resources, it is noteworthy that planning and implementation of changes continued.

Inconsistencies in the overall programme and between staff undoubtedly led to frictions, but many positive indications came from early experiences. This staff genuinely committed to the programme made immense efforts to increase their own expertise, to develop behavioural and child-care techniques and to come to terms with the necessity of negotiating within an administrative framework. The overriding emphasis on achieving for the performance of positive behaviours contributed significantly to the shaping of staff's observations and practice. Instead of assuming the traditional passive role until crises occurred, staff became increasingly able to pay attention and respond to positive behaviour and begin to discriminate what proportion of behaviour was positive rather than wait and fear difficulties.

Once staff began to realize that the data generated provided a balanced view of the reality of the centre's development, it then became possible to plan modifications to the programme in a systematic way, rather than to respond to crises or attribute change to staff or system 'failure'. This shift towards data-based, planned innovation has gone some way to shaping staff's confidence in, (a) a flexible programme, and (b) their own expertise.

From experience it became increasingly clear that the amount and type of specialist support would be needed to alter significantly. If the programme was to continue to develop and provide the flexibility necessary to meet the needs of children, staff, and, most importantly, ensure the delivery of treatment, an increased definition of the programme, speciality of individual treatment, staff training and staff reinforcement was required. These considerations were underscored in a practical sense by children and staff who recognized that basic changes in the system and delivery of treatment were necessary.

The revised system

Changes in management

In early 1979, lengthy discussions were undertaken within the centre, and the DHSS on this issue. It was decided, given staff changes, that the Assistant Director (Education) should become Deputy Director responsible for education and staffing matters and that the Principal Psychologist should move from an advising function to line management as Programme Director with responsibility for the overall treatment programme, staff training and staff recruitment. In addition, it was agreed that given the overall emphasis of a Social Learning Theory approach, two Senior Clinical Psychologists should be appointed as advisers to specific units with a general brief to contribute to staff training/advice and overall policies of the centre. From autumn 1979 the management structure of Glenthorne became (as shown in Figure 2).

Specialists then became able to offer an increasing amount of day-to-day support, advice and modelling of therapeutic techniques. Further, more detailed

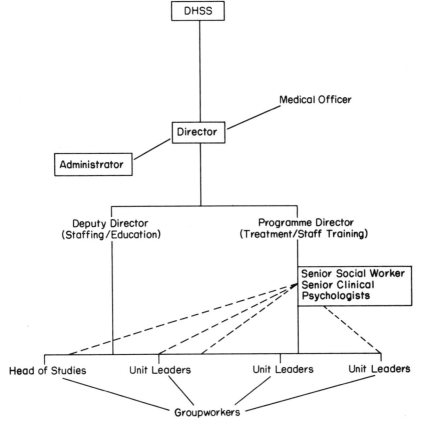

Figure 2   Management structure of GYTC

planning of medium- and long-term aims became possible given their increasing links with the Senior Social Worker and Community Education/Works Experience Department. Moreover, an increasing platform of expertise, both within specialists and staff in general facilitated the beginnings of detailed research projects which contributed significantly to changes in policy and programmes.

Research findings

Given staff's concern about the frequency and intensity of aggressive/disruptive behaviour, a study was undertaken to replicate and elaborate on the earlier work of Strain and Ezzel (1978). The original study investigated the appropriate/inappropriate behaviours exhibited by behaviours exhibited by behaviourally disordered adolescents in a residential psychiatric setting. Using observational techniques and sequential analyses they investigated, among other features, patterns of disruptive/inappropriate behaviours and their co-variation across settings. Results suggested that, (a) duration and pattern of disruptive/inappropriate (D/I) sequences of behaviour varied as a function of specific response topography that initiated such activity, and (b) the relative frequency of each D/I behaviour category varied significantly between particular settings (being most frequent during Transactional Analysis).

Using a similar experimental design, Dagnan (1979) and Tobin (1979) established some interesting findings. They found no evidence that D/I behaviours varied significantly across settings and it is hypothesized that the overall consistent structure of the system militated against such differences. In addition, the use of observational techniques made it clear to staff that valuable data on individual programmes could be obtained with relatively little additional work. Perhaps the most significant finding, particularly at a time of relatively low staff morale, was the proportion of appropriate/inappropriate behaviour. Observational data indicated that, contrary to the subjective estimates of the staff, frequency of all D/I categories was relatively low, (appropriate behaviour across situations varied between 74 per cent and 79 per cent). The authors suggest, that provision of such information went some way to encourage a more realistic and positive evaluation by staff of the relative effectiveness of the programme.

Additional positive feedback was provided by analysis of the management log which details all 'medium' and 'serious' instances of disruptive behaviour. Assessment of the data has shown a marked decrease in the frequency of such behaviour over the first $2\frac{1}{2}$ years of the centre's functioning.

Although it is important not to under-estimate the frequency and intensity of problem behaviours, judicious evaluation of the positive features of the programme certainly encouraged staff to plan confidently and implement changes in the system. Additional positive feedback came from formal evaluations of individual programmes. Stallard (1979), working with a particularly difficult girl, demonstrated the short-term effectiveness of a job-training programme. Staff were involved in both training sessions and outcome evaluation and were able, at first hand, to observe the improvements in all three target behaviours dealt with. As expected, active participation in a 'real' and successful treatment programme had a far more significant effect on staffs' confidence and behaviour than management instructions or 'talk and chalk' training sessions.

Improvements in initial assessment also began. Dissatisfaction with pre-admission procedures at a practical level, led to the development of the Glenthorne Behavioural Checklist, a comprehensive, behaviour-specific checklist covering more than one hundred items including dressing skills, social skills and general living skills. It was used to provide a more detailed and specific assessment of assets and deficits than had been possible previously, increasing individualization of programmes. Although superceded by the more comprehensive procedures of the new assessment unit, it still forms an important part of the initial assessment of all boys and girls coming to the centre.

A major contribution to improvement of the overall programme resulted from a detailed investigation of the use of Pink Cards and Time Out (Stallard, 1980). It had been realized for some time that the Pink-Card system had significant disadvantages. The time taken for its implementation in terms of substituting cards and the ritual of requiring a child to accept and operate a points 'freeze' led to problems. On occasions, extended confrontation, led to escalation of a previously minor problem behaviour and the effects of this on both young people and staff were largely negative.

Moreover, the hierarchical structure of the overall control system could result in a youngster being unnecessarily punished twice, i.e. by exclusion to time out and by a points 'freeze'. Further, the maximum penalty of 1000 points meant that access to reinforcers could be denied for up to 24 hours (the maximum 'earning off' period). This penalty, in combination with Time Out, effectively nullified the goal of the latter. In addition, the use of fixed interval Time Out may result in appropriate behaviour during the Time Out period going unrewarded; thus an individual's behaviour has little effect on his environment and as a result the emission of inappropriate behaviour during this time period may be encouraged (Hobbs and Forehand, 1975).

Therefore, more flexible, immediate and effective methods were sought. Stallard (1980) investigated the relative efficacy of three procedures; fixed interval Time Out and response cost (points freeze), fixed interval Time Out and release from Time Out contingent on appropriate behaviour. Situational variables, notably the difference· in expectations between studies and units significantly affected overall results such that there were no marked differences between the three procedures, except that the two Time Out procedures, in isolation, produced significant decreases in non-compliance. However, as staff had experienced the modified procedures for several months, on the grounds of improving their ability to deliver positive treatment and minimize unnecessary confrontation, all staff groups elected to discontinue the use of Pink Cards. Individual units were encouraged on practical and theoretical grounds to choose whether to use fixed interval or contingent release Time Out procedures. Preliminary data suggests that there has been an overall decrease in disruptive behaviours since these innovations.

The final significant research contribution to date involves the general delivery and maintenance of the therapeutic programme. In the long term this may prove to be the most crucial area for continued investigation. Fletcher (1981), is currently investigating ways of generating and maintaining treatment effort from staff. The maintenance of appropriate staff responses have been shown to be crucial to the effectiveness of Token Economy programmes (Atthowe, 1973). This appears to be an even greater problem for staff in 'corrective' institutions for juveniles particularly because peer group pressure may work actively against any treatment effort. The nature and effects of such resistance have been demonstrated by Buehler *et al.* (1966) who found that peer group reinforcement contingencies could effectively maintain inappropriate behaviour within an institutional setting. Similar evidence has been found by Sanson-Fisher and Jenkins (1978).

Fletcher (1981) has begun to investigate the generation of supportive behaviours within four separate unit staff groups. The initial 1-year pilot study on one group using an operational definition of 'support', i.e. behaviours which encourage and support staff to deliver treatment, has been completed. Using a variety of survey and observational techniques, together with contracting between staff and middle management, the pilot project produced encouraging data. Results suggest a positive relationship between staff–staff supportive behaviour and treatment orientated interactions; equally, management's commitment to encourage positive interactions also increased staff's treatment orientated interactions. As a result, investigation has now extended across the Centre. The same research design will operate but in addition, the identification of individual and group reinforcers of treatment effort and their appropriate provision within an institutional setting are now a major target.

The impact of results to date is clear. Staff are now evaluating the reinforcing effects of this intervention and, as a result, the centre now needs to think in practical terms about mechanisms for enhancing staff–staff feedback, practical skills training and rationally based individual skills development. Although the literature provides an abundance of suggestions and prescriptions to achieve these ends, their operational value is sadly lacking. The present investigation

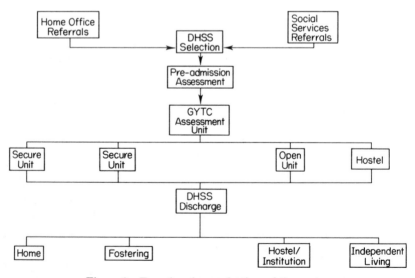

Figure 3   Functional organization of the centre

hopes to provide modest replicable indications of how change may be effected and maintained. The shift in definition of 'support' from a semantic to an operational level will make a clear and constructive contribution to the active delivery of the treatment programme.

Progress to date

Considerable restructuring has occurred in order to facilitate an overall programme which more closely approximates to the original aims of specificity, flexibility and an emphasis on positive behaviour. Continued dissatisfaction with pre-admission assessment and a general need to improve behavioural assessment and programme planning, in its broadest sense, have led to the introduction of an assessment unit for all admissions. As a result the present functional organization of the Centre is as shown in Figure 3.

In terms of treatment developments, there have been major alterations in two areas;
(a) organizational, (b) treatment technology.

Organizational. Despite prolonged discussion of the virtues of a sequential model, i.e. units with unique functions—for example, one unit for all offenders from the Home Office; in reality such rigidity, given a behavioural orientation is contrary to individual programme planning. As the overriding aim of flexibility and individualization requires assessment and treatment to be individually based, the most that specific units can legitimately expect is a broad overall management programme aimed at the client group, in the medium term, together with the discrete programmes required by each youngster. The present balance has led to three mixed units and one single-sex (male) unit. Nevertheless future admissions may well lead to alterations in distribution given their age, sex and degree of behaviour disorder. Equally, in terms of techniques used, it is probable that the continuum of artificial techniques—from star chart to written contracts could be contemplated on basic units, together with the more naturally occurring contingencies which can be operated in less secure and open conditions. To fully implement such a sophisticated and genuinely therapeutic regime requires staff competence at the highest level. The aim of the present staff reinforcement and training is to enable them to cope with the two general strands of the programme:

1. Techniques: star charts/points/contracts/verbal contracts/self-control techniques.
2. Environments: security/minimal security/open unit/hostel/fostering, other hostels, etc.

All of the planning is geared to produce positive behaviours at an acceptable level, with artificial means of necessary, e.g. points. Then, as rapidly as constraints allow, each individual is moved to lessening degrees of security with a consequent lessening of external prompts. The interaction being that behaviours once established should be maintained, as far as possible, under naturally occurring contingencies, e.g. verbal approval, self-control, etc.

Treatment technology. From the original programme where all youngsters had time-based points cards, major changes have occurred. In target terms these can now be changed on a weekly basis (given sufficient data). Moreover, even within the limitations of the secure units, individual programmes are profoundly more child-specific. A points economy system is used, on the assessment unit, as a means of establishing each young person's level of functioning. The system is one means of determining exactly how a youngster can behave within a structural environment. This is supplemented by clinical investigation and specialist teachers' assessment to provide an overall evaluation of target areas needing modification. The unit's function is also, if necessary, to begin the teaching of basic skills. From this detailed assessment, allocation of any youngster can be made throughout the centre, to secure or 'open' facilities.

The 'secure' units use elements of a Token Economy system but increasingly programmes now involve specific individual training sessions geared towards social-skills training, the teaching of self-control techniques, relaxation training, etc. Formal teaching is supplemented by the impromptu use of a variety of behavioural techniques, prompting, praise, attention, etc. On the control side, extinction is now used more systematically with contingent-release Time Out if necessary.

As the centre develops, the definition of 'security' has begun to change quite considerably. Having observed and measured behaviour systematically it is clear that movement to less secure conditions can be accelerated. Given the constraints of the building this is not easy and therefore an increasing number of youngsters go out to part-time and full-time work experience, youth clubs, etc. from the basic units. Experience to date suggests that a 'simple' definition of security, in terms of locked doors, fences, etc., is grossly inadequate. Attempts to operationalize security are taking place (see Future Plans; p. 000 and already begin to show that while the option of physical security needs to be retained, given behavioural improvements, there is every reason to move towards the techniques and conditions operating in the open unit and community placements.

In such conditions, where contingencies are more closely approximate to 'real life', it may seem a contradiction to expect the programme to be seen more clearly defined than on the secure units. However, there are several practical reasons for this:

1. The Open Unit represents the first and clearest movement away from environmental control towards self-control as the technique of choice.
2. For those whose motivation to change may remain somewhat suspect, or whose grasp of new skills in a very different environment may be suspect, staff

need to be as certain as possible of the range of contingencies (not necessarily fixed responses) which can be used to meet with wide variations in behaviour.
3. 'Open' conditions require a shift of emphasis in the operation of the programme. As the overriding aim is to develop self awareness, self-control and the generalization of new skills, considerable attention needs to be given to the definition of relevant behaviours and how these are to be encouraged.

A three-part programme has been developed on the Open Unit to meet these demands. The unit team have attempted to specify 'expected' behaviours which may be expected in 'open' conditions, e.g. possessing basic self help skills and the absence of frequent aggressive or disruptive behaviours. In the absence of artificial prompts, all youngsters are expected to be able, and agree, to perform this minimal level of competence on the unit and in studies or at work (where appropriate). Each youngster's ability to do so is assessed within a five-level system where they are rated by all staff in contact with them. Overall weekly assessment allows for monitoring of general progress and each level has specified reinforcers attached which increase in value as a youngster progresses through the levels. For example, at higher levels a youngster can achieve lengthy periods of time (alone or with friends) outside the centre. Although situational Time Out, i.e. ignoring inappropriate behaviours and on rare occasions, a secure room, can be used as control techniques, the overall emphasis is on positive, individually geared achievement.

Open conditions facilitate, and require, that an increasing emphasis needs to be placed on major and minor individual targets. The former includes the structured shaping of survival and self-help skills in as natural a setting as possible, e.g. work and school. Teaching involves self-ratings by youngsters and staff assessments, and is largely based on negotiation and agreement of those involved. In addition, 'offence behaviours' can be directly tackled in conditions of less security. Where appropriate, counselling sessions by psychologists and experienced staff are geared either to directly modify offence behaviour or provide incompatible, more appropriate responses. For example, if temper control in a work situation is a problem, specific strategies can be designed to cope with the relevant problems in the 'real' environment. Similarly, if the antecedents of fire setting are identified, intervention can be geared to teach alternative responses, e.g. increased personal assertion/avoidance techniques.

In addition, an open environment provides the opportunity to shape minor targets to the highest levels possible. Detailed assessment by both youngsters and staff enables accurate 'fine tune' evaluation of either slight problems or assets needing some improvement. This style of responding, e.g. undue sarcasm or slight lack of assertion can be quantified and by using a weekly 'percentage positive index' can be modified. Youngsters are made aware of their present functioning and provided with the skills training necessary to, (a) effect slight behaviour change, and (b) be more able to discriminate when particular behaviours are or are not appropriate. It is anticipated that the process will continue in the increasingly 'open' conditions provided by our hostel accommodation as of April 1981. As far as possible the design will follow that of the Shape Project, (Ostapuik and Reid, 1981; Ostapuik, chapter 6, this volume). The overall aim is to increasingly shape individual responsibility and behavioural competence in as wide a variety of settings (work, family, hostel, etc.) as possible. The use of hostel manager schemes, self government, etc. (see Ostapuik, chapter 6, this volume) have shown that such techniques have considerable value.

A summary of progress to date (January 1981)

There have been significant developments in the operation of the Centre in its $2\frac{1}{2}$-year life. For a variety of reasons (detailed earlier) the treatment techniques have become increasingly flexible and responsive to the needs of the individuals. The improvement in assessment techniques (observation, self-rating, etc.) have certainly contributed together with general resource development and staff expertise. The centre can now offer a wide range of educational options, work experience schemes and family therapy. All of these are recent developments and, as such, their long-term value is difficult to ascertain at this stage.

There is, however, more concrete evidence of improvement. In staff terms, the rate of staff leaving for reasons other than promotion, pregnancy, etc. has decreased markedly. The numbers leaving because of their difficulties in coping with the programme were: 1978, 11; 1979, 12; 1980, 5. It is still too early to be certain that this trend will continue but the early trend is encouraging. Similar improvements are becoming apparent in the decrease in staff sickness rate.

Data on the youngsters is more difficult to evaluate given the limited timescale of the project to date. Information is now available on the forty-two boys and girls admitted in terms of their ages, number of previous placements, etc. but data on length of time in security and follow-up information is more difficult to evaluate. Such a small group ($n = 15$) have formally left the programme and length of discharge varies so widely (from 1 month follow-up to 1 year 8 months) that it is impossible to make generalizations from the data. Four boys have been re-convicted and sent to penal establishments but these convictions occurred while they were still within the programme (two were in the early months of opening). Similarly, the limited follow-up period; within a year, the number of discharged youngsters and length of follow-up period should be sufficient to enable more detailed assessment of the efficacy of the programme.

Future plans

Generalization

It has been demonstrated many times that one of the most difficult problems for any treatment programme to come to terms with is how to maintain treatment gains following discharge from the programme. This is particularly pertinent to Glenthorne as we admit youngsters from all parts of the United Kingdom. Moves are being made to overcome the problem by:

1. Youngsters spending an increasing amount of time outside the centre from both secure and open units so that they have the maximum opportunity to practice their developing skills in the 'real' world.
2. An increasing amount of work with families, where appropriate, is being undertaken to ensure that they have the skills necessary to encourage and maintain improved behaviour.
3. The hostel, running as it will, on a self-government model will be another means of encouraging independent living skills and provide an opportunity to be practised in a natural environment.
4. Our efforts to provide counselling and support for youngsters for up to 2 years after they have left the centre. This should enable staff to identify any problems as early as possible so that remedial action may be taken. Unfortunately the constraints of long-distance travel and staff availability means that the service is not yet as well developed as is necessary.

Despite attempts to overcome the problem of generalization there are still certain outstanding problems. On occasions, it is difficult to place a youngster in outside hostels or other facilities because they have the label of having been in a Youth Treatment Centre. This fact alone, despite evidence of improvement, may be sufficient for a child to be rejected from a treatment or living provision that he or she needs. In addition, the notion of 'improvement' can often be called into question. While from a behavioural point of view one instance of minor aggression in a period of months may be seen as a dramatic improvement over preceding years of violence, others may, and have, interpreted this behaviour as yet another manifestation of some form of 'well of aggression'. When faced with such conflict of ideologies it can be extremely difficult for the centre to convince others that a youngster has improved sufficiently to return to the natural environment. It seems at present that the only means we have of improving this situation is by continued persuasion and by the youngsters managing to maintain improvement in their behaviour.

In addition, relationships between the centre and the local authorities to whom a child may return can be a source of problems. The response of local authorities varies tremendously from on the one hand, complete co-operation to the centre's programme to overt hostility often on ideological grounds. It can, therefore, be difficult to ensure that the consistent treatment approach will continue once a youngster has left the centre. Steps are being taken to attempt to resolve the position. One possible way being explored at the moment is whether or not the centre can establish formal contracts with local authorities defining the respective responsibilities of the centre and local social workers such that community targets can be continued and developed in a rational way and that the methods used to promote improvement in behaviour can be specified and adhered to. It is hoped that pilot contracts may be tested later in the year.

Developments within the centre

Although considerable strides have been made in developing the treatment model, it is still in many ways, largely initiated and carried out by staff. Assessment, target setting and therapeutic interventions are undertaken, in the main, by groupworkers. Similarly, any major programme changes tend to be decided by staff teams with little involvement of the youngsters in any formal way. In terms of good child care practice we have a responsibility to teach certain skills but increasingly, given staff's developing confidence and expertise, it is possible to consider significant alterations to the balance of the contributions of staff and youngsters. There are clear ethical considerations, including the right to treatment, informed consent, etc. (Nietzel, 1979) which would strongly support an increasing emphasis on client participation.

On treatment grounds, it is essential as early as possible to encourage the youngsters to develop their problem-solving skills and their ability and willingness to take responsibility for; (a) their own behaviour, (b) their living environment. There are several ways in which this may be accomplished:

1. Target setting by youngsters themselves. Numerous treatment programmes (Ostapuik, chapter 6, this volume) have demonstrated that clients, with support, are capable of a full contribution to the development, monitoring and evaluation of their programmes. Steps in this direction have already occurred on the open unit and ways of implementing this far earlier in a youngster's stay are now being formulated. One way may be to include them in all programme planning meetings and progress reviews. Whether this may best be achieved by staff and individual youngsters designing and monitoring programmes or whether staff/children group meetings would be the most appropriate vehicle will need to be tested and evaluated. It may well be that to shape confidence and positive problem solving skills in both staff and youngsters most effectively, an individual approach should be used in the short and medium term.

2. An increase in youngsters' contribution throughout the centre. They already have an impact in terms of determining types of reinforcers available but their influence could be extended and developed in other areas. Many crucially important areas of the children's life are directly under the control of administrative staff, sometimes within the centre, e.g. food, clothing; sometimes outside, e.g. the Department of the Environment is responsible for all repairs and decoration of centre buildings. It can be strongly argued on therapeutic grounds and the successful experiences of other programmes (Phillips, 1979) that the position should be reversed. It is essential to teach survival skills which include selection and cooking of own food, purchasing clothing, decorating one's living environment, etc.

Such a move runs counter to the tradition of many child care institutions. Giving the increasing and desirable preoccupation with treatment and cost effectiveness it is more important than ever to clearly specify the function of the institution. Is it to set targets to enable smooth running of the system and operate procedures which will train children how to live in an institution divorced from the real world, or is our primary responsibility to equip them to live in as natural an environment as possible? From any therapeutic standpoint the answer has to be the latter but to ensure its occurrence will require considerable planning and changes in traditional attitudes. One suggestion, mooted at present is for youngsters, with staff support, to meet formally with Directors to give feedback and suggest modifications throughout the centre. If such an exercise proves successful it will hopefully lead to an increasing degree of participation and control being devolved directly to individual units. Such movement will require significant organizational changes within the centre.

Although the populations of Glenthorne and Boys Town are significantly different several of their successful experiences have direct relevance to the future development of our organization. Several brief quotes from Phillips (1979) serve to illustrate improvements that could be made: 'another significant change was to remove any responsibility for planning for each youth from a large team (as many as 4–12 persons) to the teaching parents'.

Given the significantly less well developed base of behavioural expertise in the UK at present and the wide differences between our client population, a complete acceptance of the Teaching–Parent model would not be workable. Nevertheless, it has been possible to move towards co-ordinating the treatment approach to youngsters by strictly limiting the number of people involved in overall programme planning and concentrating on training staff teams in programme implementation. Whether in the future it will be possible to decrease teams to more nearly approximate to the Teaching–Parent model is difficult to assess but it will be given serious and continued consideration.

Certainly the organization of the hostel represents a pilot scheme in this direction where overall running will be the responsibility of three to four staff with specialist back-up from centre resources.

Other features of the Boys Town programme may also aid the streamlining of treatment:

the boys . . . ate adequate food and wore clean clothes but hardly in a family atmosphere.

Laundry service was centralised . . . delivered with everything pressed or folded like magic, without any involvement by the boys. (The Central Laundry was closed.)

Each cottage is now independent, responsible for its own laundry and marketing.

As Phillips acknowledges, such changes may be unpopular with some staff and do not occur without difficulties. However, their experiences suggest that control of the day to day functions including food, laundry, clothing and transport can be used to better therapeutic effect if under the control of treatment staff. Discussions are presently taking place to establish how best day-to-day budgetary control can be managed within individual units such that treatment staff and youngsters became responsible for purchasing, unit decor, etc. Overall accounting and approval of annual budgets would clearly remain with Centre Administration. Progress will be slow but it is hoped to establish a timetable for changes such that they occur in a planned and rational way. Ultimately the degree of innovation achieved will depend on the degree of support provided by central government.

Staff considerations

Any successful programme depends, to a large extent, on the performance of the therapeutic staff involved. The means of staff reinforcement are being investigated (see earlier) as are two equally improvement areas, (a) staff salaries and conditions, (b) staff training.

Staff salaries and conditions. This has been a contentious area since the first Youth Treatment Centre opened in 1971. The majority of front-line therapists, designated as 'groupworkers' are professionals drawn from the teaching, nursing or child care professions. Although they perform essentially the same job, salaries and conditions are linked to their parent professions which results, in some cases, in their receiving widely different salaries and holiday entitlements. Not surprisingly, such discrepancies lead to resentment which is compounded whenever each profession negotiates separate agreements for its members. The conditions of 'specialist' staff, studies teachers, psychologists and social workers are all subject to the same anomalies. The result is a massive organizational exercise each year when faced with the task of reconciling the demands of widely differing contracts of employment. In practice, 'specialist' staff present less of a problem than 'groupworkers' who, if they are to bear any resemblance to a team need some common core of pay and conditions.

   The Directors of the centre are presently formulating a salary structure where remuneration would be based on qualifications and experience but where greater emphasis would be placed on performance in the treatment situation, such that, major salary increases would be accorded to those showing greatest treatment effectiveness. It is proposed that there be three salary bands (irrespective of purely professional qualifications; Basic Grade Therapist, Intermediate Grade Therapist, Senior Grade Therapist. Except in exceptional circumstances all new staff would begin within the basic grouping and progression through levels would be based on annual performance evaluation. As with many other proposed changes, alterations on such a scale will require considerable negotiation on a number of fronts including; (a) fostering acceptance by centre staff,

(b) agreement from central government employers, (c) agreement from professional unions. It may be that such a proposal is based on more optimism than the appreciation of harsher realities.

Nevertheless, one measure which may go some way towards facilitating such improvements is to gear professional progress to increased training via a formal qualification. It has been found that staff secondment to a variety of partially related courses (usually of diffuse theoretical orientations) may partly meet the needs of individual staff and the centre, but, on the whole, courses geared largely to academic performance, as our own early training programmes have proved of limited usefulness to the treatment task.

Staff training. Present centre training is geared increasingly to formal skills training either by workshops or impromptu staff teaching sessions on units. It is planned to co-ordinate these developments within a 1-year Post Qualifying Certificate in Applied Behaviour Modification based at the School of Social Work, Leicester University.

Initially the course will be open to centre staff with teaching and training largely supplied by a Department of Health funded Course Director appointed to the School of Social Work. Teaching will be supplemented by experienced staff from both the school and the centre. The course will have a high-level academic component but will have a relatively stronger practical skills training emphasis. The basic syllabus is already at the advanced planning stage and under the auspices of the Department of Health, the Course Director should be appointed by January, 1982 to enable the 5-year pilot course to begin in October 1982.

Given the experiences of Achievement Place, Boys Town and the Shape Project which attest to the crucial importance of staff's personal qualities and professional expertise, the proposed course may well be one of the most significant factors in the centre's continued development and contribute towards developing a broader base of behavioural expertise within the child care system.

Consideration re: national agencies

As detailed earlier, overall functioning of the centre is determined by central government agencies and unions in London. Geographical separation and organizational procedures may, on occasions, mean that respective bodies, centre staff, government bodies, unions, etc., may have insufficient information available to be fully aware of the full implications of certain issues, and as a result unnecessary delays may occur.

One way of ensuring feedback to all concerned is to draw all executives external to, and within the centre closer to the functioning of the centre by establishing a management group from all the relevant agencies, such that executive decisions could be made at monthly meetings on all major facets of the programme, e.g. buildings, staffing, personnel, etc. If this were to occur even for a pilot period, experience elsewhere in the UK and USA would suggest that a significant improvement could be made in the effectiveness of the treatment programme.

Conclusion

It is extremely difficult to encompass and describe the progress, problems and future plans of such a complex, developing programme. It has been equally difficult to know which facets to omit in the short life of the centre. Since 1978 when an inexperienced staff in an incomplete building were expected to administer a points system few understood, major changes have been made. In treatment terms, the quality and variety of treatment techniques and specificity of individual programmes have increased dramatically. Perhaps more important; the 'delivery' of treatment is now significantly more relaxed, natural and, best of all, tinged with humour.

Most of these improvements have been achieved by committed staff learning from their experiences, seeking knowledge and more lately, having the benefit of specialist psychological advice. The full impact and benefits of increased support are still to be felt but in the final analysis continued successful development will remain, as it should, with the groupworkers, teachers and increasingly the youngsters themselves.

Perhaps one of the most encouraging developments to date, as yet unquantified, is continuing shift in staff attitudes from self-doubt and negativity to a more healthy and productive scepticism towards certain features of the treatment programme. The control method of 'Pink Cards' has already disappeared and there is an increasing demand for diversification of the positive treatment and recreational options available. Input of youngsters to their programmes is increasing and, across the centre, a film club, gym club, outdoor pursuits and a youth club are now well established. In addition, examination classes (and successes) and work experience schemes have progressed significantly and will continue to do so. In treatment terms there is a reason for guarded optimism both in terms of present development (as outlined earlier) and future plans, however, many of the means of achieving changes lie outside the direct province of the centre. To date, Children's Division and the Social Work Service of the Department of Health have played a large part in the overall development of the programme. In the earliest days it was ultimately their approval and support which allowed the unique innovation in the UK of a national resource developing purely on behavioural lines. With continued support it may well be possible to introduce many of the developments necessary to increase the immediacy and effectiveness of the treatment programme.

If most or all of the proposed developments occur, it can be realistically hypothesized that within the next 2–3 years far more detailed data will be available on the effectiveness of the programme (given the follow-up data available), the cost of the programme and several other important areas notably:

1. the nature of the overall programme and the 'delivery' of specific treatment techniques which are most appropriate for our youngsters;
2. the increasing contribution youngsters can, and should, make, to the overall running of the centre;
3. the impact of more comprehensive staff training and support systems in terms of
   (a) increased staff effectiveness
   (b) staff resistance to the 'burn out' phenomenon
4. perhaps the most contentious of areas, an increasingly clear definition of the problem behaviours which warrant secure conditions and a more lucid elaboration of the nature of 'security'.

Is it simply a fence, locked doors and a 'caring' attitude on the part of staff? Or, as we suspect, does security largely mean objective treatment planning and implementation which is negotiated by and understood by all parties involved with the notion of secure conditions if necessary?

The centre is now viable. The next 2–3 years of planning and innovation will determine the scope of its potential progress and the quality of data available to permit an accurate evaluation of its effectiveness.

Note

The views expressed in this chapter are solely those of the author and in no way represent those of the Department of Health and Social Security, the Home Office or the Department of the Environment.

References

Atthowe, J. M. (1973). Token economies come of age, *Behaviour Therapy*, **4**, 646–654.
Barlow, G. (1978). Security—a dirty word? *Journal of Adolescence*, **1**.345–351.
Barlow, G. (1979). Youth Treatment Centre, in *Caring for deprived children* (Eds C. Payne and K. J. White) Croom Helm.
Buehler, R. E. Patterson, G. R. and Furniss, J. M. (1966). The reinforcement of behaviour in institutional settings, *Behaviour Research and Therapy;* **4**, 157–167.
Cawson, P. and Martell, M. (1969). *The Children and Young Person's Act,* HMSO, London.
Cawson, P. and Martell, M. (1979). *Children referred to Closed Units,* HMSO, London.
Dagnan, J.(1979). *The Sequence and Distribution of Disruptive-inappropriate Behaviour in a Group of Behaviourally Disordered Adolescents.* Dissertation submitted for the British Psychological Society Diploma in Clinical Psychology.
Fletcher, D. S. (1981). The generation and maintenance of staff treatment effort in an

institution for severely disturbed adolescents. Glenthorne Youth Treatment Centre (unpublished).

Gibbons, D. C. (1975). Offender typologies two decades later, *British Journal of Criminology*, **2**, 140–156.

Hobbs, S. A. and Forehand, R. (1975). Effects of a differential release from Time out on children's deviant behaviour, *Journal of Behaviour Therapy and Experimental Psychiatry*, **6**, 256–257.

Martell, M. and Cawson, P. (1975). *The Development of Closed Units in the Child Care Service and its Research Implications*, DHSS Social Research Branch, HMSO, London.

Mayers, M. O. (1980). *The Hard-Core Delinquent*, Saxon House, Farnborough.

Millham, S., Bullock, R. and Hosie, K. (1978). *Locking up Children: Secure Provision Within the Child Care System*, Saxon House, Farnborough.

Nietzel, M. (1979). *Crine and its Modification, a Social learning Perspective*, Pergamon Press, Oxford.

Ostapuik, E. B. (1982). Strategies for community intervention in offender rehabilitation, in *Development in the Study of Criminal Behaviour*, Vol. 1 (Ed. M. P. Feldman) Wiley, London.

Ostapuik, E. B. and Reid, I, D. (1981). rehabilitating offenders in the community: implications for penal policy and professional practice, in *Reconstructing Psychological Practice* (Eds I. McPherson and A. Sutton) Croom Helm, London.

Phillips, E. L. (1978) *Progress Report: A 1977 Evaluation of the Boys Town Youth Care Department Programmes*, Monograph Series, Boys Town Community-Based Programmes.

Phillips, E. L. (1979) In a family way, *Innovations*, Spring, 11–18.

Reid, I. D., Feldman, M. P. and Ostapuik, E. B. (1980). The Shape Project for Young Offenders: introduction and overview. *Journal of Offender Counselling Services Rehabilitation*, **4**, 233–246.

Reid, I. D. and Wilkie, J. R. (1980). *Developing a Behavioural Regime in a Secure Youth Treatment Centre*. Paper presented at the World Congress on Behaviour Therapy, Jerusalem, July, 1980.

Ross, R. R. and Price, M. J. (1976). Behaviour modification in connections: autopsy before mortification, *International Journal of Criminology and Penology*, **4**, 305–315.

Sanson-Fisher, R. and Jenkins, H. J. (1978). Interaction patterns between inmates and staff in a maximum security institution for delinquents, *Behaviour Therapy*, **9**, 703–716.

Sereny, G. (1972). *The Case of Mary Bell*. Eyre Methuen, London.

Stallard, P. N. (1979). *The Short Term Effects of a Job Interview Training Programme with a Delinquent Adolescent Girl*, Unpublished First Year MSc. Project, University of Birmingham.

Stallard, P. N. (1980). *An Experiment to Investigate the Effects of Three Types of Time Out Procedures on the Total Frequency, Place and Type of Inappropriate Behaviour Displayed by a Group of Delinquent Adolescents*. Unpublished MSc. thesis, University of Birmingham, 1980.

Stoll, C. S. (1968). Images of man and social control, *Social Forces*, **47**, N-2.

Strain, P. S. and Ezzel, D. (1978). The sequence and distribution of behaviourally disordered adolescents' disruptive/inappropriate behaviour. *Behaviour Modification*, **2**, 403–425.

Tobin, M. R. (1979). *The Sequence and Distribution of Disruptive-inappropriate Behaviour in a Group of Behaviourally Disordered Adolescents*. Unpublished MSc. thesis, University of Birmingham.

Developments in the Study of Criminal Behaviour
Volume 1: The Prevention and Control of Offending
Edited by P. Feldman
© 1982, John Wiley & Sons, Ltd.

5

Social Skills Training with Young Offenders

Susan Spence

The role of social skills deficits in the development and maintenance of juvenile offending

It is becoming clear that the causes of juvenile offending are many and varied, with different patterns of aetiological factors being evident for different individuals. Recently, theorists and practitioners have emphasized the role played by interpersonal skill deficits in the development and maintenance of offending with some young people (Braukmann *et al.*, 1975; Goldstein *et al.*, 1978). Sarason (1968) introduced this concept by proposing that delinquent behaviour was a reflection of inadequate opportunity to observe, display and receive reinforcement for socially appropriate behaviour. Obviously Sarason's model is rather limiting as it assumes inadequate social performance for all young offenders. Similarly, it fails to consider the role of other aetiological determinants such as financial gain, peer modelling and reinforcement, motivational states and environmental opportunity.

It does seem likely, however, that inadequacy in interpersonal skill performance plays an important role in the development and maintenance of juvenile offending for many individuals. In most societies today, there is considerable pressure upon adolescents to achieve socially desirable goals such as material possessions, financial gain, educational and vocational success, peer status and popularity. Fortunately, most children develop the skills to enable them to achieve these goals by socially acceptable methods. There remains a section of the population, however, who fail to develop the necessary behavioural repertoires. If adolescents are unable to achieve such socially desirable goals by acceptable means, then it seems likely that they will do so in inappropriate ways, given the opportunity.

Inadequacy in social skills performance can have far reaching effects for adolescents. Social skills can be defined as a repertoire of basic responses and response strategies which enable individuals to elicit reinforcing consequences from a given social interaction, in a manner which is socially acceptable and does not result in harm to others. This type of definition emphasizes the situational specificity of social skills, in that the type of behaviour which is considered to be socially skilled varies according to the characteristics of the individuals and the situation involved. For example, very different skills are likely to be needed if an adolescent wishes to make friends with another child at school compared to those required for success in returning a defective article to a shop.

If a young person is deficient in terms of social skills then, by definition, he or she is going to be unsuccessful in certain social interactions. The type of situations that often produce difficulty to young people include making friends, accepting adult criticism and requests, dealing with teasing and bullying, asking for help, refusing undesirable peer influences, and dealing with police encounters and job interviews (Spence, 1979). There is now considerable evidence to support the notion that specific social skills are important in determining the outcome of social interactions. For example, studies have demonstrated the importance of various responses in determining success in peer relationships. Both Gottmann *et al.* (1975) and Hartup *et al.* (1967) demonstrated an association between peer acceptance and the frequency with which children give out positive social reinforcers such as smiling, laughing, affectionate physical contact and verbalizations.

In addition to influencing success in general social interactions, social skills are also likely to play an important role in determining the outcome of juvenile-police interactions. Evidence suggests that young people who are lacking in social skills are less likely to receive a positive outcome when apprehended by the police compared to their socially skilled counterparts. Studies have shown that a youth's style of dress and attitude (Werthman and Piliavin, 1967; Piliavin and Briar, 1964), voice intonation, facial expression and orientation (Cicourel, 1968) and posture, politeness, co-operation and response to questions (Werner *et al.*, 1975) are all important in determining what is written on police reports, whether the boy is detained, treatment in court, whether he will be stopped in the future and whether he is cautioned or arrested after an offence.

The relationship between juvenile offending and social skills deficits is therefore rather complex. On the one hand it seems likely that adolescents who are deficient in social skills may well resort to offending as a means of achieving the peer status and respect they would be unable to obtain by more socially acceptable means. Similarly, it seems probable that children who experience difficulty in interactions with teachers and/or peers at school are more likely to truant, and thereby become more likely to commit offences. To complicate matters further, evidence also suggests that when apprehended by the police, adolescents who are deficient in social skills will be more likely to be prosecuted or convicted for the offence than their socially skilled peers.

Given the importance of social skills in determining the outcome of situations such as interactions with teachers, parents, peers and coping with police encounters and job interviews, there would seem to be a good case for teaching the necessary responses to young people to maximize their chances of obtaining successful outcomes.

The social skills training approach

Sarason (1968) proposed that juvenile offenders could be taught to exhibit socially acceptable behaviour if they were provided with an appropriate learning experience. Attempts to teach social and interpersonal skills have recently been made with a variety of client populations using a technique known as social skills training (SST). Social skills training is a therapeutic package composed generally of instructions, discussion, modelling, behaviour rehearsal, feedback and transfer training. The approach was initially developed by Wolpe (1958) who attempted to teach assertive responses to unassertive psychiatric patients. Argyle (1969) expanded this model, which focused on social behaviour at a macro-level of responding, to include a complex analysis of social behaviour in terms of learned micro-level skills. He suggested that socially skilled behaviour could be broken down into component skills, such as eye contact or tone of voice, which could then be trained in the same way as any motor skills, using instructions, guidance, modelling, practice and feedback.

Since Argyle's original model, there have been several extensions of SST such as Personal Effectiveness Training (Liberman et al., 1975) and Structured Learning Therapy (Goldstein, 1973). Studies have demonstrated various versions of SST to be effective in improving interaction skills with a variety of client populations, ranging from students with dating anxiety (Curran, 1973) and unassertive college students (McFall and Marston, 1970; McFall and Twentyman, 1973) to socially inadequate psychiatric in-patients (Hersen et al., 1975; Edelstein and Eisler, 1976; Bellack et al., 1976). The results have been less dramatic, however, with psychiatric out-patients (Argyle et al., 1974; Marzillier et al., 1976).

Evidence of social skills deficits in juvenile offenders

The model proposed in this paper lays heavy emphasis on the importance of social skill deficits in the development of persistent offending. What evidence is there then to support the view that many juvenile offenders are deficient in terms of interpersonal skills? An excellent study by Freedman et al., (1978) showed that a group of young male offenders responded less skillfully on a series of role-play tests compared to a matched group of non-offenders. The tests involved a series of role-plays related to social situations which, if mishandled by adolescents could lead to conflict with the police. A wide range of possible responses were identified for each situation and each response was then rated by independent judges on a scale for appropriate behaviour. This allowed a scale to be produced on which it was possible to score responses to each role-play situation. Using this scoring system, it was found that institutionalized offenders scored significantly worse than a group of boys without criminal records who were matched for age, IQ and social background. Interestingly, Freedman and his co-workers also found that institutionalized delinquent boys who had frequent behaviour problems within the institution performed less skillfully on the role-play tests than institutionalized offenders who evidenced few behaviour problems. This study therefore provides some evidence that, in general, young offenders are less socially skilled, at least in terms of choice of response to situations, than their non-offending counterparts.

A study by Spence (1981) also investigated the differences in social skills performance between juvenile offenders and non-offenders. Eighteen institutionalized male offenders and a group of eighteen boys without criminal records, comparable in terms of age, social background and educational attainment, were videotaped during a 5-minute interview with a previously unknown adult. Each videotape was then subjected to a behavioural analysis on thirteen measures of specific micro-level responses (e.g. eye contact and fiddling movements). The tapes were also shown in random order to a group of six independent judges who rated each tape on three ten-point scales of friendliness, social skills performance and probability of being given a part-time job.

The offender group were found to show a significantly lower level of eye contact, head movements (nods and shakes) and total amount spoken plus a higher level of fiddling and gross body movements, compared to their non-offending counterparts. No differences were found in terms of gestures, smiling, speech dysfluencies, attention feedback responses, interruptions, latency of response, question asking and initiations. The teachers ratings revealed that the offender group were scored significantly lower in terms of social skills performance and employability compared to the non-offender group. No difference was found between the groups on the friendliness scale.

The studies mentioned tend to support the view that many convicted juvenile male offenders are deficient in social skills in terms of response choice, micro-level responding and the impression created during interview.

The role of educational and vocational deficits in the maintenance of persistent offending has been acknowledged in many recent intervention programmes (Cornish and Clarke, 1975). The emphasis in many community home schools in Britain is now on the development of remedial education and vocational training programmes. Less attention has been paid, however, to the systematic teaching of social and interpersonal skills. Intervention programmes with juvenile offenders have attempted to produce increases in prosocial behaviour and decreases in antisocial behaviour by a variety of means. Methods such as token reinforcement (Kirigin et al., 1979), contingency contracting (Stumphauzer, 1979), cognitive therapy techniques (Camp et al., 1977; Williams and Akamatsu, 1978), transactional analysis (Jesness, 1976) and psychotherapy (McCord et al.,

1959) have all been reported in attempts to modify delinquent behaviour. The primary assumption behind all these approaches, however, is that the adolescents concerned have the ability, when they choose, to discriminate the needs of different social situations, select socially acceptable responses and then perform these responses in an appropriate manner. Hence the majority of therapeutic approaches create an expectancy that the adolescent will behave in a socially skilled manner, and yet rely heavily on the adolescents' capabilities in areas of interpersonal functioning. Obviously, young offenders involved in such programmes are less likely to benefit from intervention if they are unable to reach the behavioural criteria set and thereby fail to obtain reinforcing consequences.

There would seem to be, therefore, a great need to consider the level of social-skills performance when assessing the behavioural repertoire of young offenders. It should then be possible to identify those adolescents who are likely to benefit most from social skills training procedures.

Applications of social skills training with juvenile offenders

Introduction to methodology

The use of social-skills training as a component of intervention is becoming increasingly popular both at an institutional and community-based level. Despite its increased popularity, relatively few studies have attempted to investigate the possible benefits of SST with juvenile offenders. There has been a tendency to assume that SST is unlikely to make a significant impact on offence behaviour if used in isolation from other intervention methods. Studies have therefore tended to investigate the benefits of SST over and above the effects produced by other ongoing regimes.

The effects of social skills training with young offenders have been evaluated by means of two types of experimental design: single-case designs and group comparisons. Single-subject designs differ from uncontrolled case studies in that they attempt to demonstrate the effectiveness of training by associating variations in the dependent measures of social skills with systematic variations in the intervention. If the dependent measure changes as the intervention is applied, withdrawn or then reapplied (withdrawal designs) or as the intervention is sequentially applied to either different behaviours, different situations or different subjects (multiple baseline designs) then it can be concluded that the intervention is associated with changes in the dependent measures (Wallace *et al.*, 1980).

Group designs on the other hand compare differences between the outcomes for groups receiving different interventions. If the groups were initially comparable then it can be concluded that differences in outcome are related to differences in the interventions.

Outcome studies using single case designs

There have been several single-case design studies reported in the literature which have attempted to assess the effects of training social skills with young offenders. Generally, these studies have focused on the short-term effects of training specific skills within the training setting, and have not considered the longer term and more generalized benefits of training.

Several such reports have been published from the Achievement Place Project, a series of family group homes, set up for young offenders and 'pre-delinquents' in Kansas, USA. For example, Minkin *et al.* (1976) reported the use of instructions, modelling, practice and feedback, combined with financial reinforcement for performance during practice, to teach conversational skills to four 'pre-delinquent' girls. Two skills, namely question asking and positive conversational feedback were trained sequentially to produce a multiple baseline design across behaviours. Although the data showed an increase in responding in both targets contingent upon the introduction of training, there was no attempt to assess whether the improvements were long lasting and generalized beyond the training setting. Similar studies have been reported from Achievement Place demonstrating that SST combined with contingent reinforcement can be effective in producing short-term improvements in heterosexual interaction skills (Braukmann *et al.*, 1973), interview skills (Braukmann *et al.*, 1974) and conversation-related skills such as posture (Maloney *et al.*, 1976). An interesting study reported by Werner *et al.* (1975) attempted to teach skills to facilitate police–juvenile encounters. The first step of the project attempted to identify some of the important responses which influenced the outcome of police–youth interactions. By means of questionnaires completed by eight police officers, four specific responses were identified as important, namely looking at the officer, making polite statements followed by a statement of respect, e.g. 'Sir' or 'Officer', making statements of reform and finally expressing understanding and cooperation. Three youths from the Achievement Place family group home who had a history of frequent contact with the police were selected for training. The SST procedure consisted of instructions with rationale, modelling and practice with feedback. The skills were trained in a sequential order, again to conform to a multiple baseline design across behaviours for each subject. The results showed marked improvements in skill performance contingent upon the introduction of training of a specific skill, for all three subjects. In an attempt to validate the benefits of training, pre- and post-training videotapes of role-played police–juvenile interactions were shown to five police officers. Beneficial changes were reported after training in terms of indices such as being labelled a trouble maker, the decision to take into custody or stop again. However, similar changes were also reported for three boys who did not receive the training procedure, which confuses the issue somewhat. The study was also limited in that it failed to consider the long-term, generalized effects of training.

This was also true of a study reported by Spence and Marzillier (1979) which assessed the short-term effects of SST on the performance of four basic social skills. A single-case, multiple baseline design across behaviours was employed in which skills were trained sequentially with five adolescent, male offenders. The results showed that SST was effective in improving the performance of certain skills such as eye contact or decreased fiddling movements. Other skills such as head movements and attention feedback responses were harder to train, with subjects varying in their response to training. Where SST was effective, the change was generally maintained at the 2-week follow-up.

The single-case literature regarding SST with young offenders only allows limited conclusions to be drawn. This type of experimental design is most suitable for assessing changes in those very specific responses which can be accurately and reliably measured, and occur with relatively high frequency. It is also difficult to extend such designs to evaluate the longer-term effects of training and determine whether the changes carry over beyond the training setting. The training of very specific micro-level responses such as eye contact or question asking would seem to be rather limited in terms of the impact on social behaviour in general. Successful performance in social interactions tends to be influenced by the choice of response strategy, in addition to the use of a wide range of basic social skills. It is much harder, however, to obtain reliable measures of social performance on a more macro-level analysis of social skills, such as response to criticism or teasing. First, the researcher is more dependent on rating scale measures or subjective reports regarding success in dealing with the situation. Secondly, it is often difficult to collect sufficient data for a single-case analysis, if the situation of interest occurs relatively infrequently. Despite these difficulties, Thelen et al. (1976) made use of a multiple baseline design across situations to assess changes in complex interaction skills, using behaviour ratings with six individual cases. After an initial 2-week baseline phase, six delinquent boys in a group home were shown videotapes of students modelling appropriate responses in a variety of interpersonal conflict situations. The boys were then required to role-play the situations with the therapist. Training was divided into two phases, with the first 5 weeks focussing on tapes dealing with conflict in the home and the final 2 weeks on conflicts in the school. Social behaviour was assessed by staff and teachers in both the house and school settings throughout the programme. Behaviour ratings within the group home suggested that SST did improve the interpersonal adjustment of three of the six boys, but these changes were not maintained at the 2-week follow-up. No changes were observed in the school behaviour ratings when training began to focus on school conflicts, possibly because the effect of training skills related to the home situation carried over to behaviour in the school with a consequential ceiling effect.

At first sight, it would seem from the single-case data that, although short-term improvements can be demonstrated in the training of very specific responses such as eye contact, the results are less encouraging for the teaching of more complex

Table 1 Single case studies

Reference	Type of design	Treatment and length	Trainees	Number of SST subjects	Setting	Targets	Generalization measures	Follow-up	Outcome
Braukmann et al. (1973)	Multiple baseline across behaviours	SST (instructions, modelling, practice and feedback). 4 sessions	Male pre-delinquents	2	Family group home	Heterosexual interaction skills (information, prompts, head nods, attention feedback)	Observation at parties	None	Increase in skills performace contingent on training. Increased female contact at parties
Braukmann et al. (1974)	Multiple baseline (a) across behaviours (b) across subjects	SST (instructions, modelling, practice and feedback). 8–14 sessions	Male pre-delinquents	6	Family group home	Interview skills (posture, eye contact, answers and appearance)	Stooge inter views	None	Increase in skill performance contingent upon onset of training
Kifer et al. (1974)	Multiple baseline across subjects	Instructions, practice and feedback. 4–6 sessions	Pre-delinquents and their parents	3	Family group home	Family negotiation skills	Home observation and 4 role play	None	Increases in negotiation responses after training
Maloney et al. (1976)	Multiple baseline across trainers	SST and contingent points reinforcement training by peers or teaching parents. 10–20 sessions	Female pre-delinquents	4	Family group home	Conversation skills (posture and volunteering answers)	None	None	Training by peers as effective as by teaching parents

Minkin et al. (1976)	Multiple baseline across behaviours	Instructions with rationale, practice with feedback plus financial reinforcement. 3–7 conversations (sessions unknown)	Female pre-delinquents	4	Family group home	Conversation skills (question asking and conversation feedback)	None	None	Increase in skill performance contingent upon training
Spence and Marzillier (1979)	Multiple baseline across behaviours	SST package (instructions, discussion, modelling rehearsal and feedback). 7–10 sessions	Male offenders	5	Residential institution	Conversation skills (eye contact, head movements, listening skills	Staff questionnaire of social behaviour	2 wks	Improvement for some skills more than others. Individual differences in response to SST

response strategies. There are, however, several criticisms of the methods employed in the Thelen *et al.* (1976) study. First there was no initial attempt in the study to carry out any initial assessment of the interaction skills of the boys involved. Rather, the study tended to assume that all young offenders are deficient in social skills and will therefore benefit from SST. This is a highly questionable assumption and it seems more likely that deficits in social skills will be evident only with some young offenders and not others. Similarly, the type of situations in which difficulties are found are likely to vary for different individuals. The targets of training should therefore be selected according to the needs of the trainees, based on carefully collated assessment data and not the clinical intuitions of the therapists (Combs and Slaby, 1977). Given that the Thelen *et al.* (1976) study did not meet this requirement, it was perhaps not surprising that significant changes were not produced.

A second limitation of the study was its failure to programme for generalization of behaviour change. For example, there was no attempt to train the care staff or peers to model, prompt and reinforce desirable social behaviour outside training sessions. Similarly, it may have been preferable to make use of peer models, rather than drama students in the videotaped demonstrations, in order to maximize the modelling effect. Bandura (1973) suggests that modelling effects are likely to be greater if peer models are used, rather than models who differ considerably from the trainees in terms of age, status and social background. Table 1 summarizes the single-case design studies available to date.

Outcome studies involving group designs

The majority of studies which have attempted to assess the benefit of training complex interaction skills have used group designs (see Table 2). Sarason and Ganzer (1973) were possibly the pioneers in this area, reporting an extensive research programme which is one of the few studies to investigate the effects of therapy on subsequent offending. The majority of studies investigating the benefits of SST with young offenders have tended to assess change purely in terms of indices such as social behaviour within the institutional setting. Few have considered whether the intervention influences the behaviour that theoretically led to the adolescent being referred for training in the first place, namely delinquent activities.

In the Sarason and Ganzer (1973) study, 192 male, first offenders were randomly assigned to three groups; a SST group, a discussion group and a no-treatment control group. The SST procedure involved the modelling of appropriate behaviour by adult students, depicting a variety of problem situations. The boys were then asked to imitate the correct way of responding, trying to approximate as closely as possible to the model's performance. Feedback was then given from the rest of the group. The boys attended fourteen, 1-hour sessions in groups of four. The discussion group on the other hand simply discussed the same problems as the SST groups, and the means of dealing with them. Both groups received the same amount of therapist contact. The no-treatment group received only the traditional regime of the institution. The results demonstrated positive changes in attitude such as shifts towards internal locus of control on the Rotter (1966) scale, positive changes in behaviour and less recidivism over the 3-year follow-up for both treatment groups compared to the no-treatment group. There were no significant differences, however, between the modelling and discussion group conditions, which suggests that the effects may have been due to increased adult contact or increased information about tactics of dealing with difficult social situations.

The Sarason and Ganzer study, however, also falls foul of the same assumption as Thelen *et al.* (1976) in that there was no attempt to screen out boys who were already adequate in terms of social skills. They tended to assume that all young offenders are deficient in social skills and would therefore benefit from SST. It is likely that, in practice, many of the subjects selected for SST were already adequately skilled. Indeed, this suggestion is borne out to some extent by Sarason and Ganzer themselves who reported that boys described as passive and deficient in verbal skills tended to respond better to the modelling procedure, whereas boys who were verbally skilled tended to respond rather better to the discussion procedure. This tends to support the view that, perhaps not surprisingly, SST procedures are most appropriate for those juvenile offenders who are deficient in interaction skills and that this is not necessarily the case for all young offenders.

In a more recent study reported by Shoemaker (1979) young offenders from a series of cottage home residential placements were selected as being suitable for SST according to their scores on a staff questionnaire and self-report question-naire of social behaviour. The thirty lowest scoring boys were randomly assigned to either an assertive training procedure, a minimal treatment group (non-directive discussion) and a no-treatment control group. The assertive training procedure involved a typical SST package designed to facilitate performance during conflict situations. The two treatment groups received eight therapy sessions, in addition to two discussion sessions occurring before and after training. The no-treatment boys attended the discussion sessions only. Direct observation of behaviour during these discussion sessions revealed an increase in assertive behaviour for the assertive training group but not for the comparison groups. Staff ratings of assertive behaviour in the cottage setting also showed a significant improvement for the assertive training procedure. No improvement was found, however, in terms of ability to discriminate between assertive and non-assertive behaviour and passing an assertive situation test. These problems were overcome in subsequent groups by differential reinforcement, to encourage the boys to discriminate between aggression and withdrawing.

A similar institutional-based programme was recently reported by Ollendick and Hersen (1979). In a previous study (Ollendick and Elliott, 1978) it had been

Table 2 Group design outcome studies

Reference	Groups	N	Treatment and length	Trainees	Setting	Targets	Generalization measures	Follow-up	Outcome
Alexander and Parsons (1973)	Family SST Client centred Psychodynamic No treatment	46 9 11 10	Instructions and discussion, modelling, practice, feedback and social reinforcement. Some token economy. 12–15 sessions	Male and female offenders	Family clinic	Family interaction skills (communication and negotiation skills)	Recidivism and videotaped family discussion	6–18 months	Lower recidivism for SST. improved interaction for SST
Ollendick and Hersen (1979)	SST Discussion No treatment	9 9 9	Instructions, peer modelling, behaviour rehearsal, feedback, social reinforcement and homework tasks. 10 sessions	Male Offenders high on external locus of control	Residential institution	Interpersonal conflict skills	Points earned in institution programme role play tests	2 weeks	Shift towards internal locus of control, positive changes on role play behaviour and points carried for SST but not discussion or no treatment
Sarason and Ganzer (1973)	SST Discussion No treatment	64 64 64	Modelling, role play and feedback. 14 sessions	Male offenders	Residential reception centre	Wide range on interpersonal situations	Recidivism rate, self-report scales, staff ratings of behaviour	3 years	Less recidivism, positive behaviour and attitude change for both SST and discussion groups
Shoemaker (1979)	Assertive training Discussion No treatment	10 10 10	Instructions, modelling, role play and feedback plus token reinforcement. 8 sessions	Male offenders. Low scoring on assertion	Residential cottages	Assertive responding	Staff ratings, peer rankings, observation of discussion sessions	None	Assertive training superior to discussion and no treatment on staff ratings and assertive behaviour in discussion. No difference on peer ratings

Reference	Type of design	Treatment and length	Trainees	Number of SST subjects	Setting	Targets	Generalization measures	Follow-up	Outcome
Spence (1979); Spence and Spence (1980)	SST, Attention placebo, No treatment	Instructions, discussion, role play, feedback social reinforcement, homework tasks. 12 sessions	Male offenders. low scoring on staff question-	32, 20, 24	Residential community home	Basic and complex interpersonal skills	Staff questionnaire, self-report social problems, recidivism, video-taped interview, social work questionnaire	6 months	SST greater shift to internal locus of control of APC and NTC. Specific improvements on basic skills. No changes on staff questionnaire or video-taped interview. SST and APC improvement on self-esteem and self-reported social problems. No difference in recidivism or social workers questionnaire.
Thelen et al. (1976)	Multiple baseline across situations plus no-treatment control (N=3)	Modelling and role playing. 9 sessions	Male offenders	7	Group home	Conflict resolution skills	Staff ratings of interpersonal behaviour	2 wks	Improvement for 3 boys only and not maintained at follow-up
Werner et al. (1975)	Multiple baseline across behaviours plus no-treatment control (N=3)	Instructions with rationale, modelling, practice with feedback. 14 sessions	Male offenders	3	Family group home	Police interaction skills (eye contact, polite responses, expressions of reform, co-operation)	Ratings of interviews with police officers	None	Improvement on specific skills. Pre-post improvement on police judgements but also found for no-treatment group

reported that juvenile offenders who scored as 'externals' on a locus of control scale showed more aggressive behaviour, were discharged after a long period from a behaviour modification programme and evidenced a higher recidivism rate after a 1-year follow-up period than their 'internal' scoring counterparts. Ollendick and Hersen (1979) on the basis of this finding, took scores on the Nowicki–Strickland (1973) Locus of Control scale for children as the criterion for selection for a social-skills training programme. Twenty seven boys were selected as scoring high in terms of external orientation and were then randomly assigned to either a SST group, discussion group or no-treatment control. The SST group received ten sessions occurring once a week in which interpersonal problems were reported by the group. Next discussions were held regarding alternative response choices and instructions were given regarding their performance. New responses were taught by means of peer modelling, behaviour rehearsal, feedback, social reinforcement and homework tasks. The discussion group received an equivalent level of therapist contact but merely discussed interpersonal conflicts and possible solutions. The no-treatment group received only the regular behaviour modification regime of the institution. The study found that the SST group showed significant shifts towards internality from pre- to post-training on the locus of control scale (Nowicki and Strickland, 1973), positive improvements on behavioural measures during role play (e.g. eye contact, latency of response and aggressive contact) and points earned in the institutional programme. No such changes were evident for either the discussion or no-treatment control groups.

Both the Shoemaker (1979) and the Ollendick and Hersen (1979) studies therefore provide evidence to suggest that SST procedures can produce positive short-term changes in certain aspects of social behaviour. Neither study, however, reported whether these changes were maintained, nor whether there was any influence on subsequent offence behaviour. It was encouraging to find that both the above studies did attempt to determine whether the behaviour change produced generalized to everyday interactions in the residential setting. The Shoemaker study made use of a staff questionnaire, as the staff were unaware of which group the boys were attending, whereas the Ollendick and Hersen (1979) study considered the number of points earned in the behavioural programme. In both cases, positive pre- to post-training changes were produced for the SST procedure on these measures of generalization.

The Tennal Project

An attempt to investigate the long-term, generalized effects of social skills training with adolescent male offenders was recently carried out in a local authority community home school (Spence, 1979; Spence and Spence, 1980). This study attempted to overcome many of the methodological inadequacies of previous studies by combining a single-case experimental design with a group design. The participants were seventy-six male offenders aged between 10 and 16 years resident in a local authority community home school as the result of a variety of offences, ranging from persistent truancy to arson and assault. Boys were considered as being eligible for the project if they were identified as experiencing interpersonal difficulties on a staff questionnaire. The targets for training related to very specific responses such as eye contact, head movements and listening skills, in addition to more complex strategies of responding such as dealing with teasing, bullying, criticism and police interactions. The curriculum for each group was determined from the outcome of an assessment battery involving a staff questionnaire, self-report questionnaire and direct behavioural analysis of a videotaped interview.

The boys were randomly assigned in groups of four to either social skills training ($N = 32$), attention-placebo comparison ($N = 20$) or no-treatment control ($N = 24$) groups. The SST group received twelve 1-hour sessions of instructions, discussion, videotaped peer modelling, behaviour rehearsal, feedback with social reinforcement and homework tasks. Several attempts were made to programme for generalization of behaviour change as suggested by Goldstein *et al.* (1978). A wide range of trainers were used, peer prompting and reinforcement was encouraged outside sessions, homework tasks were set and relevant targets were selected for training. Unfortunately, it was not possible to programme staff prompting and reinforcement outside sessions as the staff members were required to be blind to the procedure received by the boys, in order to act as independent raters of social behaviour.

Four basic skills were trained sequentially for three sessions each, so as to conform to a multiple baseline design across behaviour. A brief period was allowed at the beginning of each session in which a conversation between each boy and an adult stooge was videotaped, in order to assess basic skill performance. The attention-placebo comparison group received equivalent levels of staff contact but discussed relevant social issues such as life in borstals and racial prejudice. Films relating to these topics were shown and plays were then written and videotaped. The no-treatment group received only the traditional regime of the institution and assessment contact.

Changes in the more complex interaction skills were assessed by means of pre- and post-training and 6 month follow-up measures on a staff questionniare, a self-report questionnaire, the Coopersmith (1967) self-esteem scale, Nowicki–Strickland (1973) locus of control scale for children, social worker's questionnaire of family and social interactions, and self-reported and official offence data. The results of the single-case, multiple baseline design across behaviours of the SST subjects showed that SST led to a specific and marked improvement in the performance of certain basic social skills, such as eye contact, head movements and a decrease in fiddling movements when training was introduced, for the majority of subjects. Certain basic skills were found to be harder to train than others, with attention feedback responses proving to be particularly resistant to change. The boys were also found to vary in their response to training of basic social skills. Where improvements were produced, these changes were generally maintained at 3-month follow-up.

Assessment of the benefits of training more complex responses by means of the group design produced less encouraging results. An overall negative trend in social behaviour was found over time for all the groups in general, as reported by the staff questionnaire. The SST procedure served to limit this deterioration to some extent, but the difference was not significant and did not extend beyond the training period. A significant decrease in self-reported social problems was found for both the SST and attention placebo group, with a similar although statistically insignificant decrease for the no-treatment group. This improvement did not continue, however, during the follow-up period. In terms of self-esteem, both the SST and attention placebo group showed a significant increase from the pre- to post-training assessment but there was a subsequent reversal towards low self-esteem during the follow-up phase. The SST procedures resulted in a shift toward external locus of control during training which was not found for the comparison groups, a finding which parallels that of Ollendick and Hersen (1979). This effect, however, was again not maintained during follow-up, where there was a trend towards external locus of control for all groups. No differences over time or between groups were found in terms of self-reported or official offence data, social workers ratings of family and social relationships or independent judges ratings of pre- and post-training videotaped interviews.

It seems therefore that, despite producing significant and considerable improvements in basic social skills and attempting to train more complex strategies of dealing with problem situations, there were no marked changes in social behaviour outside the training sessions. This was particularly disappointing when attempts had been made to programme for generalization of behaviour change. Where positive changes in self-report measures were evident, these were also found for the attention-placebo group, suggesting an attention effect. Similarly, these improvements also tended to be short-lived, even on the locus of control scale. Only the improvements on specific, basic social skills such as eye contact, were of long duration and assessment of these measures was limited to the training setting. It was not possible therefore to determine whether these changes carried over to everyday interactions within the school

The findings of this study were disappointing, particularly in view of the more positive findings of other studies such as Ollendick and Hersen (1979) and Shoemaker (1979). However, several possibilities can be suggested to account for the difference in results. First, the type of institutional regime upon which the SST programmes were based varied considerably in the different studies. The institutional setting in the Shoemaker study involved a series of small cottages in which behaviour modification programmes were already operating. The training centre involved in the Hersen and Ollendick study was also operating a token economy and flexible behavioural contracting system. Both institutions therefore differed markedly from the regime operating at Tennal, where staff were less experienced in prompting and reinforcing desirable behaviour. In the Tennal project the subjects were housed in large thirty-boy units, where the emphasis was on containment, personal care and counselling rather than behaviour modification. Observation in the house units revealed that, partly due to limited staffing levels, the staff rarely prompted or reinforced appropriate social behaviour. In addition, peer influences within the units tended to be primarily of an anti-social nature, in which pro-social behaviour was frequently punished and anti-social behaviour frequently modelled and reinforced. Similar findings in this type of institutional setting have been reported by Patterson (1963), and Furness (1964). The suggestion that the grouping together of large numbers of delinquent boys in the absence of clearly defined behavioural regimes may be detrimental was supported to some extent by the deterioration in social behaviour reported from the staff questionnaire.

It seems likely therefore that the value of SST programmes within institutional settings is very much determined by the ongoing regime of the institution. Social skills training aims to increase desirable and pro-social behaviour during social encounters and this aim is most likely to be achieved in everyday interactions if the programmes are operating to model, prompt and reinforce such behaviour outside the training setting. Where staff are not already trained to carry out this function as part of the ongoing institutional regime, it seems essential that attempts are made to train staff in these areas, as part of the SST programme.

A review of the group design studies suggests that generally short-term improvements in interpersonal functioning can be produced with young offenders and these changes do generalize beyond the training setting. However, changes appear to depend upon the type of institutional regime operating outside the training setting. The adequacy of measures used to assess generalization can, however, be questioned. The use of staff questionnaires of assertive behaviour (e.g. Shoemaker, 1979), role-play techniques, and points earned outside training sessions, need further investigations as to their reliability and validity as indicators of inter personal effectiveness. It would be preferable to observe social behaviour directly in real-life situations in order to monitor behaviour change. This process for example could be achieved by means of complex coding systems (e.g. Patterson et al., 1969) but is obviously arduous and time consuming.

The long-term benefits of institution-based SST programmes were only reported in two studies (Sarason and Ganzer, 1973; Spence, 1979). In the former study, SST was found to produce limited improvements at follow-up but these were also evident for the discussion group. The latter study failed to produce evidence of long-term benefits in terms of generalized changes, although lasting improvements in skill performance were found within an interview setting. Perhaps all that can be said on the basis of the evidence available to date, is that

SST can be successful in producing short-term improvements in social behaviour but its long-term value relationship to offence behaviour remains to be adequately demonstrated.

Social skills training with young offenders and their families

Another area to which SST has recently been applied is the teaching of appropriate family interaction patterns. An excellent study reported by Alexander and Parsons (1973) attempted to teach complex interpersonal skills to young offenders and their parents. An initial study (Alexander, 1973) had provided evidence to suggest that the interaction patterns of the families of young offenders differed from the families of non-offenders, in terms of levels of reciprocal communication, equality of communication between family members and requests for clarification and feedback. Alexander suggested that maladaptive interaction patterns between family members may be a primary factor in the maintenance of adolescent offending. In order to test out this hypothesis attempts were made to train those responses that had been shown to differ for offender and non-offender families. Seventy-six families of juvenile offenders were randomly assigned to either a short-term skills training group ($N = 46$), a comparison group of either client-centered ($N = 19$) or psychodynamic ($N = 11$) orientation, or a no-treatment control group. The interaction skills training procedure made use of instructions, discussion, modelling, role-play, prompting and social reinforcement. After training, these families showed more equality of talking between family members, less silence and more interruptions for clarification, increased information and positive feedback. This pattern improved in the direction typical of families without a delinquent member. Lower recidivism rates were also found over the 6–18-month follow-up for the skills training group, compared to both the comparison groups and no-treatment control. Possibly the most important finding was that in those families that did not show any change in interaction patterns the adolescent also demonstrated minimal reduction in recidivism. This supports the notion of an association between family interaction patterns and persistent juvenile offending.

A subsequent study which also attempted to train negotiation skills to the families of predelinquent youths was reported by Kifer et al. (1974). The authors suggested that many youths make inappropriate responses to conflict situations (such as fighting, withdrawing, tantrums or verbal abuse) which consequently bring them into contact with courts, clinics and similar agencies. Negotiation is another possible response which, although more difficult to execute, is more likely to produce acceptable consequences to those involved. The study therefore set out to investigate the possibility of training the component behaviours involved in the negotiation process. Three parent–child pairs were trained in negotiation responses, using a multiple baseline across subjects. Initially, the families were observed in the home, on three occasions prior to training to enable measures of negotiation responses and agreements to be made. Further baseline data was then collected in the clinical setting. Training consisted of instructions and discussion of conflict situations, alternative responses and consequences, practice, role reversal and feedback. After training a further series of observations were made in the home, in which the families discussed conflict situations. Emphasis was placed on certain components of the negotiation process such as a statement of ones own position, requests for the other person to state his/her position, identification of the point of conflict and suggesting options.

The results showed an increase in the performance of the negotiation responses after the onset of training for each subject, within the training setting. The generalization measures within the home also showed marked increases in negotiation responses during discussion tasks. The adequacy of this type of task as being representative of natural parent–child conflict interactions, however, is rather questionable. The lack of an untreated control group also prevents conclusions that the changes produced within the home were specifically due to the training procedures. The study also failed to investigate the durability of training effects, further limiting the conclusions that can be drawn.

However, both the Alexander and Parsons (1973) and Kifer *et al.* (1974) studies provide encouraging evidence to suggest that SST procedures may be of value in teaching family interaction skills to young offenders and their parents. This would seem to be a particularly important area if the aim of intervention programmes is to re-integrate juvenile offenders into their natural homes and community. Much more research in this area is warranted.

Evaluation of studies

Methodology

Although it is encouraging to find an increased interest in research into the benefits of social skills training with young offenders, we are still a long way from being able to draw valid conclusions about its efficacy. Studies have been carried out in a variety of institutional and community-based settings but the research produced has frequently been limited by methodological inadequacies. The single-case design studies have generally been restricted to the training of very specific responses at a micro-skill level of social behaviour. Although positive improvements in skill performance have been demonstrated, the assessment of change has been limited to immediate effects and, typically, to the setting in which the training was carried out. There has been a general failure to determine whether changes in micro-level responses are maintained, carry over to everyday interactions outside the training setting and, perhaps most importantly, influence the outcome of social interactions and future offending. Studies are needed which carry out naturalistic observations of basic skill performance outside the training setting, as part of the evaluation process and also consider the influence of training on future offending.

Whereas the single-case design literature has mainly been restricted to the training of micro-level responses, the group design studies have mostly focused on the training of social skills at a more molar level (e.g. acceptance of criticism or making requests). The tendency of skills training programmes to focus on different levels of behaviour makes comparability between studies difficult. Group design studies, however, have the advantage of making the evaluation of long-term and generalized changes easier to achieve. Again, however, it is difficult to draw conclusions about the outcome data owing to a range of methodological limitations. Different studies have varied in the way in which subjects have been selected for training. The criteria for selection has varied from low scores on staff questionnaires of social behaviour (Spence, 1979), to scoring as highly 'external' in terms of locus of control (Ollendick and Hersen, 1979). Other studies have made no attempt to select participants on the basis of interpersonal skills deficits and have selected purely on the basis of offence history (e.g. Sarason and Ganzer, 1973). The failure of studies to select trainees on the basis of social skills deficits may partially reflect the lack of research and expertise in the area of assessment of social skills. Much more consideration needs to be given to the development of reliable and valid assessment tools (Spence, 1980).

Not only is there a lack of comparability between subjects in the research literature, but there is also a lack of comparability in terms of training methodology. Programmes have varied in the degree to which they have attempted to programme for generalization. Some (e.g. Spence, 1979) tried to facilitate the transfer of training effects in several ways, whereas others (e.g. Sarason and Ganzer, 1973) made little attempt to do so. Similarly, the duration and number of sessions have varied, as has the type of techniques used in training. For example, the type of modelling procedure used has varied in terms of the use of adult, student, or peer models and live versus videotaped models.

Few of the group design studies available to date have met all the requirements of adequate comparison groups, population sizes, and assessment of generalization and durability of training effects. The population sizes have been rather small in some studies (e.g. Ollendick and Hersen, 1979; Shoemaker, 1979) which limit the conclusions that can be drawn. In some cases (e.g. Shoemaker, 1979) long-term follow-up data have not been reported. Although the group design studies have attempted, in general, to determine whether the benefits of training carry over to real-life settings and influence success in naturalistic social interactions, the method of assessment has, on occasion, been rather questionable. The use of role-play and simulated interview techniques as being representative of real-life interactions is rather questionable (Bellack et al., 1978). As with the single-case design data, studies are needed which carry out extensive naturalistic observations of social behaviour, in order to assess adequately the transfer of training effects. Such evaluation should extend to community-based interactions and should not be limited to the institutional setting, if the aim of training is to teach skills to enable the adolescent to cope more successfully in interactions within the community. Similarly, if it is suggested that the social-skills training procedure should in some way act to reduce the probability of future offending, then the evaluation process should consider offence statistics, indicating both official and self-reported offence data. It is quite possible that social skills training may have the effect of reducing the likelihood of conviction for an offence, without having any significant impact on the actual frequency of offending. This possibility can only be assessed by comparison of official and self-reported offence data.

When drawing conclusions about the effectiveness of a therapeutic intervention, it is important to consider the size of the behaviour change produced. It is quite possible for studies to report statistically significant changes which are actually relatively small and of little practical relevance. If this concept is applied to the social skills training data with young offenders, the results cannot be said to have produced marked benefits of great impact even when statistically significant benefits have been shown (e.g. Sarason and Ganzer, 1973). This possibly reflects the short duration of the training programmes used. The length of training has varied across the different studies but, on average, has involved only about ten sessions. Perhaps it is unrealistic to expect extensive changes in social behaviour to be brought about after such a limited input. The training procedure is attempting to achieve effects which would generally result from several years of training from parents, teachers and peers. Research would therefore be useful which compares the long-term effectiveness of training for programmes of different lengths. It may prove necessary to incorporate social skills training sessions into the ongoing regime of the institution, in order that training becomes a continuous process, if lasting and marked changes in social behaviour are to be produced. This relates not just to the time scale of training but also to the frequency of sessions. Typically, training has been carried out on a once- or twice-weekly session basis. It may prove more effective if training is carried out on a daily session basis by the care staff or teachers who are in continuous contact with the adolescents. It would then be relatively easy for the same adults to carry out the reinforcement of desirable social behaviour outside sessions, in order to maximize the transfer of training effects. Indeed, this approach is recommended by Goldstein et al. (1978) but has not been adequately evaluated in relation to work with juvenile offenders.

Finally, it is also important to consider the type of regimes operating in addition to the social skills training procedure. As already mentioned, the type of ongoing regime has varied markedly in the different studies ranging from a counselling-based approach (e.g. Spence, 1979) to a token economy/behavioural contracting base (Ollendick and Hersen, 1979). It is essential that studies clearly report the type of ongoing regime received by the trainees, as this may have considerable influence upon the outcome of the social skills training procedure, and indeed may explain the failure to find positive effects in some studies (e.g. Spence, 1979).

Efficacy

The methodological limitations and lack of comparability between studies makes it difficult to draw conclusions about the value of social skills training as an intervention method with young offenders. However, it can be said that social skills training has been found to be effective in producing short-term improvements in the performance of certain micro-level responses, within the training setting. The only study which has attempted to evaluate the durability of training effects suggest that generally the improvements in basic skills performance are maintained (Spence, 1979). There are, however, considerable differences in the response of different trainees to the procedure. Similarly, different responses would seem to be harder to train than others. Evidence is not yet available to determine whether the effects generalize beyond the training setting nor, more importantly, whether they influence the outcome of social interactions and recidivism.

When considering the benefits of training more complex interaction skills, the results are less clear-cut. Few studies are available in this area and existing reports have produced conflicting data. Training of juvenile offenders and their parents in family interaction skills has produced perhaps the most encouraging results to date. Although more studies are required in this area, the evidence to date suggests that improved family interaction patterns can be taught and do generalize to the natural setting. In addition, such benefits would seem to be associated with a reduction in offence behaviour.

Those studies which have investigated the benefits of social skills training with juvenile offenders without the involvement of other family members have produced conflicting results. Typically programmes of this type have been carried out within institutional settings and differences in background regimes may account for the differences in outcome. Until further research into this possibility is carried out, however, conclusions cannot be drawn. Whereas some studies suggest that social skills training programmes can produce generalized improvements in social interaction performance, others have not been able to replicate this finding. In general, there has been a failure to investigate whether training programmes influence future offending and the limited evidence in this area has again produced conflicting results. Perhaps the most encouraging conclusion that can be drawn to date is that some studies have produced evidence to suggest that social skills training can produce positive changes in social behaviour that generalize beyond the training setting and produce significant reductions in offending. However, much more research is necessary before reliable and valid conclusions as to the long-term, generalized, benefits of social skills training with juvenile offenders can be drawn. Until such evidence is available, the practice of social skills training should proceed with caution, with practitioners attempting, wherever possible, to evaluate the benefits of their programmes.

Future directions of research and practice

Many important questions remain to be answered. For example, it is important to determine which aspects of the training package are necessary and effective in bringing about therapeutic change. It is also important that methods are investigated which maximize the degree of behaviour change produced and/or increase the transfer of training effects to naturalistic situations. It is essential to understand not only which types of background regimes enhance lasting and generalized changes but also which therapeutic components may be added to the training package to produce such effects. For example, recent work in the area of social skills training with adult populations has stressed the need to consider the role of cognitive components in determining social performance (Morley *et al.*, 1982). Even when an adolescent has developed an adequate repertoire of social skills, his performance may still be limited by inappropriate thoughts such as 'I'm bound to fail, so what's the point of trying' or 'Why the hell should I try, all adults are pigs anyway'. In such instances, cognitive restructuring techniques, such as those of Beck (1976) and Ellis (1958), may be of value.

In addition to techniques which may be incorporated into the training package, it is important to determine more fully the influence of different background regimes on the outcome of training. For example, the benefits of linking up token economy system targets to the targets of training in social skills programmes would be worth investigating. This may provide a useful means of facilitating the generalization process as it increases the likelihood that desirable social behaviour will be reinforced outside training sessions. However, not only is it important to determine those methods which enhance training effects within institutional settings, but it is also important to investigate the value of social-skills training programmes in conjunction with community-based programmes. Although there are many community-based projects catering for juvenile offenders, such as intermediate treatment programmes, there has been a noticeable lack of research into the value of social skills training as an adjunct to such approaches. Undoubtedly, many programmes make use of social skills training procedures to teach a variety of interpersonal and vocational skills, but few have assessed the value of these endeavours. It would be interesting to evaluate the benefits of training social skills in community programmes, as many of the problems associated with achieving generalization of behaviour change are likely to be reduced. Similarly, it would be interesting to assess the possibility of involving parents in training programmes, not just in the teaching of family interaction skills but also making use of parents as trainers to model, prompt and reinforce desirable social behaviour outside training sessions. If parents could be used in this way, lasting and generalized changes would be much more likely. As yet, there is a lack of information as to the type of adolescents who benefit most from social skills training procedures. Although it seems likely that young offenders who are deficient in interpersonal skills are more likely to benefit from the techniques than those who are already adequately skilled, this suggestion requires further investigation. It would also be useful to identify other criteria which predict a successful response to training. Only then will it be possible for trainers to select those individuals who are most likely to benefit from training.

We also need much more information as to which targets should be trained for particular individuals. There has been a tendency for many programmes to select targets for training because therapist intuitions suggest that such targets should be relevant and important. However, much more research is needed in order to clarify which responses are important in determining success in social interactions for adolescents. A prerequisite to achieving this goal is the development of reliable and valid means of assessing social skills for adolescent populations. Although initial attempts have been made in this area (Freedman *et al.*, 1978; Spence, 1979) much more work is yet to be done. Reliable and valid assessment tools would also make it much easier for trainers to identify clients for training, select appropriate targets on an individual basis and evaluate the effects of training. It also seems important that the assessment and training of social skills extends from the execution of overt responses to consider the perception of other peoples' use of non-verbal and verbal cues. For example, an initial attempt at assessing the ability to perceive emotional state from cues such as facial expression, posture, gestures and tone of voice has been reported by Spence (1980). However, much more attention needs to be paid to assessment and training in this area as inability to perceive the meaning of such cues, or indeed misperception, may have marked adverse effects on social functioning (Trower *et al.*, 1978).

On a final note, it is worth mentioning the potential role of social skills training techniques in the prevention of delinquent behaviour. Research suggests that children who experience interpersonal difficulties, in particular with their peers, are more likely to show other subsequent adjustment problems such as school maladjustment (Gronlund and Anderson, 1963), failure to attend school (Ullman, 1957) and delinquency (Roff *et al.*, 1972). It seems likely, therefore, that the development of such problems would be reduced if children could be taught those skills that increase success in social interactions. It may be possible to identify children who are deficient in terms of social and interpersonal skills and direct them into preventive social skills training programmes. Alternatively, it may prove useful to incorporate social skills training techniques into the regular school curriculum. Initial attempts to introduce preventative programmes into schools such as the use of social problem-solving techniques (Allen *et al.*, 1976) have produced encouraging results. Research into the preventive use of social skills training procedures would be of undoubted value and may even be the most important direction of future research.

Summary

This chapter has reviewed the research into socialskills training programmes with juvenile offenders. Single-case and group design studies were considered separately in order to assess the outcome and methodological adequacy of evaluative reports. An attempt was made to assess critically the contribution made by individual studies to this area of research. Conclusions about the efficacy of social skills training techniques with young offenders were difficult to draw owing to limitations in methodological design and lack of comparability between studies. Training programmes were found to differ greatly in terms of components of training, duration, micro- versus macro- level training, selection of trainees and method of assessment. There was also a failure of some studies to investigate the durability and generalization of training effects. Suggestions for future research and practice were made, with a final emphasis on the potential of social skills training in preventive programmes.

References

Alexander, J. P. (1973). Defensive and supportive communications in normal families, *Journal of Consulting and Clinical Psychology*, **40**, 223–231.
Alexander, J. P. and Parsons, B. V., (1973). Short-term behavioural intervention with delinquent families: Impact on family process and recidivism, *Journal of Abnormal Psychology*, **81**, 219–225.
Allen, G. J., Chinsky, J. M., Larcen, S. W., Lochman, J. E. and Selinger, H. V. (1976). *Community Psychology and the Schools*, Wiley, London.
Argyle, M. (1969). *Social Interaction*, Methuen, London.
Argyle, M., Trower, P. and Bryant, B. (1974). Explorations in the treatment of personality disorders and neuroses by social skills training, *British Journal of Medical Psychology*, **47**, 63–72.
Bandura, A (1973). *Aggression: A Social Learning Analysis*, Prentice-Hall, New York.
Beck, A. T. (1976). *Cognitive Therapy and the Emotional Disorders*, International Universities Press, New York.
Bellack, A. S., Hersen, M. and Turner, S. M. (1976). Generalization effects of social skills training in chronic schizophrenics: an experimental analysis, *Behaviour Research and Therapy*, **14**, 391–398.
Bellack, A. S., Hersen, M. and Turner, S. M. (1978). Role Play tests for assessing social skills: Are they valid? *Behaviour Therapy*, **9**, 448–461.
Braukmann, C. J., Fixen, D. L., Phillips, E. L. and Wolf, M. M. (1975). Behavioral approaches to treatment in the crime and delinquency field, *Criminology*, **13**, 299–331.
Braukmann, C. J., Maloney, D. M., Fixen, D. L., Phillips, E. L. and Wolf, M. M. (1974). Analysis of a selection into view training package for predelinquents at Achievement Place, *Criminal Justice and Behaviour*, **1**, 30–42.
Braukmann, C. J., Maloney, D. M., Phillips, E. and Wolf, M. M. (1973). The measurement and modification of heterosexual interaction skills of pre-delinquents at Achievement Place, University of Kansas (unpublished).

Camp, B. W., Blom, G. E., Herbert, F. and Van Doorninck, W. J. (1977) 'Think Aloud': a program for developing self-control in young aggressive boys, *Journal of Abnormal Child Psychology*, 5, 167–169.

Cicourel, A. V. (1968). *The Social Organisation of Juvenile Justice*, Wiley, New York.

Combs, M. L. and Slaby, D. A. (1977). Social Skills training with children, in *Advances in Clinical Child Psychiatry* Vol. 1 (Eds B. B. Lahey and A. E. Kazdin) Plenum Press, London.

Coopersmith, S. (1967). *The Antecedents of Self Esteem*, W. H. Freeman, London.

Cornish, D. B. and Clarke, R. G. (1975). *Residential Treatment and Its Effects on Delinquency*, Study No. 32, HMSO, London.

Curran, J. P. (1973). Correlates of physical attractiveness and interpersonal attraction in the dating situation, *Social Behaviour and Personality*, 1, 153–157.

Edelstein, B. A. and Eisler, R. M. (1976). Effects of modeling and modeling with instructions and feedback on the behavioural component of social skills, *Behaviour Therapy*, 7, 382–389.

Ellis, A. (1958). Rational psychotherapy, *Journal of General Psychology*, 59, 35–49.

Freedman, B. J., Rosenthal, L., Donahoe, C. P., Schlundt, D. G. and McFall, R. M. (1978). A social-behavioural analysis of skill deficits in delinquent and non-delinquent adolescent boys, *Journal of Consulting and Clinical Psychology*, 46, 1448–1462.

Furness, J. (1964). *Peer Reinforcement of Behaviour in an Institution for Delinquent Girls*. Unpublished Masters Thesis, Oregon State University.

Goldstein, A. P. (1973). *Structured Learning Therapy: Towards a Psychotherapy for the Poor*, Academic Press, New York.

Goldstein, A. P., Sherman, M., Gershaw, N. J., Sprafkin, R. P. and Glick, B. (1978). Training aggressive adolescents in prosocial behaviour, *Journal of Youth and Adolsecence*, 7, 73–93.

Gottman, J., Gonso, J. and Rasmussen, B. (1975). Social interaction, social competence and friendship in children, *Child Development*, 46, 709–718.

Gronlund, H. and Anderson, L. (1963). Personality characteristics of socially accepted, socially neglected and socially rejected junior high school pupils, in *Educating for Mental Health* (Ed. J. Seidman) Growell, New York.

Hartup, W. W. (1965). Peers as agents of social reinforcement, *Young Children*, 1965, 20.

Hartup, W. W., Glazer, J. and Charlesworth, R. (1967). Peer reinforcement and sociometric status, *Child Development*, 38, 1017–1024.

Hersen, M., Turner, S. M., Edelstein, B. A. and Pinkston, S. G. (1975). Effects of phenothiazines and social skills training in a withdrawn schizophrenic, *Journal of Clinical Psychology*, 31, 588–594.

Jesness, C. F. (1976). The Youth Centre Project: Transactional analysis programs for delinquents, *Behavioural Disorders*, 1, 27–36.

Kifer, R. E., Lewis, M. A., Green, D. R. and Phillips, E. L. (1974). Training pre-delinquent youths and their parents to negotiate conflict situations, *Journal of Applied Behaviour Analysis*, 7, 357–364.

Kirigin, K. A., Wolf, M. M., Braukmann, C. J., Fixen, D. L. and Phillips, E. L. (1979). Achievement Place: A preliminary outcome evaluation, in *Progress in Behaviour Therapy with Delinquents* (Ed. J. S. Stumphauzee) Charles C. Thomas, Springfield, Illinois.

Liberman, R. P., King, L. W., De Risi, W. J. and McCann, M. (1975). *Personal Effectiveness: Guiding People to Assert Themselves and Improve their Social Skills*, Research Press, Champaign, Illinois.

McCord, W., McCord, J. and Zola, I. K. (1959). *Origins of Crime! A New Evaluation of the Cambridge-Somerville Youth Study*, Columbia University Press, New York.

McFall, R. M. and Marston, A. B. (1970). An experimental investigation of behaviour rehearsal in assertive training, *Journal of Abnormal Psychology*, **76**, 295–303.

McFall, R. M. and Twentyman, C. T. (1973). Four experiments on the relative contribution of rehearsal, modeling, coaching to assertion training, *Journal of Abnormal Psychology*, **81**, 199–218.

Maloney, D. H., Harper, T. M., Braukmann, C. J., Fixen, D. L., Phillips, E. L. and Wolf, M. M. (1976). Teaching conversation—related skills to predelinquent girls, *Journal of Applied Behaviour Analysis*, **9**, 127–139.

Marzillier, J. S., Lambert, C. and Kellet, J. (1976). A controlled evaluation of systematic desensitization and social skills training for socially inadequate psychiatric patients, *Behaviour Research and Therapy*, **14**, 225–238.

Minkin, N., Braukmann, C. J., Minkin, B. L., Timbers, G. D., Timbers, B. J., Fixsen, D. L., Phillips, E. L. and Wolf, M. (1976). The social validation and training of conversation skills, *Journal of Applied Behaviour Analysis*, **9**, 127–139.

Morley, S., Shepherd, G. and Spence, S. H. (1982). Cognitive approaches to social skills training, in *Social Skills Training in Practice* (Eds S. H. Spence and G. Shepherd), Academic Press, London.

Nowicki, S. and Strickland, P. R. (1973). A locus of control scale for children, *Journal of Consulting and Clinical Psychology*, **40**, 148–154.

Ollendick, T. H. and Elliott, W. R. (1978). Locus of control as related to effectiveness in a behaviour modification program for juvenile delinquents, Indiana State University (unpublished).

Ollendick, T. H. and Hersen, M. (1979). Social skills training for juvenile delinquents, *Behaviour Research and Therapy*, **17**, 547–555.

Patterson, G. R. (1963). *The Peer Group as Delinquency Reinforcement Agent* Unpublished Doctoral Thesis, University of Oregon.

Patterson, G. R., Ray, R. S., Shaw, D. A. and Cobb, J. A. (1969). *A Manual for Coding of Family Interactions*, Microfiche Publications, New York.

Piliavin, I. and Briar, S. (1964). Police encounters with juveniles, *American Journal of Sociology*, **70**, 206–214.

Roff, M., Sells, B. and Golden, M. (1972). *Social Adjustment and Personality Development in Children*, University of Minnesota Press, Minneapolis.

Rotter, J. B. (1966). Generalized expectancies for internal versus external control of reinforcement, *Psychological Monographs*, **80**.

Sarason, I. G. (1968). Verbal learning, modeling and juvenile delinquency, *American Psychologist*, **23**, 254–266.

Sarason, I. G. and Ganzer, U. J. (1973). Modeling and group discussion in the rehabilitation of juvenile delinquents, *Journal of Counselling Psychology*, **5**, 442–449.

Shoemaker, M. E. (1979). Group assertion training for institutionalized male delinquents in *Progress in Behaviour Therapy with Delinquents* (Ed. J. S. Stumphauzer) Charles C. Thomas, Springfield, Illinois.

Spence, A. J. and Spence, S. H. (1980). Cognitive changes associated with social skills training, *Behaviour Research and Therapy*, **18**, 265–272.

Spence, S. H. (1979). *The Long Term Generalized Effects of Social Skills Training with Adolescent, Male Offenders in an Institutional Setting.* Unpublished Doctoral Thesis, University of Birmingham.

Spence, S. H. (1981). Differences in social skills performance between institutionalized juvenile male offenders and a comparable group of boys without offence records, *British Journal of Clinical Psychology*, **20**, 163–171.

Spence, S. H. (1980). *Social Skills Training with Children and Adolescents: A Counsellor's Manual*, NFER Publishing Co., Windsor.

Spence, S. H. and Marzillier, J. S. (1979). Social skills training with adolescent, male offenders: 1. Short-term effects, *Behaviour Research and Therapy*, **17**, 7–16.

Stumphauzer, J. S. (1979). *Progress in Behaviour Therapy with Delinquents*, Charles C. Thomas, Springfield, Illinois.

Thelen, M. H., Frey, R. A., Dollinger, S. T. and Paul, S. C. (1976). Use of videotaped models to improve the interpersonal adjustment of delinquents, *Journal of Consulting and Clinical Psychology*, **44**, 492.

Trower, P., Bryant, B. and Argyle, M. (1978). *Social Skills and Mental Health*. Methuen, London.

Ullman, C. A. (1957). Teachers, peers and tests as predictors of adjustment, *Journal of Educational Psychology*, **48**, 257–267.

Wallace, C. J., Nelson, C. J., Liberman, R. P., Aitchison, R. A., Lutoff, D., Elder, J. P. and Ferris, C. (1980). A review and critique of social skills training with schizophrenic patients, *Schizophrenia Bulletin*, **6**, 42–62.

Werner, J. S., Minkin, N., Minkin, C. J., Bonnie, L. (1975). 'Intervention package': an analysis to prepare juvenile delinquents for encounters with police officers. *Criminal Justice and Behaviour*, **2**, 22–36.

Werthman, C. and Piliavin, I. (1967). Gang members and the police, in *The Police: Six sociological essays* (Ed. D. Bordua) Wiley, New York.

Williams, D. V. and Akamatsu, T. J. (1978). Cognitive self guidance training with juvenile delinquents: Applicability and generalization, *Cognitive Therapy and Research*, **2**, 285–288.

Wolpe, J. (1958) *Psychotherapy and Reciprocal Inhibition*, Stanford University Press, Stanford.

Developments in the Study of Criminal Behaviour
Volume 1: The Prevention and Control of Offending
Edited by P. Feldman

6

Strategies for Community Intervention in Offender Rehabilitation: An Overview

EUGENE OSTAPIUK

Failure of traditional approaches

The debate concerning traditional approaches and methods in offender rehabilitation has been wide ranging and long standing. The variety of methods conventionally used, including probation, fines, and the variety of forms of custodial detention, each have their supporters and opponents both amongst the concerned general public and professionals who work within existing systems. And yet, it seems, despite the abundance of arguments there is a scarcity of well-documented evidence that traditional systems have made significant inroads in staunching the trend towards an increase in crime in general and in reducing the unacceptably high rate of recidivism in particular. Schur (1965) has put this point very succinctly:

No research has been done to date which enables us to say that one treatment programme is better than another or that enables us to examine a man and specify the treatment he needs. There is no evidence that probation is better than institutions, that institutions are better than probation ... [so] much of what is now being done about crime may be so wrong that the net effect of that action may be to increase rather than decrease crime ... none of the researches conducted to date answers these questions.

It is, therefore, worrying that emphasis is still placed by the 'law and order' lobby on unproven methods based on punishment and deterence, and institutional incarceration.

Although this chapter does not set out to critically survey traditional approaches, the inadequacies and disappointing results of which have been extensively reported elsewhere (Bailey, 1966; Logan, 1972; Feldman, 1977), it is necessary to briefly comment on the two significant factors that have typified such approaches, namely their underlying psychotherapeutic philosophy, and their emphasis on delivery of rehabilitative services in an institutional context, as these factors are in sharp contrast to the promising recent developments which this chapter hopes to illustrate. The relevance of the psychotherapeutic approach to offender rehabilitation has been seriously questioned (Feldman, 1977), while the demonstrable lack of efficacy of the 'psychotherapies' in general has also been addressed (Eysenck, 1960; Rachman, 1972). As Feldman (1977) points out there are a number of premises that undermine the credibility of the psychotherapeutic approach. First, there is the questionable assumption that offenders are necessarily disturbed or maladjusted and that by removing the root causes of such disturbance one will cure the problem of offending. The direct connection between offending and psychological disturbance still remains to be demonstrated. Secondly, if the psychotherapies have proven largely ineffective in treating willing, co-operative and articulate individuals who unquestionably suffer and have sought help themselves, then it is unlikely that individuals who do not seek help, nor consider themselves in personal distress will benefit. To date, it seems, the psychotherapeutic approach has largely failed to demonstrate a significant contribution to the prevention or treatment of offenders, despite many attempts to do so (Reid et al., 1980). Another trend that has characterized traditional provisions for offender rehabilitation has been the emphasis on institutional incarceration. Here again there is hardly any objective evidence available on the effectiveness of punitive, custodial deterrence. On the contrary Feldman (1977) has suggested that institutional systems have little or no training effect on delinquents in terms of within-prison behaviour, and may, indeed, have negative long-term consequences in terms of further development of pro-deviant skills and attitudes. The net result may be that while a very small proportion of offenders may be deterred from reoffending, others are more likely to reoffend following penal, institutional treatment. Stumphauzer (1970, 1973) has shown that offenders in institutions encourage further offending by providing inmates with new deviant skills and ample reinforcement for using them. Perhaps the most significant shortcoming of institutional provisions is that they are highly artificial environments usually isolated from the community hence less likely to prepare individuals for the stresses of the real world, for there is sufficient evidence that skills taught in a highly artificial learning situation are exceedingly difficult to transfer to the subject's natural environment. Thus prison inmates are more often trained to fit neatly into the institution rather than their local community and neighbourhood. Despite these serious drawbacks the use of large institutions has constituted the mainstay of penal policy and traditional attempts at offender care and rehabilitation to the extent that the criminal justice system in the UK is facing a serious crisis. The very recent report of the Parliamentary All Party Penal Affairs Group (1980) entitled *Too Many Prisoners* highlighted the potentially explosive situation in the grossly overcrowded, seriously deprived and antiquated prison establishments. The recommendations of the report were laudable, for example, shorter sentences, and educating the judiciary to send to prison only those most likely to benefit from such provision. However, it failed to consider and recommend preventative measures in order to reduce the prison population nor did it stress the need for non-institutional alternatives and methods of dealing with offenders based on more effective, current, innovative approaches. Perhaps the most promising and vigorous development of the past 10 or 15 years in the field of offender rehabilitation has been the growth and application of behavioural procedures and methodology, based on the principles of both respondent or classical and operant or instrumental learning. Characterized by the rejection of the 'disease model' as inappropriate, if not irrelevant, to the conceptualization of human problems which occur in a social context, the behavioural approach postulates that much of 'abnormal' or 'deviant' behaviour is developed, maintained, and can be modified in the same way as normal behaviour. Accordingly, 'normal' and 'abnormal', 'healthy' or 'deviant' are best considered labels which do not reflect intrinsic differences in social behaviour as much as they represent arbitrary decisions by medico-legal professionals, and society at large, about whether or not the behaviour of a given person is appropriate at a given time or place. The behaviour modification approach has drawn widespread, often controversial, interest from practitioners, the lay public and the media. Its critics have ranged from those who have questioned its application to offender care (Burgess, 1965; Sage, 1974) or have stressed its vulnerability to abuse by institutional staff or the system (Mitford, 1973; Trotter, 1975), to those who maintain that the application of behavioural techniques are unconstitutional or an infringement of civil liberties (Start, 1974). Despite the doubters, there is by now a mass of literature illustrating not only the well-founded promise of behavioural psychology for more effective intervention with offenders, but also the hope of an effective technology of prevention.

Most of the research effort and resultant exciting developments have occurred in the USA. A wide range of behavioural principles have been scrutinized and tried in effecting behaviour change with delinquents. Positive reinforcement and negative reinforcement, modelling and behaviour rehearsal, aversion techniques and response cost, token economies, level systems and time-out are a few examples in a long list of behavioural techniques investigated and, in some cases, applied successfully in intervention programmes undertaken in a variety of treatment environments ranging from penal institutions (Milan et al., 1974) correctional schools (Jesness, 1975b), community based teaching-family homes (Phillips, 1968), local neighbourhoods (Schwitzgebel, 1964; Stumphauzer et al., 1977), to family and even recreational settings (Stuart and Lott, 1972; Fo and O'Donnell, 1974, 1975). By comparison the winds of change have been slow to blow in the UK. Where change has occurred, it has been more a question of re-organizing existing resources than of trying out new approaches. The application in the UK of behavioural technology and methodology to the problem of offender rehabilitation has been sporadic at best. There has been little co-ordination of effort and a dearth of useful research or evaluation reports. The rare attempts at behavioural interventions have been limited to small-scale experimental studies within the parameters of traditional, usually institutional programmes. Nonetheless, there is a perceptible and ever growing emphasis on behavioural alternatives which has gathered momentum throughout the 1970s and, hopefully, heralds the awakening of interest in, and a willingness to apply more extensively, the principles of behavioural psychology to the treatment and prevention of offending.

Behavioural beginnings—an emphasis on institutional programmes

The early attempts to apply behavioural principles to the problem of delinquency were restricted to case studies which had little impact on the rehabilitation scene. However by 1964, Schwitzgebel and his colleagues were already pursuing the kind of enquiry and intervention that 15 years later appears not only relevant but, indeed, innovative. He and his colleagues tackled the problem of attendance at therapy sessions by paying volunteers money. They extended their 'street corner' approach to recruiting delinquent clients directly from the street and set up their project in an old storefront in a high crime area. They were first to point out the uses of contingency contracting with delinquents in their natural environment well before it became a major component of current behavioural practise. By emphasizing the role of modelling and imitation, and paying attention to problems of generalization Schwitzgebel laid the foundation for the current trend towards direct community intervention. However, most of his contemporaries were engaged in more modest treatment programmes. Wetzel (1966) demonstrated that compulsive stealing by a 10-year-old could be controlled by withdrawal of attention, and Tyler (1967) was able to significantly improve the academic performance of a delinquent in an institution through the use of tokens. It is, perhaps, ironic that at this time several commentators deliberating on the application of behaviour modification techniques to the treatment of delinquents, concluded that apart from aversive conditioning other specific techniques would prove of limited usefullness to offender rehabilitation (Jones et al., 1965), for the next decade was to witness a veritable explosion of interesting, if not always successful developments of behavioural intervention programmes. Most of the larger-scale studies were undertaken in an institutional context which still remained the primary locus of treatment efforts.

Among the earliest attempts is the work of Cohen and Filipczak (1971) who were involved in the CASE II project. Working with an institutionalized juvenile population they were able to demonstrate positive improvement in educational standards and indices of intelligence following a token reinforcement programme. In an early attempt to evaluate behavioural against traditional intervention methods Jesness (1975a) compared a token economy programme run at the Karl Holton School for Boys with transactional analysis, the treatment approach at nearby OH Close School for Boys. He and his colleagues found similar recidivism rates for both groups after 1-year follow-up, though both were better than comparison institutions. A lack of treatment effects was also reported by the Rehabilitation Research Foundation (1974) who looked at the impact of a token economy system on a vocational training programme. On the positive side,

Allison *et al.*, (1979) provide evidence for the efficacy and cost-effectiveness of a behavioural treatment programme in a 'juvenile hall' or remand home, utilizing a token or points economy system and contingency contracting. Similar positive results are reported for the 'Learning House' project (Thoresen *et al.*, 1979). This is a behavioural programme for young problem children, using a progression from a points system to contracting, self-control, academic skills training, self-rating, parent counselling, and continuing after-care. The goal of the programme is to help the child develop self-control and to ensure that the home and school environment will continue to support this self-control. In the UK reported studies of behavioural programmes for offenders have also been largely based in institutions of some form. Brown (1977) described the implementation of a token economy scheme for delinquent boys at Gilbey House, a fifteen-bed unit in Tennal Community Home School. The treatment programme comprised of three distinct phases: the daily token programme, the merit programme, and the graduate programme. A youth progressed from daily token earnings which could be cashed in for back-up reinforcers depending on progress in specified target behaviour areas, through a period of fading out of token reinforcement and the introduction of normal social reinforcers, to weaning the youths completely away from dependence on token earnings and substituting target setting and progress evaluation on a contractual basis. The programme extended into the family of the youths by obtaining the parental co-operation from the outset and by incorporating assessments and feedback by parents in the overall evaluation of a youth's progress. (In chapter 5 Spence describes a programme of training in social skills for young male delinquents she established, at Tennal School).

Perhaps the earliest example of an institutional behavioural programme in the UK is reported by Burland (1978). He described the evolution of a token economy programme at Chelfham Mill School, a private residential school for maladjusted and pre-delinquent boys aged 7–12 years. The school was established in 1966; during the first years of its existence behavioural principles were used unsystematically and there were many inconsistencies. Initial emphasis was placed on shared responsibility between staff and kids as important in establishing the ethos of the school and securing a good basis for behaviour change. From the early days of praising any appropriate behaviour when it occurred and providing specific positive feedback at the same time, the programme has developed to the point where rigorous analysis of behaviour and more efficient formulation and implementation of behaviour modification techniques is now possible. Burland and his colleagues have investigated a great number of issues relating to the application of behavioural techniques to different children at Chelfham Mill. Some of these include preference for different forms of tokens, novelty effects on token earnings, voluntary versus coerced participation in token earnings, and the effects on token earnings of displaying reinforcers. One of the most ambitious projects undertaken within the context of an established treatment facility is reported by Hoghughi (1980). Based on a pilot token economy and self-government programme for young offenders in Franklin House, a house unit of a large training school at Aycliffe (Hoghughi *et al.*, 1977), the comprehensive behavioural programme of the recently built Special Unit at Aycliffe School is one of only two projects known to this reviewer spanning the entire treatment regime of an institution. The programme is on a sequential treatment model operating in three house units. In the first of these, Merlin House, a token system is used to improve general behaviour and help the youths achieve individual and group objectives. Daily group meetings review the youths' past 24 hours and provide staff and the peer group feedback on behaviour as well as setting targets for the next day. The second house, Siskin, operates a contingency contracting system aimed at individual and group behavioural objectives. In the third house, Heron, the youths operate a self-government system. At this stage the youths may be spending more time out of the house unit, whether out in the community or other parts of the school. Throughout the sequential treatment programme emphasis is placed on intensive group and individual feedback, positive peer culture, and differential reinforcement. The use of punishment, whether token earnings loss or seclusion is kept to a minimum. As a youth progresses through the system he enjoys more relaxed supervision, increased pocket money, more flexible bed time and increasing access to external activities. Treatment evaluation is based on daily house meetings, regular staff meetings, staff ratings, and self-report measures by the youths. The programme is in its early days and there are no data available yet regarding the efficacy of the programme. The only other comprehensive institutional behavioural programme reported to date in the UK is that of Glenthorne Youth Treatment Centre, run by the Department of Health and Social Security and dealing with seriously disturbed, dangerous and delinquent children aged 10–18 years (Reid and Wilkie, 1980). Details of this programme are described in chapter 3 of this volume.

Most of the UK programmes so far have yet to produce detailed data on the efficacy of the behavioural programmes. However, there have been a number of reviews published which have addressed the question of treatment effectiveness of behavioural interventions in the USA. Martinson (1974) surveying all types of programmes up to the late 1960s concluded that there was little evidence that any of these had a significant impact on recidivism. A similar conclusion was reached by Emery and Marholin (1977). Reviewing a representative sample of behavioural programmes with delinquents from the late 1960s to the middle 1970s, they suggested that these interventions may be producing first-order changes only. In their opinion, the lack of individual target behaviours, the absence of adequate follow-up data, and the failure to show the relationship between successful behaviour change efforts and a subsequent reduction in measures of delinquency, are among the most important critical ommissions commonly found in these interventions. Such criticism appears well founded and justified, even in the case of the best examples of behavioural programmes. In most cases, where the efficacy of the techniques used has been demonstrated in small scale projects within existing institutional facilities, practitioners have been keen to demonstrate the usefulness of their behavioural technology and their ability to change specific behaviours, rather than restructuring the overall framework of rehabilitation. Even more important, as Johnson (1977) points out, the failure of behavioural practitioners to evaluate separately the effects of existing traditional penal strategies has significant implications for the reliability of the behaviour change resulting from behavioural procedures, in that the former may be compounding the effects of the latter. Perhaps the most significant criticism levelled at behavioural programmes has been their failure to address themselves to the actual offence behaviours of their client population, with the result that illegal acts *per se* have seldom been considered the target of behavioural intervention (Emery and Marholin, 1977; Feldman, 1977; Johnson, 1977). Hall and Baker (1973) have pointed to another problem which often plagues behavioural programmes in institutions—the adequacy of training received by treatment staff, who are charged with the responsibility for determing client target behaviours that are to be reinforced, extinguished, shaped, punished, etc.

However, the lack of staff skills necessary for teaching appropriate social behaviours means that tackling the clients behavioural deficits and excesses by modelling or providing consistent contingency consequences often remains a pious hope rather than a practical reality. Staff turnover, shift work, and institutional priorities often conspire against consistency in treatment effort, and in the end lead to inadvertent reinforcement of deviant behaviour and dependence. Thus, while the behavioural approach has brought with it an emphasis on informed innovation and the goal of prevention as well as rehabilitative change, the mixed results of behavioural programmes in institutional settings, and the growing conviction in the need for carefully planned after-care support for released offenders, have provided the rationale for the growth of community based offender rehabilitation programmes.

Community alternatives—a climate of change

The late nineteenth and early twentieth century was characterized by a growing social and political concern with the moral welfare of society both in the USA and UK. Historical overviews of the development of social policy designed to tackle the pressing social problems of this period are well documented elsewhere (Levine and Levine, 1970; Zax and Specter, 1974, in the USA; Wootton, 1959; West, 1967, in the UK). The more enlightened approach of policy makers of this era helped to ameliorate the lot of both adolescent and adult offenders and went a long way to determine the pattern of offender care and rehabilitation well into the latter half of this century. The 1960s, in turn, signalled a dissatisfaction with traditional treatment delivery systems and an increased willingness to pursue new avenues of investigation and practice. This decade saw the confluence of two trends which have, since, set the scene for innovative alternatives in tackling delinquency, namely the conviction that the community from which an offender comes should be the proper focus of treatment effort, and the acceptance of the need for a new treatment technology and methodology, based on the principles of social learning. O'Donnell (1977) describes this new trend in terms of the use of quasi-institutional settings to facilitate transition from institutional to community placements; the treatment of persons in settings in which problems occur; attention to problems affecting other members of the community rather than only the client receiving treatment; attempts to identify sources of community problems; the use of indirect services through consultation and education rather than direct services; and the promise of developing means of prevention to replace treatment of behavioural problems.

The application of reinforcement principles and operant techniques to wider society, however, is not new. In 1948, Skinner offered a blueprint for restructuring society, based upon operant technology. The focus of contemporary extensions of reinforcement to society has been the implementation of specific intervention programmes in a community setting where social problems occur rather than effecting gross social change. For example, Risley (1972) has demonstrated that behavioural principles can be applied very successfully to solving some of the problems of a neighbourhood community. He reported his involvement with a typical US government housing project, Juniper Gardens, which had begun as a well-planned scheme, but after a number of years had deteriorated into a community with several problems—delinquency, vandalism, litter, abandoned cars, fighting, loud parties, etc. Risley began by attending monthly tennant association meetings, listening to the community's concerns and finally offering practical advice as a consultant for the residents to help themselves. The worsening financial and economic climate of the last half decade has certainly not stifled the American imagination which continues to generate new programmes for handling the juvenile offender. Walk-in day centres for juvenile delinquents run by the Probation Department of New York as alternatives to detention, the innovative use of methods such as restitution, weekend incarceration, halfway houses, deferred prosecution, work and educational release, and residential support services, are but a few examples of new alternative strategies being pursued in preference to institutional programmes (Nelson et al., 1979). With such a growth of non-institutional projects for offender rehabilitation in the USA it is perhaps not surprising that the total number of residents in juvenile detention facilities has steadily declined throughout the 1970s. The increase in the total number of open facilities is consistent with officially stated goals of diverting juveniles from institutions altogether, or of placing them in small community based residences near their homes (US Bureau of the Census, 1979).

By comparison with the USA, discussion of the need for a new perspective on

Table 1 Home Office Assisted, non-statutory projects dealing with offenders in the UK (1980)

Type of project	N	Total places	Offenders	Non-offenders	Comments
Accommodation	82	3134	1660	1474	1. Hostel and/or self-catering accommodation 2. No structured programme 3. 'Basic' support and supervision
Specialized	15	300	225	75	1. Mainly hostel accommodation 2. Care and support for 'special need' groups, i.e. drug and alcohol addicts, gamblers, epileptics. 3. Unspecified intervention programme
Rehabilitative	20	786	603	183	1. Hostel and/or self-catering accommodation 2. 'Rehabilitative' support; mainly work preparation and basic self-help skills training 3. Programme unclear; no adequate evaluation
Total	117	4220	2488	1732	

treatment of offenders in general, and juvenile delinquents in particular, and the exploration of non-institutional alternatives for the care and rehabilitation of law breakers, are recent phenomena in the UK (Curtis, 1976; Probyn, 1977; Stern, 1979). Despite the growing number of proponents of community based programmes (King and Young, 1976; Harding, 1977; Hodgkin and Hodgkin, 1978; Corden *et al.*, 1979), theirs appears to be a minority viewpoint in the current climate of 'get tough' policies, characterized by the prevailing and fashionable 'short, sharp, shock' approach. The latter is itself both a statement of disappointment with traditional penal methods and a search for new alternatives. Unfortunately, this emphasis on a punitive, highly regimented corrective programme is not based on sound evidence of effectiveness, and thus appears a rather desparate measure which is likely to set the clock back in terms of offender rehabilitation. In chapter 1, Tutt discusses this current British climate as well as the recent American emphasis on the 'justice' model of juvenilecare.

There are at present comparatively few non-institutional, community-based schemes in the UK offering rehabilitative support to young offenders. A recent report by the Manpower Services Commission (1979) lists twenty-eight projects under the broad heading of provision for offenders, ex-offenders, and those considered 'at risk'. Most of these projects seem to concentrate on tackling the core problem of offender behaviour by concentrating on teaching work skills and habits and by providing some form of accommodation. Only five of these schemes are offered as alternatives to custodial detention.

It is perhaps, significant that much in the way of alternative rehabilitative efforts in the UK has been undertaken by the voluntary care sector of the personal social services. While government funding for experimental offender support projects is available, the total number of offenders, both juvenile and adult, who are provided for in this way, largely by non-statutory charitable organizations, is small when compared to the current prison inmate population of more than 40 000. The number of projects financially assisted, in whole or in part, by the Home Office, for example, is small; there are even fewer schemes which, according to details available on the nature of support and programmes they provide, can truly be classified as rehabilitative (Table 1). There are 117 projects listed, offering a total of 4220 places; less than one-third of them, i.e. 15 'specialized' and 20 'rehabilitative', provide, between them, almost 34 per cent of the places available for officially designated law breakers. Furthermore, while the 'specialized' and 'rehabilitative' project offer not only accommodation but also some measure of support and training in basic self-helf and work skills, there are very few that can demonstrate a clear, structured treatment programme or attempt to evaluate carefully their rehabilitative support and treatment effort.

If one considers the growing dissatisfaction with traditional approaches to offender care and rehabilitation, and the realization that institutional interventions are at best ineffective, and at worst, harmful, then it is all the more surprising that greater emphasis on community-based facilities has been so slow in arriving. Moreover, it is disappointing that there has been a lack of clear and concise conceptualization and implementation of alternative treatment technologies in the UK, particularly in view of recent, promising developments in community-based behavioural interventions.

Community-based behavioural programmes in the USA and UK

The last 15 years has witnessed a rapid growth in behavioural intervention programmes undertaken in non-institutional, community-based treatment settings. Many of the published studies conducted by behavioural practitioners have demonstrated the application and efficacy of specific treatment techniques, while others have described how a variety of behavioural treatment methods aimed at different target behaviours can be combined in multicomponent broadly based intervention programmes. Furthermore, while some studies have concentrated on working with offenders in their homes and neighbourhood, others have made use of residential settings in their treatment efforts. Despite the effort and ingenuity which has gone into many of the reported studies, it is true to say that only a handful, to date, have demonstrated some effect of the treatment beyond the intervention period, although most can demonstrate some measure of success during the intervention programme itself. The use of behavioural contracting, perhaps, best illustrates this point. Stuart and Lott (1972) looked at behavioural contracting with families of delinquent youths but found no relationship between content of contracts, length of treatment, client or therapist characteristics, and outcome. Alexander and Parsons (1973) applied a broad spectrum behavioural approach, including contingency contracting with families of young offenders. They found lower rates of behavioural problems and non-indictable offences at follow-up for the treatment group compared with control groups. However, the rates of criminal offences did not differ among the groups. Fitzgerald (1974) and Polakow and Doctor (1974) have reported improvements on behavioural targets during contracting, but Weathers and Liberman (1975) using contingency contracting with probation referred families, found no improvement among those clients who completed treatment. On the positive side, Fo and O'Donnell (1974, 1975), using mediators or 'buddies' trained in contingency contracting, were able to demonstrate significant reduction in a variety of targeted problem behaviours of their clients. Although offence behaviours were not tackled directly, they also found a significant reduction in delinquent behaviour during the project year. O'Donnell (1977) suggests a possible reason for such mixed results. Reviewing contracting studies with offenders, he concluded that greater success might be expected if youths contracted directly with probation authorities rather than with their families, since the former have the authority and access to an important and sought-after reward (time off probation) that families lack.

Such mixed results are, perhaps, typical of the early attempts at community interventions. However, more recent developments have given cause for greater optimism. There has been no lack of more ambitious, larger-scale community projects. The authors of one such project, Davidson and Robinson (1975) described the Kentfield Rehabilitation Program for relatively serious, hard-core offenders, which demonstrated both the efficacy of the behavioural treatment methods, and the fact that it could be carried out for less money than existing options. This project, undertaken in Kent County, Michigan, attempted to provide a comprehensive community-based programme which included keeping youths in their own homes, public works participation each morning for wages, an afternoon school programme based on programmed instruction as well as performance contracts, behavioural group sessions twice a week, and an overall level and points system. The staff involved in the project were able to convince community leaders and the courts to refer virtually every youth to this programme who otherwise would be institutionalized. Local government sceptics were so impressed with the results and the money saved, that the programme now continues with local financial support. Another highly successful example of a behavioural programme which has made a significant impact on the local community which is host to it, is that at Hunt Youth Centre in Burlington, Vermont, described by Stahl et al., (1979). The intervention was based in one of the many 'youth service bureaus' supported by the National Council on Crime and Delinquency, who run a network of community-based youth centres offering facilities to volunteer clients with the aim of preventing antisocial and other problem behaviours. Some of these centres are used as alternative placements for first time offenders, while others are more open to the community catering for a wide set of needs and with more general aims (NCCD, 1970). This project indeed represents a novel departure from traditional programmes in that the authors have made use of behavioural principles with existing facilities and volunteers directly in the community in an open social system. Not only did they show that problematic behaviours could be reliably changed by using access to preferred activities as reinforcers within a token system, they were also able to demonstrate the value of enlisting and training members of the community as aides to the programme. The authors described how their work achieved a significant and practical impact on the local community by providing effective reinforcers for programmes designed to improve school performance of problem youths, and by providing recreational and educational resources for all the youth of the community.

Perhaps the most famous and widely reported experiment in community-based behavioural interventions is that of Achievement Place, Kansas, which has served as a model for hundreds of replications throughout the USA, and as a springboard for the 'teaching-parent' concept in delinquency prevention programmes. Since several reviews of this project are available elsewhere (Davidson and Seidman, 1974; Braukmann and Fixsen, 1975; Feldman, 1977), it is not proposed to described this project in detail here. Suffice it to say that despite its originality and preeminence in this field, the results of the Achievement Place programmes have been, at best, mixed. Some reviewers have gone so far as to suggest that as yet there is no evidence that the variety of target behaviours studied at Achievement Place are related to subsequent offence behaviour nor that improvements within the programme are significantly related to lowered rates of re-offending. As early as 1975, Eitzen found no differences between Achievement Place and another correctional training school in terms of the number of police and court contacts at follow-up. Quoting more recent reviews Johnson (1977) has suggested that this picture has not improved significantly.

Another residential, community-based project which has received a great deal of attention lately is the remarkable experiment at Father Flanagans Boys Home, popularly referred to as Boys Town (Phillips, 1978). Established over 60 years ago, this world famous home for boys, which has been the focus of public attention and support from its inception, was forced some 10 years ago to undergo dramatic reorganization following a public exposé of its enormous wealth, and change from the old institutional methods which had led to a deterioration in care standards. The appointment, in 1973, of E. L. Phillips, of Achievement Place fame, as director of youth care, heralded a remarkable experiment not so much in the application of behavioural principles and methodology *per se*, but in the use of these principles to redesign the structure and social fabric of the institution and rejuvenate an institutional programme which had lost its way. Phillips and his colleagues, many of them co-workers at Achievement Place, have demonstrated clearly that the disease of traditional institutions—'hardening of the attitudes'—could be dealt with effectively by a variety of means. These included decentralizing most of the institutional support systems, i.e. laundry service, kitchen, etc.; shifting from the large and impersonal block dormitory system to an intimate family atmosphere in smaller 'cottages'; drastically reducing the number of care staff and abolishing the multidisciplinary team approach, replacing them with teaching parents; redefining divisions of responsibility; and introducing the Family and Community Skills Curriculum developed by Boys Town staff. Many questions have yet to be answered, not least of which are those concerning the effectiveness of the teaching family training, and the future of boys who leave Boys Town. However, although the long-term effects of this experiment are not yet known, the immediate effects have been dramatic enough to stimulate the interest of group homes and other offender care institutions around the USA. One of the most exciting community-based delinquency intervention projects to be reported over the past few years is the work of Stumphauzer *et al.*, (1977). In a unique attempt to tackle the core problem of offender behaviour, they have expanded the behavioural model to understand delinquent behaviour where it occurs, directly in the open community, by analysing a particular high juvenile crime community, and by doing a behavioural analysis of the violent youth gang which dominates it. Their work shows clearly that individual treatment, if indicated, and if clients were to co-operate and participate, would not be able to keep up with the recruitment and 'teaching' programmes the authors observed to operate in the prevailing gang culture. They concluded that rather than treating a few individuals after they are in trouble, the community approach must plan for wider-scale changes in local neighbourhoods, utilizing natural mediators of behaviour change—parents, teachers, local businessmen, and non-delinquent or ex-delinquent peers. The same authors have attempted to expand their behavioural analysis of high juvenile crime communities by looking at the naturally occurring self-control and trouble-avoidance strategies, as well as other adaptive behaviours already existing among non-delinquent peers in the high crime areas (Aiken *et al.*, 1977). They put forward the well-founded argument that an effective prevention programme could be implemented, based on identifying and teaching both the non-delinquent behaviours which are being learned in areas of high delinquency and the strategies that maintain them in the face of strong delinquent gang culture. In doing so they offer hope of finally achieving the long advocated goal of prevention rather than belated intervention in coping with the growing problem of delinquency.

There are as yet few reported attempts at implementing behavioural programmes in community settings in the UK. Only two such projects are known to the author—the Birmingham Action for Youth (BAY) Centre study (McGivern, 1980) and the Shape Project (Ostapiuk, 1977; Reid *et al.*, 1980; Ostapiuk and Reid, 1981). The BAY experiment was conducted at an 'intermediate treatment' centre, one of numerous such centres which sprang from and are based upon the concept of 'intermediate treatment' (IT) introduced by the Children and Young Persons Act (1969), itself an innovative piece of legislation that recommended radical changes in the juvenile justice system in England and Wales. IT is a form of intervention with young offenders which falls midway between incarceration and supervision in the community. Unfortunately it has no clear theoretical basis nor a precise methodology for application. McGivern has shown that a social-learning model can be effectively applied in a project otherwise lacking in a clear treatment technology. The project is in its early days and there is not a great deal of data available on treatment effectiveness. Nevertheless, early results look promising (see chapter 7 this volume for details).

The Shape programme

Outline

The earliest example of a comprehensive, multicomponent, community-based behavioural intervention programme in the UK is that of Shape. The development of the Shape Project and descriptions in detail of the programme components have been reported elsewhere (Ostapiuk, 1977; Reid *et al.*, 1980; Ostapiuk and Reid, 1981). A brief summary of the intervention programme is given in Table 2. The experimental behavioural programme developed at Shape under the auspices of the Shape Trust, a registered charity, has been financed from a variety of sources, some statutory—the Department of Employment and Home Office—and some not—voluntary organizations, individual donations, and payments for work projects undertaken by Shape clients.

All programme clients, who are aged between 16 and 24 years are, with one or two exceptions, adjudicated offenders who have been referred to the project from Probation or Social Services departments in the West Midlands area of the UK, although some referrals are from much further afield. They typically come from low income, social problem families, in which other family members have often been the focus of statutory agency intervention and support. The overriding rehabilitative goal of the Shape Programme is to provide phased living accommodation, some work experience, work skills training and preparation for employment, together with social or rather 'survival' skills training, for adolescent and young adult offenders in a treatment setting which closely mirrors the environmental and social conditions of the local community from which clients come and to which they will return.

The accommodation and life skills components of the Shape project are considered particularly important in view of the background of clients. For most of the Shape Programme clients a return to their families is impossible, either because they are no longer welcome at home or the clients themselves do not wish to return there, or because they have, in effect, no home to which they can return, having spent most of their lives in the care of statutory agencies. Furthermore, most of the referrals to the programme who have been released from custodial detention have clearly demonstrated a lack of basic self-help skills which have seriously jeopardized their independent survivial in the community, and compounded the effects of further delinquent activities. Therefore, a major emphasis of the Shape Rehabilitation Programme has been to provide the structure and conditions in which clients can learn the necessary survival and personal effectiveness skills in a sequential progression from a structured, communal hostel environment, through the semi-independent stage of shared accommodation in smaller house units, to the final stage of fully independent, non-shared accommodation. By specifying clearly both the areas that need to be kept clean and maintained tidy, and the level of proficiency in these tasks that is considered reasonable, the hostel upkeep programme prompts the clients performance and provides an opportunity to reinforce the acquisition of useful skills. The hostel manager scheme not only allows more accomplished clients both to model appropriate task-related behaviours and to provide support and reinforcement for other residents, but also provides staff an opportunity to assess the manager's readiness to take on greater responsibility in other programmes. The hostel programme operates a self-government system, where residents are encouraged and expected to participate fully in decision-making processes where these concern day-to-day running of the hostel, rules, sanctions for non-

Table 2 Shape Programme: summary

Programme components	Description	Comments
Pre-admission 1. Application sift	'Client selection' Acceptance profile: offence history; no serious violence or aggression; age 16–24 years; no drug or alcohol abuse; no serious sexual offences, willingness to change	Acceptance criteria are very flexible and rejections are few
2. Interview	Familiarization of client with programme, client voluntarily agrees to participate in programme	A high proportion of clients accepted to the project are unwilling to come due to the less than adequate physical conditions and provisions
Stage 1 *Hostel programme* 1. Hostel manager system	'Observation, assessment, and target setting' Clients accommodated in small communal hostel setting; high level of supervision Hostel manager is elected by residents; supervisory and spokesman role	Assessment measures include: Shape Behaviour Rating Scale; Self Reported Offence Questionnaire; Reinforcement Survey Schedule; Social Skills Rating Scale; Credit Earnings Checklist; Work Performance Survey
2. Hostel cleaning programme	Residents assigned areas of hostel to keep clean on weekly basis	
3. Credit earnings system	Clients performance is reinforced by allocation of 'credits' which are converted to pocket money on 'pay day'	
4. Workforce programme	All residents participate in voluntary work: neighbourhood clean-ups, renovation of old properties, transportation of good, etc	
5. Leisure activity programme	Two days per week reserved for hostel cleaning, meetings, visits to/by probation officers or social workers, sporting and recreation activities	
Individual programme 1. Self help/management	Teaching and monitoring of basic skills; handling money, budgeting, buying food, personal appearance and hygiene	Video and audio feedback is used in personal effectiveness training sessions

2. Job preparation and job finding — Investigating job leads, job interview skills, work routines and habits

Behavioural contract — Assessment period is concluded by a review conference including the client. Problems and targets, duties and privileges are drafted into contract

Stage 2

1. Independence skills — Clients transfer to small house unit with own bedsit, sharing kitchen, bathroom with one or two other residents; medium supervision level

   Client cooks for himself, looks after own washing, laundry, etc. He is responsible for paying rent

2. Work programme — Clients encouraged to obtain own job, if not—back to Stage 1 work programme

3. Personal effectiveness — Social skills training including: dealing with authority figures, appropriate assertiveness, alternatives to offence behaviours

4. Behavioural contract — Clients completing this phase of programme undertake to provide assistance with new clients in Stage 1, and to furnish self-report data

Stage 3

1. Independent accommodation — Clients are transferred to own independent accommodation, i.e. council flat, Shape provide apartments; minimal supervision level

2. Work — Client is in full-time work

3. Graduate system — The client is now considered to have graduated from the programme but undertakes to provide assistance where and when possible with programmes for new entrants to Stage 1

Emphasis is given to incorporating external community resources into programme, i.e. local employers, employment agencies, local policemen, university sports facilities, ect.

Follow-up measures include: Self reported offence questionnaire; Independent assessors rating scale compliant residents, etc. Regular meetings, called by the staff or hostel manager, are a useful vehicle for reinforcing appropriate problem solving behaviour of clients and for shaping up their social interaction skills. Throughout the hostel phase of the project, the clients performance is monitored and at the same time reinforced by the use of points or credits, which are converted to spending money at the end of the week.

The next major component of the Shape Programme is the work experience scheme, aimed at encouraging normal work habits, basic work skills and preparing clients to obtain and successfully hold down a regular full-time job. In order to achieve this a client's week in Stage 1 of the project is divided between two hostel activity days and three normal work days. On hostel activity days clients can participate in hostel meetings, major repairs to the hostel, organized leisure activities, or they may visit or receive visits from probation officers, social workers, etc. On normal work days programme clients are expected to participate in voluntary work projects ranging from neighbourhood clean-ups, painting and decorating and fairly simple handyman chores, to larger-scale renovation of short-life property, either new accommodation units for the Shape Trust, or for needy families in the inner-city area. Once again a clients performance in a number of set target areas is carefully monitored and reinforced by points or credit earnings. For example, clients are checked for being up on time and ready for work in the morning; while at work they are checked for complying with supervisor's instructions, achieving set job targets and appropriate social behaviour in the work setting. Those clients who perform at a reasonable standard within the Shape Works Programme are encouraged to seek full-time employment. They are put through a job finding and 'preparation for employment' package which includes job interview-skills training, employment related knowledge, i.e. wages, tax, redundancy and unemployment, etc.

The third major component of the Shape Programme deals with the clients presenting problem behaviours, social skills deficits and offence behaviours. The goal of intervention here is to teach acceptable and appropriate alternative coping behaviours that could successfully compete with previous responses and be reinforced at sufficient frequency to ensure maintenance and generalization. Each client's target behaviours are clearly stated in a behavioural contract, which also outlines the nature and content of the specific techniques and methods that will be used. Some client target behaviours are tackled in one-to-one teaching sessions, others in group sessions. Role play, modelling and behaviour rehearsal are used widely in programmes designed to improve appropriate assertive responses and social interaction skills, to teach clients how to resolve interpersonal conflicts, and deal effectively and appropriately in confrontations with the police and other authority figures. Behavioural counselling, both on an individual and group basis, is used as a vehicle to shape up clients attitudes towards acceptable alternatives to offending and anti-social behaviour in general. Throughout the programme the clients performance is carefully assessed

Table 3 Shape Programme: client variables

	N	Entry age (years)	Court contacts	Pre-admission period of insti-tutionalization (years)	Average treat-ment duration
All applicants	93	18.11	3.5	2.7	—
Rejected applicants	16	20.3	3.9	3.1	—
Accepted/non-arrivals	41	18.1	3.1	2.6	—
Programme clients	36	18.5	3.4	2.5	25.6 weeks

on a number of measures, including general measures such as staff ratings, self-report, credit earnings, and specific measures designed to reflect improvement in specifically targetted problem areas. In addition to these within-programme measures, assessment and evaluation of a clients progress is encouraged from outside sources, such as probation officers, social workers and local employers; even from the local 'beat' policeman (patrolman), who is also encouraged to participate in a modelling and teaching role in the Shape Programme. Having progressed through the sequential programme, clients who have 'graduated' are encouraged where possible to feedback their experiences, skills and practical help into the Shape project, where their value as powerfull models for new entrants is thus capitalized upon. These assessments form part of an overall evaluation of the project which has been undertaken, under the auspices of Birmingham University, since the project's inception in 1977.

Results

The total number of referrals to the Shape Programme between October 1977 and September 1979 was ninety-three (see Table 3) almost two-thirds of these were probation referrals, the remainder were from social services or voluntary agencies. More than 80 per cent of all applications were accepted as suitable for inclusion in the programme, but less than half of these joined the project as programme clients. The reasons for such a high attrition rate are twofold. Some of the clients were discouraged from joining the programme due to the poor physical conditions obtaining at the time. Others did not arrive because alternative placements were found for them, or they were, in the meantime, sentenced by the courts to custodial detention. Less than 20 per cent of referrals made between October 1977 and September 1979 were rejected as unsuitable. The reasons for rejecting these applicants included their age, dependence on drugs or alcohol, a history of serious violence, or an absence of need for the behavioural intervention offered. The total number of programme clients over the evaluation period was thirty-six. The median age for this group was 18 years

Table 4   Follow-up of Shape Programme clients

	N	Time since completion of programme (months)	Follow-up period (months) in which offences committed 0–6	7–12	13–18	Total	Percentage success
Group A	14	18	2	1	1	4	71
Group B	10	12	2	1	—	3	70
Group C	12	6	1	—	—	1	92
Total	36	—	5	2	1	8	78

and 5 months and the group was made up fairly evenly from probation and social services referrals. The average length of stay of programme clients over the evaluation period was approximately 26 weeks. With few exceptions all the clients actually admitted to the programme had a history of offences and previous custodial institutionalization, ranging from approved schools (now called Community Home Schools with Education or CHEs), borstals and prisons. Table 4 gives follow-up details on programme clients, who have been grouped according to the length of time since completion of the programme. Thus Group A clients ($n = 14$) have been out of the programme an average of 18 months; group B clients ($n = 10$), an average of 12 months; and group C clients ($N = 12$) have only been out of the programme an average of 6 months. Since the period of time from completion of the programme is not the same for all clients, the data presented are analysed for each group separately, and the percentage success figures reported at different follow-up periods relate to individual follow-up groups and not to the total sample ($N = 36$). The data clearly show that most of the clients who re-offend do so within 6 months of leaving the project, and suggest that the longer a client remains out of the programme without offending the better his chances in the long term. A clearer picture will emerge only once all clients have been out of the programme at least 18 months. Nevertheless the overall figure of 78 per cent success for all clients taken together is impressive.

Community-based intervention: strategies and issues

Perhaps the most important advantage of siting a rehabilitation programme in a community setting is that it facilitates generalization of newly acquired skills. The need to programme generalization of behavioural changes from the treatment environment to the client's natural environment is now widely recognized. It is clear that the probability of adequate generalization is increased if the behaviours targetted for change are likely to meet with reinforcement in the client's natural environment. By making the client's current treatment setting as similar as possible to his post treatment environment we increase the likelihood of generalization. However, the successful implementation of behavioural programmes, or any treatment programmes for that matter, in community-based voluntary projects is predicated upon the successful solution of a number of problems in addition to those which face traditional treatment programmes. While the behaviour modifier, engaged in rehabilitative programmes outside the available statutory provisions, may be sure that the problem of delinquency is being tackled in the relevant environment, i.e. the local neighbourhood where offenders live and engage in antisocial behaviour, he still has to answer a number of crucial questions. What are the relevant behavioural targets of intervention and which interventions work best? What are the relevant reinforcers to be used? How is the change agent to make best use of the limited resources available to him in order to maximize the effectiveness of his treatment efforts?

The effective utilization of limited resources is perhaps the single most pressing problem facing a community-based voluntary project, which requires just as much attention as the development of the therapeutic programme itself. Funding non-statutory projects is possible despite the fact that government departments are cautious, and are willing to provide grant aid only to those programmes that have demonstrated some degree of efficacy. This 'vicious circle' effect of needing money to operate a project but only receiving it once positive results have been shown often means that projects survive on inadequate funds, limited in the scope and quality of provisions for programme clients. Finding suitable premises to house the project is another problem that often plagues rehabilitation programmes in the non-statutory sector. In addition to competing with other agencies and private individuals for housing, the voluntary project is in a relatively weak purchasing position because of limited finances. Limited finances and housing shortages make it imperative to look carefully at what facilities are already available in the local community which could be harnessed to the advantage of the treatment programme. Conditions obviously vary from area to area but several examples from the Shape Programme, described earlier, highlight the kinds of resources that can be utilized. In the absence of purpose-built accommodation facilities, the Shape Project has concentrated on renovating old, short-life properties. This not only provides badly needed living accommodation for programme clients but also affords an opportunity to observe and evaluate client work skills, and preparedness and motivation for regular employment. Informal links with local employers and government job-finding centres has enabled the development of an invaluable client assessment procedure where information about job interviews and work performance can be fed back into the programme. Similar links with the local police force have led to the incorporation of the local 'beat bobby' into Shape's treatment and leisure programmes. He has been involved in the social-skills training of clients both as participant in role play and modelling seessions and as an evaluator of clients performance and progress. In an unprecedented move, he was allowed, on one occasion, to accompany Shape clients on a camping holiday as a staff auxiliary, while on police time. Another useful link has been established with the Physical Education Department of Birmingham University. Staff and students of this department and of the Sports Centre have helped to devise leisure and recreation programmes for Shape clients, which have served not only as useful reinforcers, but have also provided an opportunity to assess the clients' behavioural competence in a wider social context. From the above examples it is clear that the limited resources available to a community-based intervention programme can be augmented by tapping into already existing facilities and provisions. However, in order to do so it is imperative that projects make every effort to gain the goodwill and co-operation of potential benefactors and resource allocators. Furthermore, one needs to pay attention to ensuring the credibility of the project and its acceptance by the local community. Significant community impact can be achieved by involving programme clients in voluntary work in the local neighbourhood and by inviting comments from local residents about aspects of the programme and how they might contribute to it. Such an approach is supported by Nietzel (1979) who has stressed the need for the general public to increase its input into the discussion of values and policy as these relate to offender rehabilitation. He argues for increasing the input of the community into neighbourhood projects and for establishing citizen-professional review boards for local programmes.

Of no less importance than making best use of limited resources is the question of *relevance* of the behaviours targeted for intervention, the suitability of the intervention methods themselves, and whether *relevant* reinforcers can be made available contingently upon positive behaviour change. Several authors have pointed out that behaviour modifiers have shied away from tackling the core problem of offence behaviours *per se* (Emery and Marholin, 1977; Feldman, 1977; Johnson, 1977). If, as Feldman (1977) argues, treatment outcome measures must be in terms of reoffending, then looking closely at the specific offence behaviours and demonstrating control in this area must be of prime importance in offender rehabilitation programmes. Clearly, if the behavioural change agent is to reduce criminal behaviours rather than simply remedy educational deficits or improve social skills, then he must both inhibit offending behaviour and enhance alternative acceptable behaviours. The latter have, typically, been the focus of behavioural interventions, where the emphasis has been on equipping the delinquent with a wide range of 'survival' skills designed to make him independent of statutory agency support and thereby less likely to be in conflict with the authorities and society in general. There are several examples of interventions geared to improving the offenders skills in areas relevant to his daily survival in the community, i.e. obtaining employment, enhancing job performance, handling conflict situations with police and other authorities, etc. Jones and Azrin (1973), for example, increased information seeking about jobs among their clients by token reinforcement. Azrin et al. (1975) developed a successful job-finding club, where clients discussed methods of obtaining employment, shared any job leads, and role-played job interviews. A behavioural employment intervention package is described by Mills and Walter (1979) which involved recruiting and training local employers, contingency contracting, shaping clients pro-employment behaviours, and actually placing delinquents in jobs. The authors claim that the project was successful not only in keeping clients in their jobs, but also in reducing rates of arrest and institutionalization for experimental subjects. Actual job performance has also featured as the target of behavioural programmes. Punctuality of workers in an industrial setting has been increased by the use of tokens (Herman et al., 1973); absenteeism has been successfully reduced by using a lottery based on playing cards which make up a poker hand at the end of the week (Pedalino and Gamboa, 1974). The quality of work output has been improved by making pay contingent upon the number of tasks completed to criterion level, by providing explicit job descriptions and instructions to perform the tasks (Pierce and Risley, 1974). Since the alternative for unsatisfactory work performance is the termination of employment, the development of desirable performance and related work skills has 'survival' value, in that it increases the likelihood of keeping ones job and thus developing further skills. It is clear from the above examples that obtaining job leads, finding jobs, ensuring punctuality, attendance and high levels of job performance can be successfully altered by contingent consequences and other behavioural techniques. Another area that has received considerable attention from behavioural researchers due to its high loading in terms of survival in the community relates to handling interactions with police and other establishment figures.

Some studies have reported success in teaching delinquents the acceptable alternatives they need to display in place of their aggressive or inappropriate behaviours by using behavioural rehearsal and role playing (Kaufmann and Wagner, 1972). Others have utilized a combination of techniques including instructions, role playing and motivational procedures to teach delinquents how to accept criticism and negative feedback without engaging in arguing and verbally aggressive behaviours (Timbers, et al., 1973). One of the most detailed studies demonstrating the impact of social skills training on effective behaviours required to interact with the police is reported by Werner, et al., (1975). Based on available evidence that an offenders social behaviour often determines decisions regarding his pre-court handling, the authors attempted, first, to identify the important components of behaviour for youths to engage in when interacting with police officers and, then, to teach these appropriate behaviours to those youths who lacked them. A series of questionnaires completed by police officers, and self-reports from delinquent youths helped to identify several important interactive behaviours which subsequently served as targets for training. These included: looking at the police officer, listening attentively, not interrupting the officer when being spoken to, and showing respect by addressing the officer as 'sir', and were agreed upon by police and youths alike. Prior to training it was stressed that these behaviours were considered important by the police, not that they would necessarily get the youths out of trouble; they might help youths avoid more severe consequences such as being detained. Training consisted of instructions with rationales, demonstrations, and practice with feedback. During training the youths interacted with experimenters playing the role of police officers; however pre- and post-treatment measures of efficacy and generalization included interactions with uniformed police officers in a simulated setting where youths were 'suspects'. The social validity of the behaviour change resulting from the training package was further tested by a panel of policemen viewing videotaped pre- and post-tests for the experimental and control groups and rating each interaction on a number of dimensions. The results demonstrated that the trained youths showed significantly greater improvement over the control group as assessed both by within-training measures and by police-officers ratings.

The relevance of appropriate reinforcements in community-based programmes has been addressed by several authors (Kazdin, 1977; O'Donnell, 1977; Emery and Marholin, 1977). Kazdin (1977) has pointed out that certain features of the clients natural environment lend themselves well to effective implementation of reinforcement procedures; some potent reinforcers are already available within the social system, i.e. money, wages, etc. The problem which faces the behavioural change agent is making use of reinforcers which are relevant to the offender and that might encourage positive behaviour change and subsequently maintain it. Reduced contact with and harassment by the police, reduced interference in the offenders day-to-day life by probation officers and other establishment figures, reduced discrimination by prospective employers, etc. are all potentially potent reinforcers. However, it is questionable whether there are sufficient incentives with the existing social system to allow such reinforcers to operate. While it is true to say that an intervention programme based in the relevant environment—the offenders local neighbourhood and community—will have greater access to more relevant reinforcers, the people, places, activities important to the offender, its ability to call upon some of the most relevant incentives to non-offending behaviour will depend upon a change in the climate of current social thinking and practice of policy makers, and a change of attitude of the general public.

Assuming that the problems mentioned above have been dealt with successfully, there still remains the difficulty of staffing rehabilitative programmes with personnel adequately trained to implement treatment and evaluate programme effectiveness. Identifying the skills needed to design and implement therapeutic programmes is less problematic than identifying and selecting those individuals who are *actually* socially skilled enough to serve as acceptable models for programme clients, and resilent enough to demonstrate their skills in the frequently demanding and occasionally adverse conditions that typify community-based voluntary projects. This is not intended as a criticism of the staff currently to be found in such projects, so much as an indictment of the system which requires enthusiastic and idealistic individuals, ill prepared to address themselves to the problems discussed above, and thus more likely to persist with and less likely to question ill-considered even harmful interventions. The need for effective and practical staff training in order to teach project staff the skills involved in maximizing treatment efficacy has been clearly demonstrated (Hall and Baker, 1973). A number of researchers have shown that this need can be satisfied in a variety of ways; for example, by modelling required skills, guiding trainer practice to criterion level, and differential feedback (Gardner, 1973), while others have underlined the importance of maintaining learned skills by monitoring staff behaviour and providing differential feedback and consequation (Kazdin and Bootzin, 1972).

Related to the issue of training of project staff in relevant skills, is the problem of consistent handling of project clients outside the programme proper. In this respect the co-operation of other agency personnel is important. Probation officers and social workers who are likely to be involved with clients both during their period of rehabilitation and after their departure from the programme not only need to be familiar with the behavioural methods used in treatment, but also should be prepared to maintain consistency in client support by utilizing the same behavioural methods. This requires training statutory agency personnel in behavioural techniques throughout their contact time with project clients and gradually shaping up their practice of relevant client support skills. This is not quite as simple as it sounds. Burkhart *et al.*, (1976) trained juvenile probation officers in behaviour modification principles, behaviour analysis of probation cases and behavioural contracting over a period of 6 weeks. Immediate post-training effects were promising in showing an increment in behavioural skills. However, Stumphauzer *et al.*, (1976) following-up the same trainees at 6 months found that the probation officers were utilizing their training only to a limited degree. They suggested that we must look closely at the variables controlling the behaviour of change agents and should not expect new systems to be used if there is no ongoing modelling and reinforcement from the trainers, or if the new techniques mean more work! Further evidence for the efficacy of non-specialist change agents in contributing to positive behaviour change in delinquents is provided by Fo and O'Donnell (1974) who showed how volunteers could be used effectively, while Tharp and Wetzel (1969) have made a strong case for using 'natural mediators'—parents, peers, teachers, employers, etc. It is clear that the chances of success of any behavioural intervention programme, but especially that situated in a community setting, can be increased through the co-operation of informed natural mediators and trained non-specialists from the local community.

In the face of considerable difficulties which challenge the implementation of effective offender care and rehabilitation programmes, it becomes all the more important to demonstrate clearly that treatment efforts can produce positive results and positive social impact. The question remains, however, what yardstick will satisfy these criteria? In terms of treatment effectiveness a number of yardsticks suggest themselves. Recidivism measures, or whether offenders are reinstitutionalized after release from a treatment programme, may not on their own be an adequate indication of programme effectiveness. They are not sensitive to new law-breaking behaviour; as an all or nothing measure, recidivism provides no qualitative feedback following treatment (Costello, 1972). While police and court contacts are a more sensitive index of offender post-treatment behaviour, and can be made even more sensitive by a separate measure of the seriousness of the offences leading to such contacts, they remain, unfortunately, better indices of failure than success. On the positive side a variety of evaluative measures have been suggested. Among these have been: educational indices, for example, attendance records, suspensions, academic achievement, measured intelligence, etc.; indices of social functioning and adjustment, e.g. ratings completed by parents, peers, and other community members; employment and work-related indices, i.e. time-keeping, absenteeism, job performance; and in some cases attitude and personality measures. None of the measures mentioned so far on their own constitute a sufficient, let alone adequate, yardstick of treatment effectiveness; however, used together they may go some way to fulfilling the minimum requirements for programme evaluation. Several other criteria have been proposed as necessary for scientific acceptability in outcome studies of treatment efficacy (Logan, 1972; Feldman, 1977). However, there are, as yet, few reported studies that could stand up to the rigour of closer examination on even a few of the proposed criteria. In recent years there has been an increasing interest in, perhaps, the most relevant and unavoidable programme evaluation criterion given the current financial climate—that of cost effectiveness.

There are several good reasons for including a monetary criterion in the evaluation of offender treatment programmes. It is now widely recognized that not all offenders are suited to, nor benefit from penal provisions. In this case, custodial detention is needlessly inefficient and a waste of scarce resources, since the offenders economic status and potential is reduced and his family and community are punished indirectly (Adams, 1967). Instead of contributing to the state as worker and taxpayer, the offender-inmate becomes the object of state spending and his family the recipient of state aid. Since the cost of providing for the upkeep of incarcerated offenders is continuously escalating and in view of the low success rate for custodial provisions, it will not, perhaps, be too long before

Table 5:   Comparison costs of Achievement Place and UK Treatment/Custodial
           Facilities (1978/79 prices)

	Achieve-ment Place	BAY Centre (Intermediate Treatment)	Borstal Dentention Centre	CHE	Shape Trust
Capital investment per youth	£3158 $6000	No data	No data	No data No data	£263 $500
Yearly operating costs per youth	£2895 $5500	£2333 $4432	£5400 $10260	£5400 £5720 $10260 $10868	£1684 $3200
Youths 'treated'	16	24	2117	6303 5500	18
Youths 'successful'*	13	19	318	1576 No data	14
Costs per 'successful' youth	£3563 $6769	£2947 $5599	£35949 $68303	£21579 No data $41034	£2165 $4113

*18-months follow-up in all cases

the policy-makers ask the question 'can it be done cheaper?' In these
circumstances, the comparison of relative costs would, at worse, allow for a valid
and acceptable choice between programmes where there are insignificant
differences in treatment outcome, and at best dictate the intervention programmes of choice both in terms of treatment and cost-effectiveness (see Table
5). However the issue of cost-effectiveness is not a straightforward one. There
has, to date, for example, been no way to compare meaningfully the reported
costs and effects of treatments. Different programmes have, typically, used
somewhat different means of estimating cost-effectiveness, with many factors
going into totalling their individual cost figures. In addition, there remains the
problem of comparing different treatment locations whose cost of living are
substantially different, and of comparing figures from different years. However,
some researchers have attempted to present a rationalized approach to the
assessment of treatment cost-effectiveness. Yates *et al.*, (1979) provide a
preliminary but thorough model of cost-effectiveness analysis which allows for
sensitive feedback, improvement, and 'fine tuning' for programme evaluation.
Their model is detailed enough to give a breakdown of costs for behaviour
treated as well as cost-effectiveness for each programme client. It remains to be
seen whether, in future, treatment programme evaluators will submit their efforts
to such detailed scrutiny.

Concluding comment

Traditional approaches have failed to make significant inroads into the ever
pressing problem of delinquency and anti-social behaviour. Behavioural approaches on the other hand have brought a more functional and pragmatic

perspective on the offender problem and a more promising technology to deal with it. However, so far, these alternatives represent more a promise than an established and proven fact. There are several reasons why this is the case. Institutional intervention programmes face the problems of generalization and have yet to demonstrate lasting effects of their treatment efforts. There has been a general reluctance to tackle the problem of offending behaviour *per se*, which will continue to call into question the credibility of treatment programmes in an age when the general public are more interested in whether the offender stops transgressing against them, rather than whether he is a nicer, more socially-skilled offender. The credibility of intervention programmes is further called into question by the lack of agreement on adequate evaluative criteria, and their failure to address the question of 'value for money'. The days of 'treatment at any cost' are numbered and, in the worsening economic climate, the reality of limited finances and resources has significant implications for future developments in offender rehabilitation. This is particularly relevant to community-based, voluntary projects for whom limitations in terms of funding, physical resources and adequate staffing pose severe restrictions on the quality of treatment provisions they can afford for their clients. Nevertheless the case for an increase in community-based facilities is strong, and is supported by a number of reported examples of treatment-effective and cost-effective programmes both in the USA and UK.

References

Adams, S. (1967). A cost approach to the assessment of gang rehabilitation techniques, *Journal of Research in Crime and Delinquency*, **4**, 166–182.

Aiken, T. W., Stumphauzer, J. S. and Veloz, E. V. (1977). Behavioural analysis of non-delinquent brothers in a high juvenile crime community, *Behavioural Disorders*, **2**, 212–222.

Alexander, J. F. and Parsons, B. V. (1973). Short-term behavioural intervention with delinquent families: impact on family process and recidivism, *Journal of Abnormal Psychology*, **81**, 219–225.

Allison, T. S., Kendall, S. and Sloane, D. (1979). New directions in a juvenile hall setting, in *Progress in Behaviour Therapy with Delinquents* (Ed. J. S. Stumphauzer), Charles C. Thomas, Springfield, Illinois.

Azrin, N. H., Flores, T. and Kaplan, S. J. (1975). Job-finding club: a group-assisted program for obtaining employment, *Behaviour Research and Therapy*, **13**, 17–27.

Bailey, W. G. (1966). Correctional outcome: an evaluation of 100 reports, *Journal of Criminal Law, Criminology and Police Science*, **57**, 153–160.

Braukmann, C. J. and Fixsen, D. L. (1975). Behavior modification with delinquents, in *Progress in Behavior Modification*, Vol. 1 (Eds M. Hersen, R. M. Eisler and P. M. Miller). Academic Press, New York.

Brown, B. (1977). Gilbey House: a token economy management scheme in a residential school for adolescent boys in trouble, *B.A.B.P. Bulletin*, **5**, 79–89.

Burgess, A. (1965). *A Clockwork Orange*, Ballantine, New York.

Burkhart, B. R., Behles, M. W. and Stumphauzer, J. S. (1976). Training juvenile probation officers in behavior modification. Knowledge, attitude change, or behavioral competence? *Behaviour Therapy*, 7, 47–53.

Burland, J. R. (1978). The evaluation of a token economy in a residential school for maladjusted junior boys, *Behavioural Psychotherapy*, 6, 97–104.

Cohen, H. L. and Filipczak, J. A. (1971). *A New Learning Environment*, Jossey-Bass, San Francisco, California.

Cordon, J., Kuipers, J. and Wilson, K. (1979). Accommodation and homelessness on release from prison, *British Journal of Social Work*, 9, 75–86.

Costello, J. (1972). *Behavior Modification and Corrections*. The Law Enforcement Assistance Administration, Washington, DC.

Curtis, D. (1976). Aftercare now, *New Society*, 38, 131–132.

Davidson, W. S. and Robinson, M. J. (1975). Community psychology and behavior modification: a community-based program for the prevention of delinquency, *Journal of Corrective Psychiatry and Behavior Therapy*, 21, 1–12.

Davidson, W. S. and Seidman, E. (1974). Studies of behavior modification and juvenile delinquency: a review, methodological critique and social perspective, *Psychological Bulletin*, 81, 998–1011.

Eitzen, D. S. (1975). The effects of behavior modification on the attitudes of delinquents, *Behavior Research and Therapy*, 13, 295–299.

Emery, R. E. and Marholin, D. (1977). An applied behavior analysis of delinquency. The irrelevancy of relevant behavior, *American Psychologist*, October, 860–873.

Eysenck, H. J. (1960). The effects of psychotherapy, in *Handbook of Abnormal Psychology* (Ed. H. J. Eysenck), Pitman Medical, London.

Feldman, M. P. (1977). *Criminal Behaviour: A Psychological Analysis*, Wiley, London.

Fitzgerald, T. J. (1974). Contingency contracting with juvenile offenders, *Criminology*, 12, 241–248.

Fo, W. S. O. and O'Donnell, C. R. (1974). The Buddy system: relationship and contingency conditions in a community intervention program for youth with nonprofessionals as behavior change agents, *Journal of Consulting and Clinical Psychology*, 42, 163–169.

Fo, W. S. O. and O'Donnell, C. R. (1975). The Buddy system: effect of community intervention on delinquent offences, *Behavior Therapy*, 6, 522–524.

Gardner, J. M. (1973). Training and trainees: a review of research on teaching behavior modification, in *Advances in Behavior Therapy* (Eds. R. D. Rubin, J. P. Brady and J. D. Henderson), Academic Press, New York.

Hall, J. and Baker, R. (1973). Token economy systems: breakdown and control, *Behaviour Research and Therapy*, 11, 253–264.

Harding, J. K. (1977). The place of the voluntary hostel within the community, *International Journal of Offender Therapy and Comparative Criminology*, 21, 124–130.

Hermann, J. A., de Montes, A. I., Dominguez, B., Montes, F. and Hopkins, B. L. (1973). Effects of bonuses for punctuality on the tardiness of industrial workers, *Journal of Applied Behavior Analysis*, 6, 563–570.

Hodgkin, E. C. and Hodgkin, N. I. (1978). *The Involvement of the Community in Criminal Justice and the Treatment of Offenders*, Barry Rose, London.

Hoghughi, M. S. (1980). The treatment system, in *Aycliffe School Special Unit—The First Year* (Ed. M. S. Hoghughi) Aycliffe Studies of Problem Children, Aycliffe.

Hoghughi, M. S., Cumiskey, P. D., McCaffrey, A. and Muckley, A. (1977). *The Franklin Token Economy*, Aycliffe Studies of Problem Children, Aycliffe.

Jesness, C. F. (1975a). Comparative effectiveness of behaviour modification and transactional analysis programs for delinquents, *Journal of Consulting and Clinical Psychology*, 43, 758–779.

Jesness, C. F. (1975b). The impact of behaviour modification and transactional analysis on institution social climate, *Journal of Research in Crime and Delinquency*, **12**, 79–91.

Johnson, V. S. (1977). Behaviour modification in the correctional setting, *Criminal Justice and Behaviour*, **4**, 397–428.

Jones, R. J. and Azrin, N. H. (1973). An experimental application of a social reinforcement approach to the problem of job finding, *Journal of Applied Behavior Analysis*, **6**, 345–353.

Jones, H. G., Gelder, M. and Holden, H. M. (1965). Symposium on behaviour and aversion therapy in the treatment of delinquency, *British Journal of Criminology*, **5**, 355–387.

Kaufmann, L. M. and Wagner, B. R. B. (1972). A systematic treatment technology for temper control disorders, *Behavior Therapy*, **3**, 84–90.

Kazdin, A. E. (1977). Extensions of reinforcement to society, in *Progress in Behavior Modification*, Vol. 4 (Eds M. Hersen, R. W. Eisler and P. M. Miller), Academic Press, New York.

Kazdin, A. E. and Bootzin, R. R. (1972). The token economy: an evaluative review, *Journal of Applied Behavior Analysis*, **5**, 343–372.

King, J. F. S. and Young, W. (Eds) (1976). *Control Without Custody*, Cambridge University Press, Cambridge.

Levine, M. and Levine, A. (1970) *A Social History of Helping Services: Clinic, Court, School and Community*, Appleton, New York.

Logan, C. H. (1972). Evaluation research in crime and delinquency: a reappraisal, *Journal of Criminal Law, Criminology and Police Science*, **63**, 378–387.

Manpower Services Commission (1979). *The Relevance and Application of the M.S.C. Special Programmes for the Unemployed to Ex-offenders, and those Non-offenders 'At Risk'*. New Opportunity Press, London.

Martinson, R. (1974). What works?—Questions and answers about prison reform, *Public Interest*, **35**, 22–54.

McGivern, M. A. (1980). Intermediate treatment—the development and assessment of an approach to community care. Paper presented at the World Congress on Behaviour Therapy. Jerusalem, July 1980.

Milan, M. A., Wood, L. F., Williams, R. L., Rogers, J. G., Hampton, L. R. and McKee, J. M. (1974). *Applied Behavior Analysis and the Imprisoned Adult Felon. Project 1: The Cellblock Token Economy*, Rehabilitation Research Foundation Montgomery.

Mills, C. M. and Walter, T. L. (1979). Reducing juvenile delinquency: a behavioral-employment intervention program, in *Progress in Behavior Therapy with Delinquents* (Ed. J. S. Stumphauzer), Charles C. Thomas, Springfield, Illinois.

Mitford, J. (1973). *Kind and Unusual Punishment*, Knopf, New York.

National Council on Crime and Delinquency (1970). *The Youth Service Bureau: A Brief Description of the Current Programs*. NCCD, Paramus.

Nelson, E. K., Ohmart, H. and Barlow, N. (1979). *Promising Strategies in Probation and Parole*, LEAA Report, US Government Printing Office, Washington DC.

Nietzel, M. T. (1979). *Crime and its Modification. A Social Learning Perspective*, Pergamon Press, New York.

O'Donnell, C. R. (1977). Behavior modification in community settings, in *Progress in Behavior Modification*, Vol. 4. (Eds M. Hersen, R. M. Eisler and P. M. Miller). Academic Press, New York.

Ostapiuk, E. B. (1977). *Behaviour and Attitude Change Following Institutional and Community Based Treatment Programmes for Delinquents*, Unpublished M.Sc. thesis, University of Birmingham.

Ostapiuk, E. B. and Reid, I. D. (1981). Rehabilitating offenders in the community:

implications for penal policy and professional practice, in *Reconstructing Psychological Practice* (Eds I. McPherson and A. Sutton), Croom Helm, London.

Parliamentary All Party Penal Affairs Group (1980). *Too Many Prisoners*, HMSO, London.

Pedalino, E. and Gamboa, V. U. (1974). Behavior modification and absenteeism: intervention in one industrial setting, *Journal of Applied Psychology*, **59**, 694–698.

Phillips, E. L. (1968). Achievement Place: token reinforcement procedures in a home style rehabilitation setting for pre-delinquent boys, *Journal of Applied Behavior Analysis*, **1**, 213–223.

Phillips, E. L. (1978). *Progress Report: A 1977 Evaluation of the Boys Town Youth Care Department Programs*, Boys Town Community-Based Programs Monograph Series.

Pierce, C. H. and Risley, T. R. (1974). Improving job performance of neighborhood corps aides in an urban recreation program, *Journal of Applied Behaviour Analysis*, **7**, 207–215.

Polakow, R. L. and Doctor, R. M. (1974). A behavioral modification program for adult drug offenders, *Journal of Research in Crime and Delinquency*, **11**, 63–69.

Probyn, W. (1977). Whose welfare? *Community Care*, November, 29.

Rachman, S. J. (1972). *The Effects of Psychotherapy*, Pergamon, Oxford.

Rehabilitation Research Foundation (1974). *The Post-prison Analysis of Criminal Behavior and Longitudinal Follow-up Evaluation of Institutional Treatment*, R. R. F., Montgomery.

Reid, I. D., Feldman, M. P. and Ostapiuk, E. B. (1980). The Shape Project for young offenders: introduction and overview, *Journal of Offender Counseling, Services and Rehabilitation*, **4**, 233–246.

Reid, I. D. and Wilkie, J. R. (1980). Developing a behavioural regime in a secure Youth Treatment Centre. Paper presented at the World Congress on Behaviour Therapy. Jerusalem, July 1980.

Risley, T. (1972). '*Juniper Gardens*'. American Psychological Association Convention, Honolulu, September 1972.

Sage, W. (1974). Crime and the clockwork lemon, *Human Behaviour*, **9**, 16–25.

Schur, E. M. (1965). *Crimes Without Victims: Deviant Behaviour and Public Policy: Abortion, Homosexuality, Drug Addiction* Prentice-Hall, Englewood Cliffs, New Jersey.

Schwitzgebel, R. K. (1964). *Street Corner Research: An Experimental Approach to Juvenile Delinquents*, Harvard University Press, Cambridge, Massachussetts.

Skinner, B. F. (1948). *Walden Two*, Macmillan, New York.

Stahl, J. R., Fuller, E. J., Lefebre, M. F. and Burchard, J. (1979). The token economy community youth center: a model for programming peer reincorcement, in *Progress in Behavior Therapy with Delinquents* (Ed. J. S. Stumphauzer), Charles C. Thomas, Springfield, Illinois.

Start (1974). Start Unconstitutional, *A.P.A. Monitor*, **5**, (12).

Stern, V. (1979). The care and rehabilitation of prisoners after discharge, *Royal Society of Health Journal*, **99**, 161–165.

Stuart, R. B. and Lott, L. A. (1972). Behavioural contracting with delinquents: a cautionary note, *Journal of Behavior Therapy and Experimental Psychiatry*, **3**, 161–169.

Stumphauzer, J. S. (1970). Behavior modification with juvenile delinquents: a critical review, *F. C. I. Technical and Treatment Notes*, **1**, 1–22.

Stumphauzer, J. S. (1973). *Behavior Therapy with Delinquents*, Charles C. Thomas, Springfield, Illinois.

Stumphauzer, J. S., Aiken, T. W. and Veloz, E. V. (1977). East Side Story: behavioral analysis of a high juvenile crime community, *Behavioral Disorders*, **2**, 76–84.

Stumphauzer, J. S., Candelora, K. and Venema, H. B. (1976). A follow-up of probation officers trained in behavior modification, *Behavior Therapy*, **7**, 713–715.

Tharp, R. G. and Wetzel, R. J. (1969). *Behavior Modification in the Natural Environment*, Academic Press, New York.

Thoresen, K. E., Thoresen, C. E., Klein, S. B., Wilbur, C. S., Becker-Haven, J. F. and Haven, W. G. (1979). Learning house: helping troubled children and their parents change themselves, in *Progress in Behavior Therapy with Delinquents* (Ed. J. S. Stumphauzer), Charles C. Thomas, Springfield, Illinois.

Timbers, G. D., Timbers, B. J., Fixsen, D. L., Phillips, E. L. and Wolf, M. M. (1973). Achievement Place pre-delinquent girls: modification of inappropriate emotional behaviors with token reinforcement and instructional procedures, Paper read at American Psychological Association, Montreal, Canada, 1973.

Trotter, S. (1975). Token economy program perverted by prison officials, *A.P.A. Monitor*, **6**, 24–27.

Tyler, V. O. (1967). Application of operant token reinforcement to the academic performance of an institutionalized delinquent, *Psychological Reports*, **21**, 249–260.

US Bureau of the Census. (1979). *Children in Custody: Advance Report on the 1977 Census of Public Juvenile Facilities*, US Government Printing Office, Washington DC.

Weathers, L. and Liberman, R. P. (1975). Contingency contracting with families of delinquent adolescents, *Behavior Therapy*, **6**, 356–366.

Werner, J. S., Minkin, N., Minkin, B. L., Fixsen, D. L., Phillips, E. L. and Wolf, M. M. (1965). 'Intervention package': an analysis to perpare juvenile delinquents for encounters with police officers, *Criminal Justice and Behavior*, **2**, 55–83.

West, D. J. (1967). *The Young Offender*, Pelican, London.

Wetzel, R. (1966). Use of behavioral techniques in a case of compulsive stealing, *Journal of Consulting Psychology*, **30**, 367–374.

Wooton, B. (1959). *Social Science and Social Pathology*, Allen & Unwin, London.

Yates, B. T., Haven, W. G. and Thoresen, C. E. (1979). Cost-effectiveness analysis at Learning House: how much change for how much money? in *Progress in behavior therapy with delinquents* (Ed. J. S. Stumphauzer), Charles C. Thomas, Springfield, Illinois.

Zax, M. and Specter, G. A. (1974). *An Introduction to Community Psychology*, Wiley, New York.

Developments in Study of Criminal Behaviour
Volume 1: The Prevention and Control of Offending
Edited by P. Feldman
© 1982, John Wiley & Sons, Ltd.

7

Intermediate Treatment: A New Approach to Community Care

MARY ANN PRESTON

Introduction

One of the major issues fought at the last General Election in Great Britain was the issue of law and order, and in particular the rising official statistics on juvenile crime. This topic has gained momentum over the last couple of decades, influenced not only by the escalating criminal statistics, which are almost certainly an under-estimate of offences committed (Hood and Sparks, 1970), but by the very high recidivism rates for traditional interventions—79 per cent for borstal trainees and 70 per cent for junior detention centres (NACRO, 1977)—and the increasing cost of keeping an individual in an institution.

Historically attempts to deal with this problem have led to changes in penal legislation, with the general aim of punishing the offender, deterring would be transgressors and protecting society. Hence the principal form of intervention has tended to be incarceration of one form or another, for example, borstal and detention centres. However, the failure of these traditional punitive approaches is now well documented (Hood and Sparks, 1970; Cornish and Clarke, 1975; Feldman, 1977), with Hood and Sparks (1970) providing a convincing summary of the failure, not only of incarceration but also of other traditional methods such as probation, fines, etc.

One of the latest legislative initiatives in response to the problem of juvenile crime in this country emerged in the Children and Young Persons Act (1969). Known as 'Intermediate Treatment' (IT), it represents a radical departure from previous legislative strategies, although in common with the earlier developments it owes less to a coherent model of delinquent behaviour than to the social, moral and financial pressures on policy makers.

During the 1960s, many practitioners were expressing concern about the 'inhuman' locking up of juveniles, while the politicians were becoming acutely aware not only of the increasing numbers of juveniles appearing in court but also of the increasing financial burden of keeping young people in institutions. At the same time however, they were under pressure not to weaken on the issue of juvenile justice, as they did have an obligation to 'protect society' and indeed the escalating criminal statistics may have indicated that tougher measures were required. The policy on juvenile justice at the time was confused to say the least. In an effort to find a solution that would satisfy some and placate others, the Government set up a series of enquiries and Parliamentary Committees to investigate this 'new social problem', which resulted in a proposal for a 'new alternative' form of intervention with juveniles—*Intermediate Treatment.*

The term first appeared in a Government White Paper—*Children In Trouble,* (1968)—and, as the name would suggest, it was proposed as a form of intervention with juvenile offenders that would be midway or intermediate between incarceration in a detatched residential establishment, and what is known in Great Britain as 'supervision in the community'. The White Paper pointed out that the existing forms of intervention for juvenile offenders available at that time distinguished sharply between those which involved complete removal from home and those which did not. The paper therefore proposed that 'some form or forms of intermediate treatment' should become available that would allow the child to remain in his own home, but would also bring him into contact with a different environment for a specified period of time.

This new 'community based' proposal was quite innovative, and indeed many members of parliament considered that the move was too radical. However, it was accepted, and IT was introduced formally into the legislation in 1969. It was incorporated into the juvenile justice system as a sentencing possibility for juvenile offenders, to intensify supervision in the community and to deflect the majority away from residential establishments.

In essence, therefore, the proposal was a change in 'location' from institution to community rather than a change in 'treatment' or method of intervention. National guidelines were produced on the form this new 'treatment' should take, but these were very broad and vague, and focused largely on administrative and legal aspects of the intervention. The use of 'activities' as the therapeutic medium was proposed (DHSS Circular, 1972), but the exact nature of these, and the planning, implementation and evaluation of the 'treatment' programme was left to Regional Planning Committees and individual supervisors in the local agencies involved.

What has emerged during this last decade, therefore, is central government and legislative commitment to a new alternative form of intervention with juveniles, with rather less general agreement at local level on the potential usefulness, or indeed viability, of such a move to the community. Developments therefore, have been varied ranging from, on the one extreme, the provision of lists of youth clubs, to on the other, the establishment of specialized groups to work with young offenders. There is, to date, no cohesive approach to the 'treatment' aspect of the intervention.

In sum, the new policy of the Children And Young Persons Act (1969) indicated a move to the community, not the introduction of a 'new method' of intervention As Feldman (1977) has pointed out in his discussion of the penal system in general, and IT is yet another example, the methods used have developed empirically and have not been influenced to any great extent by the findings of sociological or psychological research. They are not based on any firm model of human behaviour.

In terms of IT the exact methods and techniques used depend to a large degree on individual initiative, training and skill.

Historical perspective

While IT has emerged in Great Britain at the end of what O'Donnell (1977) has termed 'the activist reform decade' of the sixties, its origins go back at least to the nineteenth century, with roots that are many and varied (Tutt, 1976a, 1979). To try to understand the confusion of the sixties and to illustrate the rationale behind the various projects that have emerged since then under the title 'Intermediate Treatment', it may be useful to trace some of these roots.

Tutt (1979) outlines six major origins. The oldest and most established of these was a social attitude dominant in the early nineteenth century and linked closely to the Protestant Ethnic that 'the Devil makes work for idle hands'. The idea here is that boredom or idleness 'breeds' delinquency so one must 'keep them off the streets and occupied'. As Tutt points out, it is significant that the White Paper, *Children In Trouble* (1968), actually states that 'organised work activity' may be one form of IT, and this has indeed shaped many current developments.

The second root that Tutt suggests is the youth club model, tracing this back to 1906 when Charles Russell, the Chief Inspector of the Children's Department in the Home Office, advocated the establishment of youth clubs in the child's neighbourhood, to try to deal with any difficulties on the spot. These were to be an on-going, ever present facility where the child could attend for pleasure as well as advice and understanding at times of crisis. The idea of training or teaching children about 'personal relationships and social responsibility' in such an informal setting also grew from here, and this has influenced greatly many modern IT projects.

With the third root, Tutt points out that IT is linked firmly to the penal system, highlighting the fact that it was to replace the Junior Attendance Centres. These had been established as a sentencing option for the Juvenile Court, to operate at a time that was inconvenient to the offender. The White Paper, however, suggested that while these orders did allow a child to remain in his own home and at the same time experience a different environment, the time spent there was too short and this facility was limited to large urban areas. The proposal therefore was that: 'A new legal and administrative framework will be established for the development of a variety of forms of IT for children and young persons placed under supervision by the courts.'

Here we can see the origins of potential confusion over the client population of

IT. The first two roots suggest that IT may be open to non-offenders and children in the locality of the project, while the third suggests that it should deal primarily with those under court orders.

The fourth origin that Tutt describes adds to the confusion. He highlights one of the early major sociological explanations for delinquent behaviour—that deprivation is one of the principal causes. The theory behind this is that the low rate of delinquency generally found in the middle to upper classes, suggests that they have the finance and resources to 'enrich the lives and broaden the horizons' of their offspring. It follows therefore, that the opportunities should be open to all, and the 1968 White Paper proposed that the child should remain in his own home but that he should 'be brought into contact with a different environment'.

Here we see the origin of the theory that IT should offer a wide range of activities to all deprived children, i.e. not just those on court orders. In fact, the DHSS circular (1972) on IT projects, added to this confusion over potential clientele by stating that the facilities offered should 'normally be of a kind in which other children can participate, and not (be) confined to children under supervision through court orders'.

This fourth root has influenced significantly the development of IT schemes throughout Great Britain, with the focus of many projects emphasizing work with the deprived child to prevent future delinquency, rather than focussing on current offenders.

The fifth root adds to the debate. In order to reinforce this proposed move to community intervention in the form of IT, the White Paper in 1968 advocated the phasing out of Junior Detention Centres. The aim was that IT would cater for the *majority* of juvenile offenders in their own communities. This was quite an innovative proposal, and perhaps the most controversial aspect of IT. While such decarceration projects have met with success in some parts of the USA (e.g. Massachusetts, see Ohlin *et al.*, 1974) this was not generally welcomed in Great Britain. A political compromise was therefore reached, whereby the proposal to phase out detention centres was incorporated into the Children and Young Persons Act (1969), but the section of the act that contained it would remain unimplemented until an appropriate time could be reached. This section of the act has not yet been brought into force.

This has been an unfortunate ommission, as the non-implementation of this part of the act has confused practitioners as to the aim of IT, and reinforced many field workers in preferring to work with younger juvenile in a preventative capacity.

The final root that Tutt discussess is the concept of 'treatment'. This stems from a form of intervention with offenders that has been introduced in recent years, not as a result of legislation, but rather originating from the psychotherapeutic model of human behaviour and the influence this has had on current models of deviance.

The concept of 'treating' offenders is based on the view that delinquent or deviant behaviour is a symptom of some underlying 'disease' or 'personality defect' which can be 'cured' through an individualized treatment programme. This model has greatly influenced the content of professional training courses for the majority of practitioners who work with juveniles in this country, and many 'therapeutic' interventions have been introduced into institutions (Cornish and Clarke, 1975; Tutt, 1976a).

This model has also shaped 'treatment' interventions with offenders in the USA (Teuber and Powers, 1953; Grant and Grant, 1959; Jesness, 1965; Warren et al., 1966) but in both countries the results produced have been inconclusive. In a British example Cornish and Clarke (1975) carried out a major study comparing the effects of two regimes at the Kingswood Training School. One regime was a 'therapeutic community' involving twice-daily discussion groups, while the other was the traditional, formal, highly structured training regime. Both interventions resulted in a 70 per cent reconviction rate. In another British study, Tutt (1976b), reported that the new therapeutically based community home school system, also introduced by the Children and Young Persons Act (1969), had equally high reconviction rates.

However, despite these unimpressive results, the psychotherapeutic model continues to influence the general approach to 'treatment' intervention with offenders in Great Britain. In terms of IT, the major premise is that the activities used in the treatment programme are unimportant except as catalysts and that the real therapeutic medium is the relationship between adult and child. Exactly what can be achieved by moving the location of this 'therapeutic relationship' from an institution to the community has yet to be established, as the focus of such therapeutic intervention is the individual himself and not his environment. However, hopes were high for IT in 1969.

This very brief summary of a number of the origins of IT has highlighted some of the major problems facing the *practitioner*. The target population is not clearly defined, and the treatment methods and aims of intervention in IT are vague and open to broad interpretation. Even where treatment techniques are specified, these do not appear to be based on any recent research or results of similar intervention.

It is not surprising therefore that IT schemes vary greatly, from playgroups for the under fives, through evening groups for young people who go to school, to day-care facilities for school truants and/or young offenders. The professionals who administer these interventions are also a varied group, taking recruits from education, youth and community work, social work and residential care. The result is an amalgamation of skills and methods of intervention that requires careful management and administration.

Intermediate Treatment schemes in Great Britain

The Intermediate Treatment Schemes (ITS) that have developed in this country can be divided broadly into two approaches, those that provide new facilities in a community (rarely purpose-built premises, more usually the renovation of old buildings) aimed primarily at the day care of juvenile offenders; and those that use already established facilities to provide evening and weekend intervention for young people who attend school or work. Some projects have combined both approaches to provide a broad spectrum of intervention (e.g. 870 House, Birmingham; Norman, 1977).

Most of the projects, when stating a therapeutic medium, have used the psychotherapeutic model, in particular group therapy, with the use of activities 'to develop systematically more positive self concepts, thereby increasing social adjustment' (Thorpe, 1978).

The Hammersmith Teenage Project (Whitlam, 1977; Covington, 1979) was one of the early experimental IT projects established in London in 1975, under the management of NACRO (The National Association for the Care and Rehabilitation of Offenders) and it is one of the few projects that has attempted an evaluation of the work. The project was set up to work with boys and girls of 12–16 years of age, and the overall aim was to 'reduce delinquency both within the individual and the community' (Covington, 1979).

This was to be accomplished through the development of four different aims: the diversion of juveniles from the justice system—the project was to become a direct alternative to incarceration; the use of people with similar backgrounds or experiences, i.e., delinquent histories, to work with juvenile delinquents, while embarking on new careers themselves; the development of community links; and the facilitation of inter-agency co-operation.

The project provided a variety of activities for its clients, including a basic skills programme for non-school attenders, and organized projects and activities in the evenings, ranging from sports and expeditions, to local community work, to learning a particular skill such as woodwork or dressmaking.

The project ran until 1978 when it was accepted into the Hammersmith Social Services Department range of facilities, and it is now financed by them. This in itself was a limited measure of success, although in her conclusion to the evaluation of the project, Covington (1979) states, that due to methodological difficulties, 'it is impossible to determine whether or not it [the project] had an effect on reducing delinquency'.

This rather unsatisfactory conclusion highlights one of the major problems facing IT projects in this country. They tend to set very broad aims that are often both difficult to quantify and therefore to achieve, so that the overall impression tends to be one of zealous participation in a variety of diversionary activities, without any particular structure or coherent methodology.

An example of this is the ITS set up in 1973 by Lambeth Social Services Department, London—the Salamanca House project (Staples, 1977). Here the stated aims were to establish contact and work with the 'unclubbable' youngsters in the area, and to enable the community to take part in the development of services for youth in the area. Four years later, Staples (1977) reports that the project had set up two new youth clubs, a range of street-based adventure and sporting activities, two education and training schemes and the 'beginnings' of an employment service. This was quite an achievement, but unfortunately he states that: 'No one particularly cared whether we were doing youth work, community work, advice work, education or job creation, provided some energy was being expended.' He finally concludes that 'it is impossible to quantify the effect of any one of these [smaller projects]'.

An example of an IT project using existing facilities to run small 'therapeutic groups' is the project described by Flynn (1977), financed by the Thameside Metropolitan Borough. This is the Moorlands Young People's Scheme, and the object of this is 'to run several types of adolescent groups'. One group involves about twelve children referred by probation and social services and another involves a larger group of children who attend the centre on a regular basis, where they can be 'observed in informal surroundings and assessed for suitability for the first group'. The specific aim of the first group is not stated, nor are the methods of observation and assessment used in the second group. It is stated, however, that the emphasis is on 'enhancing social functioning of a young person by creating a facility which will help develop a better relationship between the supervisor and the supervised'. The study does not report any results.

Many other IT projects have been set up throughout the country e.g., Wandsworth Social Services Department's Intermediate Treatment Project; Haringey Intermediate Treatment Scheme; The Woodway Centre, Coventry and the Islington Family Service Unit Intermediate Treatment Centre. All have reported a variety of schemes and individual approaches which on the surface would appear excellent, but unfortunately overall evaluation of the projects has been very limited.

It is not surprising therefore that almost 10 years after the implementation of the Childrens and Young Persons Act (1969), IT is still not viewed as a viable alternative to incarceration for the majority of juvenile offenders in this country. Only 25 per cent of the approximate 25 000 young people in IT programmes in Great Britain are on IT Orders or Care Orders from the juvenile court, i.e. they could have been placed in residential establishments (Tutt, 1979), while the remainder are on Supervision Orders or have not been through the justice system at all—it is unlikely that these young people would have been incarcerated. As the number of young people in institutions continues to increase, it is clear that IT is not serving the offender population.

However, we now face the circular argument. Until Central Government and the administrators of the Juvenile Justice System receive evidence of the efficacy of IT in dealing with offenders, the current lack of credibility surrounding this 'new alternative' will remain. Equally, as long as the uncertainty surrounding the proposed clientele of IT reigns, practitioners will continue to take the often easier and more rewarding avenue, of preventive work with 'at risk' juveniles. Until a central directive is received, IT schemes will continue to emerge in the form of individual initiatives, founded on that legislative 'White Elephant' (in terms of

IT), the Children and Young Persons Act (1969), with its broad directive to community-based intervention.

A decision is therefore needed that will permit a national, cohesive scheme to be developed. Many involved in IT have already called for this (NACRO, 1977; Tutt, 1979), proposing a national programme of decarceration of the majority of juveniles, with the increased involvement of IT in offender rehabilitation. We have now several models of this type of programme run in individual states in North America, and it would perhaps be an opportune time to learn from our colleagues overseas. Indeed, developments in the USA have not stopped at a change in location from institution to community, as several promising pieces of work with juvenile offenders have emerged, which make full use of a developing treatment technology aimed specifically at community intervention.

IT in this country requires, not only a directive on clientele, but also some indication of how to deal effectively with them. It would seem that we may have several lessons to learn.

The behavioural approach

Dissatisfaction with the 'macro-failure' (NACRO, 1977) of traditional penal methods also developed in the USA during the 1960s and early 1970s. There, as in Great Britain, it became increasingly important to find a new, more effective avenue of intervention, and in parallel with developments in this country, a move to the community was advocated. As each State has its own individual policy governing offender intervention, the total decarceration of juveniles was initiated in some States, e.g. Massachusetts, while in others, the move was gradual and experimental, e.g. California, Kansas.

At the same time yet another parallel development was taking place, principally in the USA. Interest was growing in a new method of intervention with offenders—the use of behaviour modification or behaviour therapy. While they initially developed separately, it is essentially the confluence of these two trends that has shaped the latest experimental projects in community intervention with juvenile offenders in the USA.

It has taken behaviour therapy some time to achieve this move to a community base. As early as 1948 Skinner had advocated societal reform based on operant technology, but it is now generally held that Tharp and Wetzel (1969) were two of the initial promotors of the use of behaviour therapy in the community.

For many years behaviour therapy has been accepted in institutions (Karacki and Levinson, 1970; Cohen and Filipczak, 1971; Jesness and De Risi, 1973; Allison et al., 1979, in the USA; Chelfham Mill School, Burland 1978, and Glenthorne Youth Treatment Centre, Reid, 1981 (see chapter 3 this volume), in Great Britain), principally in the form of token economy systems. Generally, there has been some demonstrated effect of these interventions while the individual has remained in the institution, but one of the major problems is the generalization of the skills acquired to the home environment (Feldman 1977; Stumphauzer, 1979b). As Ostapiuk and Reid (1981) point out, the institution is a highly artificial environment, isolated from the community, with varied and often conflicting influences on the individual. The generalization of any appropriate skills taught during incarceration is often striving in direct opposition to the equally newly acquired more sophisticated deviant skills that juveniles can also learn in institutions (Stumphauzer, 1979b).

Obviously these observations relate to the more traditional penal and therapeutic models of intervention, as well as behaviour therapy, but it is perhaps no surprise that an increasing number of community projects using behaviour therapy have emerged. As Stumphauzer (1979a) points out, the move is an obvious one for behaviour therapists 'finally, we are heeding our own dictum that environment controls behaviour, and are doing something *in* that environment'. Taking this one step further, Preston (personal communication), in his proposals for the establishment of generalizable skills training programmes using behaviour therapy outlined three essential components to improve treatment efficacy: working in a relevant training environment, setting relevant target behaviours and using relevant reinforcers. These '3 Rs' of rehabilitation would suggest that an individual's own community or home environment would provide the most comprehensive and useful behavioural analysis, and provide the most relevant environment or setting for intervention.

Community approaches using the behavioural model—USA

Apart from a few isolated projects in Great Britain, e.g. The Shape Project, Ostapiuk and Reid (1981) (see chapter 6 this volume) most of the new developments using behaviour therapy in the community have occurred overseas, principally in the USA. Several interesting and promising studies with juvenile offenders have emerged, reporting not only improved treatment efficacy but also increased cost effectiveness compared to institutional intervention. Many of the projects are very similar in concept to IT in this country and in particular day-care centres, although, of course, the methodology is very different.

Davidson and Robinson (1975) describe the Kentfields Rehabilitation Program in Michigan. This is a non-residential, community-based programme for 'hard-core', i.e. relatively serious and repetitive, male offenders. Their comprehensive community-based programme includes keeping youths in their own homes, public-works participation each morning for wages, an afternoon school programme based on programmed instruction as well as performance contracts, behavioural group sessions twice a week and an overall level and points system.

Initially, the project staff were able to convince community leaders and the courts to refer to Kentfields the majority of young people who otherwise would have been incarcerated (125 out of 131), and their subsequent results demonstrated that a higher percentage of those boys who had completed the programme successfully returned to school or employment and stayed out of penal institutions, compared with those who had dropped out. There are no data concerning an *untreated* comparison group. Local government sceptics were so impressed with these results and the money saved by such non-institutional intervention, that the programme now has local financial support.

The Kentfields project has several aspects in common with many day-care IT schemes in this country; it deals with identified juvenile offenders (only a small number of IT schemes attempt this), keeps them in their own homes, and makes excellent use of already established facilities, e.g. public-works projects and Community Action Programs. The impressive results obtained at Kentfields would suggest, however, that the overall methodological differences are significant and that IT could indeed benefit from such a structured approach.

Several other authors have reported a slightly different community approach, again using behaviour therapy, but this time working through the families and/or supervising officers of juvenile offenders. The principal method used here is contingency contracting, and this has produced interesting, although differing, results (Alexander and Parsons, 1973; Stuart and Lott, 1972; Weathers and Liberman, 1975). O'Donnell (1977), in his review of the majority of these studies suggests that greater success is likely when youths contract directly with probation officers, or an agency that can control some sought-after reward (e.g. time off probation), than with their families. Probation officers (and in Great Britain, social workers) would have both the authority and the access to the reward that families would not have. To enable this approach to work in IT, the IT Order would have to be used more often and carry more weight in the Juvenile Court.

Fo and O'Donnell (1975), reported an interesting approach to contract work with juveniles. They employed indigenous non-professionals as mediators or 'buddies' to work with young offenders. This is similar to the 'tracker' system used by the Key Agency in Massachusetts, however, in this case, the 'buddies' were trained in the use of contingency management. Fo and O'Donnell report a significant reduction in a variety of targeted problem behaviours and while offence behaviours were not specifically dealt with, a significant reduction in delinquent behaviour was also noted.

It is unfortunate that more follow-up data are not available on these contract studies, as, while most can demonstrate some measure of success during intervention, only a few have shown some effect beyond this period. Yet another project using behaviour therapy that could be paralleled in terms of location and general aims of intervention, by some IT projects in Great Britain, is a programme called PREP—Preparation through Responsive Educational Programs (Filipczak et al., 1979). This scheme highlights the potential value of the established educational system in preventing delinquency and makes excellent use of existing state-school facilities. The project has four basic elements, individualized programming in Maths and English for both referred and volunteer students, group interpersonal-skills classes, a behavioural, educational and counselling programme for parents and teacher-staff training. The scheme is run in state schools and the authors differentiate between short- and long-term goals for each individual.

The project reports on a 5-year period, over which some 600 students had been through the scheme. Significant short-term goals were achieved in academic tests, overall class grades, discipline and school attendance. In addition, this improvement generalized to other classes in which these PREP students participated.

One-year follow up showed that these effects had been maintained, although the data on the possible generalization of this to delinquent behaviours are not yet available. However, the early indications from this study would suggest that this link between school efforts and juvenile problems should receive greater attention, and that intervention should take place relatively early on in the individual's school career.

Once again the similarity to some IT schemes is striking. Many British projects attempt to deal with young school refusers or truants, with the very difficult goal of returning them to full-time normal schooling. The general aim, as in PREP, is prevention of future delinquency, but as yet there are no data available on success rates.

The community projects discussed so far have relied on established facilities and worked through significant individuals in the natural environment. However, another major approach to community intervention using behaviour therapy has been the setting up of new facilities, and the establishment of residential community resources or family group homes. This has been pioneered by Achievement Place Studies (Phillips, 1968; Fixsen et al., 1973; Braukman and Fixsen, 1975).

Achievement Place is a community based, family style, group home for six to eight delinquent or pre-delinquent males from 12 to 15 years old. The programme is directed by members of the community and the treatment element is administered by a resident couple called 'teaching parents'. The 'teaching parents' have had at least 1 year of training in behavioural techniques before commencing in a group home.

The goal of treatment in Achievement Place is to establish through reinforcement, modelling and instruction, behavioural competence in social, academic, pre-vocational and self-care skills, and success in these areas is now well documented (Phillips, 1968; Bailey et al., 1970; Fixsen et al., 1973).

A further goal is to decrease the likelihood that Achievement Place boys will commit future offences and/or proceed to institutions. Kirigin et al., (1979) report 2-year follow-up data, with fewer Achievement Place boys incarcerated than a comparison group who had originally been treated in an institution. These results are clearly promising, although she also reports that the number of police and court contacts at follow up are similar for both groups, which would suggest that the link between behaviours targeted in the programme and offence behaviour need greater clarification.

However, the early promising results of Achievement Place, coupled with the fact that it is considerably less expensive than institutional treatment, have been welcomed across the USA, and over thirty-five other group home programmes have been developed using the behavioural approach of the teaching family model. As the model itself is continually under scrutiny and evaluation (Kirigin et al., 1979) the quality of the service Achievement Place and its subsequent developments provide, will hopefully retain this initially high standard.

The above reports are only a very few of the numerous community-based projects that are developing along behavioural lines in the USA. As Stumphauzer (1979b) states 'there is a rapid, yet almost deliberate evolution taking place, with a united move to intervention in the natural environment.

Not only has this led to direct intervention with young offenders or potential offenders, but increasingly, interest is growing in the non-delinquent and the variables that maintain his behaviour, especially in a high juvenile crime community (Aiken et al., 1977). These authors believe that the study of non-delinquents could provide the key to the elusive repertoire of behaviours that are relevant and essential to the survival of the non-delinquent living within a network of criminal activity.

This would hold vital implications for offender rehabilitation in general as well as preventive work with juveniles, and future developments from this team are eagerly awaited.

Developments in Great Britain: the BAY centre

Introduction

In contrast to the upsurge of interest in the behavioural approach to offender rehabilitation in the community, in the USA, and the concomitant decrease in the number of juveniles incarcerated (US Bureau of Census, 1979), the trend in this country has been less promising. The number of young people in institutions has continued to rise (NACRO, 1977) and as Ostapiuk and Reid (1981) point out, the application of behavioural methods to the treatment of offenders has been sporadic and piecemeal, and has relied very much on individual interest and initiative.

Several rehabilitative community-based programmes with adult offenders have been set up, notably the Shape Project (Ostapiuk and Reid, 1981), which is a community-based facility providing accommodation and work, social and general 'survival' skills training for young adult offenders, in conditions closely approximating those of the local community from which the clients come and to which they are likely to return. A number of other community-based projects also provide accommodation, although in these the emphasis tends to be principally on training employment and work-survival skills (Manpower Services Commission, 1979).

In the field of IT very few projects use any version of the behavioural approach. Even when included, it tends to be part of a conglomerate of techniques and methods that are tried, with a consequent lack of structure or overall commitment to any one.

However, despite this general lack of interest, one experimental project has emerged in IT, where the potential input of behaviour therapy has been recognized. The project is still in its infancy, but it has already drawn favourable interest from both practitioners and those influencing policy. It is essentially an attempt to introduce some structure and consistent programming into an already established, multi-purpose IT project, dealing principally with young offenders.

In 1977, a major ITS was developed by Birmingham Social Services called The Birmingham Action for Youth Project. This has several aspects, one of which is a centre aimed at providing day care for juvenile offenders who live at home—The Birmingham Action for Youth Centre (BAY Centre).

In the autumn of 1978 a clinical psychologist (M.A.P) was invited to become involved and it was essentially through this link that the approach adopted at the centre began to develop along behavioural lines.

The BAY Centre had been set up as a direct alternative to residential care, i.e. it was to deal with young people on court orders who would otherwise have been incarcerated. This has not been adhered to strictly, due to the pressure on the centre to keep its numbers up, regardless of the referral source or history. However, generally, the majority of young people referred have been through the juvenile court.

The centre is located in an old renovated school building in an inner city part of Birmingham, an area with a high crime rate and rising unemployment. Originally this 'community based' project was to act as a resource for the whole of the City of Birmingham (over 1 million population) which led to many difficulties and problems, and inhibited any efforts to integrate into the local environment. However, in the last 18 months, two other Social Services Centres have been opened, and the BAY Centre has now a more realistic catchment area.

The BAY Centre began with at least seven distinct aims: to stop young people offending; to provide day care for young people aimed at returning them to ordinary secondary schooling; to provide day care as an introduction to employment; to provide long-term day care as an alternative to prolonged residential care; to provide summer and holiday play schemes for the local community; to provide evening activities for the local community including a youth club open to all young people in the vicinity, and to act as a resources centre for the whole Birmingham Action for Youth project.

The BAY Centre therefore, had a very wide brief and an initial analysis showed that few of these aims were being achieved. The effect on offending was monitored only during the programme, no follow up was carried out; no young person had been returned successfully to school; programmes for long-term intervention were proving to be a strain on resources and the mix of short- and long-term clients led to inconsistencies and disruptions.

The only aspect of the day-care intervention that provided positive results was the introduction to employment programme for 15–16 year olds, in that 65 per cent of the group attending from September 1978 to May 1979 left the centre into employment.

The centre provided the building and limited staffing for summer play schemes, and an open youth club was run one evening a week by the warden. Unfortunately this led to his absence one day a week from the day-care programme, and as the clientele were different, there was no continuity between these two aspects of the overall programme.

Due to this rather unsatisfactory set of circumstances therefore, it was decided in September 1979 to narrow the aims of the day-care centre and deal exclusively with 15–16 year olds who had a history of offending, who would be in their last year of official schooling, and who would therefore participate in the preparation for employment programme. This decision was facilitated by the opportune increase in the numbers of young people of this age group who were referred at the time, so the Social Services Department accepted this new proposal, to provide work, social and general survival skills training for this specific group.

From September 1979, therefore, the administrative criteria for acceptance into the project were narrowed to: the young person must be 15–16 years of age; there must be an immediate probability that he or she will be taken into residential care; and there must be some support, however minimal, from a parent or guardian. These were not based on individual problem behaviours or indeed a history of offending, as some young people referred had been before the courts for non-school attendance only: However, as the BAY Centre is part of a statutory organization, they are obliged to consider all juveniles who fulfill these criteria, regardless of their specific problems, and at times, exceptions may have to be considered.

The centre can take up to thirty young people, and it is staffed by seven full-time and two part-time IT Workers. The professional background of the staff is varied—one probation officer, two youth and community workers, one teacher, one social worker, two full-time and two part-time craft instructors. No staff member had had any previous experience of behavioural therapy, so the initial stages of the present project involved staff training.

All young people are referred initially by their Supervising Officer from the Court, which in the majority of cases is a social worker.

From September 1979 to May 1980, the centre ran the following programme.

Assessment period

This was an induction period, lasting 3 weeks, during which an individual's level of competence in general educational skills, work skills, social skills and overall self-management skills were assessed. As the majority of young people referred had not only been before the courts for criminal offences, but had also been long-term truants from school, basic self-management skills in terms of personal hygiene and time keeping emerged as major problem areas.

During this assessment period the young people were introduced to a wide variety of work and activity situations and behavioural competence checklists were introduced to supplement the educational tests and direct observations of behaviour. The assessment was carried out by as many members of staff as possible and a concensus was reached on relevant targets for intervention.

Review system-contract

At the end of the assessment period a review was held, and a contract, detailing as far as possible short- and long-term goals, was drawn up and agreed with the young person, his supervising officer and his parent or guardian. Reviews were then held every 2–3 months, and these occasions were used as a forum for discussion of the individual's participation and progress in the programme, as well as a review of the goals stated in the contract.

Parents were encouraged to attend, and were often pleasantly surprised to hear positive comments from staff on their offspring.

General centre programme

After the assessment period, the young person began on Stage One, which was a General Centre Programme. This ran in conjunction with an individual educational programme and applied equally to all young people. It was based directly on principles of learning and was a system where each individual could earn points for achieving a variety of set targets, which were clearly stated and explained to everyone.

A pilot scheme in June/July 1979, coupled with both a follow up of previous young people who had attended the centre and the data from the Assessment Period, suggested that areas such as self management and work routine were good starting points, so Stage One was designed to build up these skills. The points earned were exchanged daily for special activities, e.g. ice skating, swimming, snooker, etc., which took place at the end of the day. While all these special activities were chosen by the young people, and obviously linked to available resources, care was taken to ensure that the majority were available in the local community and were therefore attainable when the young person left the BAY Centre.

Individual centre programme

When an individual was earning points consistently on Stage One, he moved on to an individual programme where the emphasis was on building up specific work and social skills. On average it took between 6 and 8 weeks to move to this stage, and the targets set were linked directly to the initial Assessment Period, as well as the ongoing monitoring during Stage One. The young people were still on a points system, and while daily activities in exchange for points were used, emphasis was also put on a long-term reinforcer to encourage the budgeting and saving of points.

Work experience

The aim of this part of the programme was to generalize the skills acquired at BAY into an actual working situation as well as providing first-hand experience of the type of employment that the young people could expect when they left. Unfortunately, progress to this stage depended not only on performance on their individual targets, but also on the availability of placements with local firms. However, the response from employers was excellent and the majority of young people had at least 1 week's experience in an employment situation, with some remaining for 3–4 weeks. Throughout this time the staff liaised directly with the employer, who was asked to assess the young person's work and self-management skills.

Feedback on performance in Work Experience was provided by centre staff, and any difficulties that had arisen were dealt with in individual training and counselling sessions. Throughout this stage, the young people were on a weekly points earning system which was designed to resemble a weekly wage packet. Budgeting and saving were ongoing aspects of the programme.

This Work Experience stage proved to be particularly useful in providing a realistic view of potential employment for these young people. They did not have state examinations to impress employers, and as the majority had criminal records many firms were reluctant to employ them. Relevant work experience was therefore very enlightening and their subsequent aspirations were much more realistic.

The overall programme at the BAY Centre lasted 8 months and throughout this time, intervention at the centre was from Monday to Friday only. Each young person lived at home, and any evening or weekend intervention was left to their supervising officer. Twenty-four young people participated in the programme.

Assessment and follow-up

The progress of the young people was closely monitored while at BAY, and in addition to the daily and weekly points earnings, behavioural checklists were completed regularly.

The follow up is limited to 6 months at the moment, but this will continue for at least 2 years. The principal comparison group is a set of twenty-six young people

Table 1   Employment figures—on leaving the centre

	Group one (n = 24)		Group two (n = 26)		City of Birmingham
Employment	63%	(15)	65%	(17)	45%
Further training	12%	(3)	0		12%
No employment	25%	(6)	36%	(9)	43%

(For Tables 1–3 group one is the behavioural programme; group two is the pre-behavioural programme)

Table 2   Employment figures—Follow up

	Group one (n = 24)				Group two (n = 26)			
	0–3 months		3–6 months		0–3 months		3–6 months	
Employment	63%	(15)	4%	(1)	27%	(7)	23%	(6)
Training	17%	(4)	4%	(1)	0		0	
Unemployed	20%	(5)	54%	(13)	62%	(16)	50%	(3)
Redundant	0		13%	(3)	0		0	
Residential establishments	0		8%	(2)	4%	(1)	8%	(2)
Not available	0		17%	(4)	8%	(2)	19%	(5)

who had been through the centre in the year prior to the present intervention. Table 1 indicates the initial success achieved by the BAY Centre in placing their young people in employment. Both groups who had attended the BAY Centre had higher employment rates than those generally achieved by 16-year-old school leavers in the City of Birmingham as a whole, and three from Group One went into local government Training Schemes. Table 2 illustrates the situation with both the BAY Centre groups at 3 and 6 months, Group One had maintained the high initial employment rate with yet another of the young people joining a training scheme. At 3 months, the figures for Group Two were not as promising with 62 per cent unemployed.

However, the situation at 6 months presented a different picture. Group Two had the higher employment figures, although it should be noted that three from Group One had lost their jobs through redundancy, i.e. they were the last employees to take up a post, so that when the current economic recession hit their firms, these young people were the first to go. In all other cases, in both groups, the loss of employment was due to the individual young person involved.

In both groups two young people were in residential establishments due to further offences committed, and the overall unemployment rates were around 50 per cent—not very satisfactory considering the initial employment figures on

Table 3   Offence rate

| | Group one ($n = 24$) | | Group two ($n = 26$) | |
	One offence	Two plus	One offence	Two plus
Pre-intervention	54% (13)	33% (8)	53% (14)	31% (8)
During	25% (6)	0	27% (7)	0
3 months post-inter- vention	0	0	12% (3)	0
6 months post-inter- vention	21% (5)	0	23% (6)	0

leaving the centre, and for Group One, the promising trends at the 3-month follow up. Indeed, this trend of increasing unemployment for Group One would suggest that while work and work-related skills can be generalized and maintained to some degree—in this case, for about 3 months—further intervention and support is required to maintain this over a longer period of time.

At the moment, this follow-up supervision is left to the individual supervising officer, who unfortunately, often views placement at the BAY Centre as fulfillment of their obligation to the client, and subsequent intervention can be sporadic and very limited. There is, therefore, scope for further involvement of the BAY Centre beyond Stage Three of their programme, perhaps establishing something like a drop in day centre for young people who are experiencing difficulties at work or home. Table 3 illustrates figures on rates of offending. It can be seen that both groups were similar in terms of previous known offences—the figures do not add up to the totals as there were some young people who were subject to Court Orders for non school attendance only. The number of offences committed while on the programme were also similar.

At 3-month follow up, a parallel improved trend to the employment figures can be noted for Group One, with no known offences at that time. In Group Two three young people had at least on known offence, and one boy was in a residential establishment.

However, once again, at 6 months the groups show very similar trends, with two from each group incarcerated and over 20 per cent of the total with at least one known offence. This adds further weight to the proposal for continued involvement of the BAY Centre after the initial programme, to reinforce and aid the generalization of the alternatives to offending behaviour that they introduce the young people to. Increased liaison with local clubs and other community facilities would be an important aspect of this, as would police involvement. The latter does happen at the moment, but to a very limited degree.

It has, in fact, been proposed that a planned programme run in parallel to the work experience scheme, but involving a range of community facilities, be incorporated into the next centre programme, to facilitate the generalization of alternative, recreational activities. Obviously, as it would appear from the follow up of Group One that this could be achieved in the short term, the future maintenance of community involvement with the young people would be vital and could indeed provide excellent models for subsquent IT referrals.

The future

The developments at the Birmingham Action For Youth Centre are promising, when one considers that the project is just over 1 year old. The Social Services Department is interested, although their strong commitment to social-work theory based on the psychotherapeutic model of human behaviour, will take time to change. The production of promising results, however, coupled with the very favourable cost of running an IT venture compared to a residential establishment, has attracted much local interest.

While it must be acknowledged that the BAY Centre only provides day care, i.e. it deals with the young people on week days only, it can be seen from Table 4 that IT is much less of a financial burden than the residential alternatives for juvenile offenders in this country. The principal residential establishments are the community home schools with education on the premises, which are essentially 'welfare' resources rather than penal establishments, with emphasis on the therapeutic community approach, and the 'treatment' of juvenile delinquency; and detention centres and borstals which are detached penal establishments. Indeed, the figures suggest that were the latter to be phased out, in line with the original proposal in the Children and Young Persons Act (1969), the finance available from this would more than adequately cover the increase in numbers in IT Schemes similar to the BAY Centre.

In Table 4, the definition of 'successful' is that a young person has not been incarcerated at a follow up of 2 years, with the BAY Centre data referring to known offences at 6 months.

Included in Table 4 is the cost of keeping a young person in Achievement Place, the community group home approach now adopted in several states in the

Table 4   Comparison costs of the BAY Centre and other treatment facilities (1979)

	BAY Centre	CHE	Detention centre	Borstal	Achievement Place
Yearly operating cost per young person	£2895	£5720	£5400	£5400	£2895
	$5500	$10868	$10260	$10260	$5500
Number 'treated'	24	5500	6303	2117	16
Number successful	19	No data	1576	318'	13
Cost per 'successful' young person	£2947	No data	£21579	£35949	£3563
	$5599		$41034	$68303	$6769

USA. Obviously the principal difference to the BAY Centre is that the young person lives in Achievement Place, and the nearest British comparison we have is the community home school with education.

It can be seen that Achievement Place compares very favourably with all British residential establishments in terms of yearly operating costs per young person. Unfortunately the community home schools do not keep follow up data, but certainly in relation to detention entries and borstals, Achievement Place has an impressive success rate, and is therefore much more cost effective. This must surely merit further attention from both practitioners and politicians in this country, and may provide a natural extension for IT centres.

In terms of the immediate furture of the BAY Centre programme, increased involvement with local community facilities has already been mentioned. Another obvious avenue of development is work with the families of the young people referred. If the BAY Centre is to become a viable alternative to residential care, in both the short-term and long-term for juveniles, then it must involve the family. At the moment, the social worker at the centre does visit the home, and the parents or guardians are invited to the reviews. However, there is no real participation by the family in the programme, or any attempt by the centre to broaden the programme into this sphere.

Unfortunately, here we see one of the major difficulties of working in a statutory organization—the boundaries of involvement are very firmly set and it is consequently often difficult for one part of this organization to carry involvement through to its logical conclusion. In terms of the BAY Centre, therefore, family work is left to the individual supervising officer and is completely divorced from anything that the young person may be doing in his programme at the centre. The anomaly is, that one of the most important, and in 1969, innovative, aspects of IT, is that the young person lives at home; yet many IT schemes fail to recognize the home environment as part of their 'therapeutic domain'.

Before the BAY Centre could develop in this direction therefore, a policy decision would have to be taken on the overall aim and responsibility of the IT scheme in relation to juveniles referred.

The future of IT

The future of IT, like its history, is an uncertain one. Commitment to it as an alternative to incarceration for juvenile offenders remains sporadic, and many in the juvenile justice system continue to view it as a 'soft option'.

Even where a relatively comprehensive IT facility has been developed, many professionals involved with juveniles do not know what IT means or how it could potentially be used. This was highlighted in a study by Cross (1979), in which juvenile magistrates, social workers and probation officers were tested on their knowledge of IT facilities in their area. The general conclusion was that the magistrates knew very little (and they are in a position to make an IT Order on a juvenile), the social workers knew a little more (and they are in a position to recommend an IT Order to the Court) and the probation officers had a reasonable knowledge (they are also in a position to recommend IT Orders).

This was a rather unsatisfactory outcome for IT. Unfortunately it reflects the general lack of involvement it has in the juvenile justice system nationally. The trend of increased involvement of IT workers with the younger 'at risk' juveniles, has not only widened the net of statutory recognition (making it very much earlier for many young people) but has also weakened the case for IT as an alternative to residential care for the majority of older offenders.

A streamlining policy is therefore required, to narrow the approach, so that specific aims can be set and worked towards. As Tutt (1979) points out, the main problem in IT is one of overall strategy—the 'deep or shallow end' dilemma. Should it deal with the very difficult young offenders—the 'deep end'—or should it adopt a 'shallow end' strategy and work with the younger individual in a preventitive capacity. Many local agencies have chosen the latter, so that IT has become just another form of social work, rather than a 'new alternative' form of intervention with established offenders.

This debate has, of course, been overshadowed by the question of methodology. How could a community approach, which would have very few controls, succeed, where a residential one, which had all the controls, had failed? This is an understandable question, and as we saw earlier, there is no logical reason to predict success by merely changing location.

New methodology must also be considered and attempted in a realistic and professional fashion. The experimental project at the BAY Centre was carried out almost against all odds, with a Social Services Department who where looking for energy expenditure and good public relations, and a staff team, who, although extremely interested and enthusiastic, were not initially trained in behavioural techniques. It survived because of individual staff commitment to the centre, concern for the young people involved and therefore a willingness to look for a more effective way of working.

If this could be translated into national policy, we would have a cohesive strategy for IT, relevant training schemes for IT workers and a 'new alternative' form of intervention that could begin to command a definite place in the juvenile justice system.

Conclusion

In the last decade we have seen a general move, both in Great Britain and the USA, to community intervention with juvenile offenders. However, it would appear that the paralled growth of interest in behaviour therapy and the subsequent extension of this to the natural environment, principally in the USA, has provided the most promising developments in terms of treatment efficacy and significantly, cost effectiveness.

In Great Britain, IT was introduced in 1969 as an innovative 'alternative' form of intervention with juveniles, without however, any prior or indeed subsequent, consideration of its methodology or training of personnel. IT has developed, therefore, as a hybrid of social work and community work, with teething troubles over clientele that have grown into major issues, with the now ever present possibility that IT will lose sight of the offender population and blend into the numerous other activity-based community facilities available to all.

IT must look seriously at its aims and objectives. It must clarify the question of client population nationally, and consider carefully the methods and techniques it uses. The project at the BAY Centre has provided some indication of what can be achieved with a consistent approach, based on planned and systematically applied behaviour therapy. It is only the beginning, and should pave the way for the future involvement of clinical psychologists, not only in individual IT projects, but also in national training schemes for IT workers. The policy of employing trained personnel from other professions may have its merits, but to bring together such a disparate group of individuals and individual skills, without any further training, can only add to the confusion over methodology.

The future, as always, is in the hands of policy makers. In making their decisions, however, they must recognize that IT has not, to date, failed to deal successfully with juvenile offenders—it has not been given a chance. National policy on IT must be clarified, relevant training schemes must be set up and policy makers must begin to take responsibility not only for major changes in legislation but also the practicalities of implementing such changes.

References

Aiken, T. W., Stumphauzer, J. S. and Veloz, E. V. (1977). Behavioural analysis of non-delinquent brothers in a high juvenile crime community, *Journal of Behavioural Disorders*, **2**, 212–222.

Alexander, J. F. and Parsons, B. V. (1973). Short-term behavioural intervention with delinquent families: Impact on family process and recidivism, *Journal of Abnormal Psychology*, **81**, 219–225.

Allison, T. S., Kendall, S. and Sloane, D. (1979). New directions in a juvenile hall setting, in *Progress In Behaviour Therapy with Delinquents* (Ed. J. S. Stumphauzer), Thomas, Springfield, Illinois.

Bailey, J. S., Wolf, M. M. and Phillips, E. L. (1970). Home based reinforcement and the modification of pre-delinquents' classroom behaviour, *Journal of Applied Behaviour Analysis*, **3**, 223–233.

Braukman, C. J. and Fixsen, D. L. (1975). Behaviour modification with delinquents, in *Progress In Behaviour Modification*, Vol. 1 (Eds M. Herson, R. M. Eisler and P. M. Miller), Academic Press, New York.

Burland, J. R. (1978). The evaluation of a token economy in a residential school for maladjusted junior boys, *Journal of Behavioural Psychotherapy*, **6**, 97–104.

City of Coventry Social Services Department (1977). The Woodway Intermediate Treatment Centre. In *Intermediate Treatment, 28 Choices* (Department of Health and Social Security), August.

Cohen, H. L. and Filipczak, J. A. (1971). *A New Learning Environment*, Fossey-Bass, San Francisco, California.

Cornish, D. B. and Clarke, R. V. G. (9175). *Residential Treatment and the Effects on Delinquency*. Home Office Research Studies No. 32, HMSO, London.

Covington, C. (1979). *Evaluation of The Hammersmith Teenage Project*, NACRO Publication.

Cross, P. (1979). *Knowledge of and Attitudes to Intermediate Treatment in the Major Referral Agents*. Unpublished BSc. Project, University of Birmingham, England.

Davidson, W. S. and Robinson, M. J. (1975). Community psychology and behaviour modification: a community-based program for the prevention of delinquency, *Journal of Cognitive Psychiatry and Behaviour Therapy*, **21**, 1–12.

Department of Health and Social Security (1972). *Intermediate Treatment: A Guide for the Regional Planning of New Forms of Treatment for Children in Trouble*, HMSO, London.

Feldman, M. P. (1977). *Criminal Behaviour: A Psychological Analysis*. Wiley, London.

Filipczak, J. Friedman, R. M. and Reese, S. C. (1979). PREP: educational programming to prevent juvenile problems, in *Progress In Behaviour Therapy With Delinquents* (Ed. J. S. Stumphauzer), Thomas, Springfield, Illinois.

Fixsen, D. L., Phillips, E. L. and Wolf, M. M. (1973). Achievement Place: experiments in self-government with pre-delinquents, *Journal of Applied Behaviour Analysis*, **6**, 31–57.

Flynn, S. (1977). *The Moorlands Young People's Centre*, Tameside Metropolitan Borough, England.

Fo. W. S. O. and O'Donnell, C. R. (1975). The Buddy System: effect of community intervention on delinquent offences, *Journal of Behaviour Therapy*, **6**, 522–524.

Grant, J. D. and Grant, M. A. (1959). A group dynamics approach to the treatment of non-conformists in the navy, *Annals of the American Academy of Political and Social Science*, **322**, 126–135.

Haringey Social Services Department. (1976). *Intermediate Treatment*. London Borough of Haringey, England.

Home Office (1968). *Children In Trouble*, HMSO, London.

Home Office (1969). *Children And Young Persons Act*, HMSO, London.

Hood, R. and Sparks, R. (1970). *Key Issues In Criminology*, Weidenfield & Nicoloson, London.

Islington Family Service Unit (1971–76). *Intermediate Treatment Centre*. Islington Family Services Unit Papers, London.

Jesness, C. F. (1965). *The Fricot Ranch Study*. Research Report No. 47. California Youth Authority: Sacramento.

Jesness, C. F. and DeRisi, W. J. (1973). Some variations in techniques of contingency management in a school for delinquents, in *Behaviour Therapy with Delinquents* (Ed. J. S. Stumphauzer), Thomas, Springfield, Illinois.

Karacki, L. and Levinson, R. B. (1970). A token economy in a correctional institution for youthful offenders, *Howard Journal of Penology and Crime Prevention*, **13**, 20–30.

Kirigin, K. A., Wolf, M. M., Braukman, C. J., Fixsen, D. L. and Phillips, E. L. (1979). Achievement Place: A preliminary outcome evaluation, in *Progress In Behaviour Therapy with Delinquents* (Ed. J. S. Stumphauzer), Thomas, Springfield, Illinois.

Manpower Services Commission (1979). *The Relevance and Application of the MSC Special Programmes for the Unemployed to Ex-offenders and those Non-Offenders 'at risk'*, New Opportunity Press, London.

National Association for the Care and Resettlement of Offenders (1977). *Children and Young Persons in Custody: Report of a NACRO Working Party*. Rose, London. 1977.

Norman, J. (1977). 870 House—Birmingham, in *Intermediate Treatment, 28 Choices*, Department of Health and Social Security, August.

O'Donnell, C. R. (1977). Behaviour modification in community settings, in *Progress in Behaviour Modification*, Vol. 4, (Eds M. Herson, R. M. Eisler and P. M. Miller), Academic Press, New York.

Ohlin, E. L., Miller, A. D. and Coates, R. B. (1974). Juvenile correction reform in massachusetts, *National Institute for Juvenile Justice and Delinquency Prevention.* United States Department of Justice.

Ostapiuk, E. B. and Reid, I. D. (1981). Rehabilitating offenders in the community: Implications for penal policy and professional practice, in *Reconstructing Psychological Practice* (Eds I. McPherson and A. Sutton), Croom Helm, London.

Phillips, E. L. (1968). Achievement Place: Token reinforcement procedures in a home style rehabilitation setting for pre-delinquent boys, *Journal of Applied Behavioural Analysis*, **1**, 213–223.

Skinner, B. F. (1948). *Walden Two*, MacMillan, New York.

Staples, A. (1977). Intermediate treatment: the community approach, *Concern* No. 24, Summer.

Stuart, R. B. and Lott, L. A. (1972). Behavioural contracting with delinquents: a cautionary note, *Journal of Behaviour Therapy and Experimental Psychiatry*, **3**, 161–169.

Stumphauzer, J. S. (1979). Modifying delinquent behaviour: Beginnings and current practices, in *Progress In Behaviour Therapy with Delinquents* (Ed. J. S. Stumphauzer, Thomas, Springfield, Illinois.

Stumphauzer, J. S. (1979). *Progress In Behaviour Therapy with Delinquents* Thomas, Springfield, Illinois.

Teuber, N. and Powers, E. (1953). *Evaluating Therapy In A Delinquency Prevention Programme*. Proceedings of the Association for Research in Nervous and Mental Diseases, **3**, 138.

Tharp, R. G. and Wetzel, R. J. (1969). *Behaviour Modification In The National Environment*, Academic Press, New York.

Thorpe, D. (1978). Intermediate treatment, in *Alternative Strategies for Coping with Crime* (Ed. N. Tutt), Martin Robertson, London.

Tutt, N. (1976a). Intermediate treatment, *Social Work Service Journal No. 11*, DHSS, October.

Tutt, N. (1976b). Recommittals of juvenile offenders, *British Journal of Criminology*, **4**, 16.

Tutt, N. (1979). 'Once Upon A Time'. Paper presented at the first North West Intermediate Treatment Association Study Day. Lancaster University, 1979.

US Bureau of the Census (1977). *Children in Custody: Advance Report on the 1977 Census of Public Juvenile Facilities*. US Government Printing Office, Washington DC.

Wandsworth Social Services Department (1977–78). *Day Care In Intermediate Treatment*, London Borough of Wandsworth, England.

Warren, M. Q., Palmer, T. B., Neto, V. and Turner, J. K. (1966). *Community Treatment Project: Research Report No. 7*. California Youth and Adult Correction Authority, Sacramento, California.

Weathers, L. and Liberman, R. P. (1975). Contingency contracting with families of delinquent adolescents, *Journal of Behaviour Therapy*, **6**, 356–366.

Whitlam, M. R. (1977). The Hammersmith Teenage Project, in *Intermediate Treatment, 28 Choices*, Department of Health and Social Security August.

Developments in the Study of Criminal Behaviour
Volume 1: The Prevention and Control of offending
Edited by P. Feldman

8

The Treatment of Sex Offenders

DEREK PERKINS

The socio-cultural context of sexual offending

The theme of this chapter, the treatment of sexual offenders, is a subject which has the potential to arouse a wide range of emotions—disgust, anger or sympathy in relation to the offender, anxiety about our own sexual attitudes and behaviour and general public concern that effective action should be taken to combat the problem. Theoretically, sexual offending has been viewed in a number of ways. Systems of analysis range from the socio-cultural correlates of sexual offending to the idiosyncratic patterns of sexual arousal displayed by individual offenders. Each level of analysis is relevant to a full understanding of the other levels. A number of ethical issues surround the treatment of sexual offenders and, as treatment research proceeds, these are becoming increasingly recognized. In some cases these issues have been underlined by legal action taken by offenders who regarded the conditions of their treatment as having violated their rights. A fine balance exists between the need to return incarcerated offenders to the community, the rights of those offenders and the need to protect the public.

The various models of sexual offending are tapped by different methods of analysis. Socio-cultural theories are usually supported by data from criminal statistics and community surveys. Psychological theories tend to rely most heavily on self reports, psychometric assessments and observations of interpersonal behaviour. At the level of sexual interests and arousal, psychophysiological assessment is the procedure most commonly used. As far as specifically treatment research is concerned, Abel, *et al.*, (1976b) note that three, increasingly sophisticated, methods of evaluation have been used. The first method, case reports although able to identify potentially valuable therapeutic leads, cannot provide aduquate evaluation data. The controlled, single-case experimental design goes one stage further by allowing the efficacy of individual therapy techniques to be tested. At the most powerful level is the control group experimental design within which the relative effects of different treatments can be compared. It is with the behavioural treatment techniques that the most powerful methods of evaluation have been used, and it is therefore in discussing these that greatest confidence can be expressed. This is not to say that non-behavioural techniques are necessarily ineffective, simply that evidence of their effectiveness is often not available.

Two general points, perhaps obvious in themselves, are relevant to any consideration of sexual offender treatment. First, like other crime, sexual offending is legally defined and as such can be eliminated by changes in the law. A notable example is homosexuality between consenting adults in England and Wales. The changes in the law which followed from the Wolfenden Report of 1957 redefined homosexuality both legally and socially and had an enormous impact on the behaviour of both homosexuals themselves and the wider public. The second point concerns the ways in which we gain our knowledge about sexual offences and sexual offenders. Descriptive and research data are arrived at after a variable number of social and legal filtering processes; the most obvious ones are the reporting of an offence to the police, apprehension of the offender, police discretion on whether to proceed, acquittal or conviction in court and the likelihood and type of custodial disposal. Results and conclusions will vary according to the point in these filtering processes at which data is sampled.

Data on sexual offences and sexual offenders come from a variety of sources. In England and Wales, indictable offences known to the police, reported in *Criminal Statistics*, is one major source of offence information. In the USA, similar information is available in the Department of Justice's *Sourcebook of Criminal Justice Statistics* and the FBI's *Uniform Crime Reports*. Such statistics are, of course, only samples, and often quite unrepresentative samples, of crimes actually committed. In England and Wales in 1978 there were over 22 000 indictable sexual offences recorded by the police. Over half of these were, and had been for the preceding 10 years, indecent assaults on females. Offences of rape amounted to 6 per cent of the total, having risen gradually from under 4 per cent in 1969. A growing willingness of rape victims to report offences now that they remain anonymous in court—Sexual Offences (Amendment) Act (1976)—may have contributed to the 22 per cent increase in rape reports from 1977–1978.

The USA criminal statistics are more complex and there is evidence (Curtis, 1976) that considerable variability exists in the reporting practices of different police departments. One aspect of the American situation which is of particular interest is the extensive use made of community surveys of victimization. For rape, Ennis (1967) reports from a sample of 10 000 interviews in the USA in 1966 that between three and four rapes are committed for each one officially reported to the police. Burnham (1974), on the basis on half-a-million annual interviews, reports a ratio 2.1 : 1 for rapes reported to survey interviewers in contrast to those reported to the police. Comparable under-reporting was also present for robbery (2.3 : 1) and burglary (2.7 : 1) but not for auto theft (1 : 1). To add a further degree of complexity to the situation, it seems that those individuals who report rapes to the police are not necessarily contained within the numbers reporting crimes to the survey interviewees. Some victims, although unwilling to acknowledge to themselves or to others that a crime has taken place, may nevertheless be prepared to discuss the incident in the context of interviews about recent 'injuries suffered' or 'sexual experiences' (Curtis, 1976).

Information about sexual offenders is subject to even more filtering and distortion than information about their offences. Consequently, very little comparability exists between studies of sexual offenders, either within the community or in institutions. With these, and the previous qualifications in mind, it can be summarized that in England and Wales, and in the USA, the majority of sexual offences known to the police involve relatively minor incidents of indecent assualts on females. The majority of convictions in this category are dealt with by non-custodial means. Reconvictions for further sexual offences are rare in this group. Hence, for sexual offenders as a whole the behaviour is neither dangerous nor likely to be repeated. However, there are categories of sexual offender who repeatedly re-offend and it is on these that most attention will be focused as far as treatment is concerned.

Descriptive studies of rape, paedophilia and exhibitionism

At the statistical level of analysis, Amir (1971) in a large-scale study of rape in Philadelphia between 1958 and 1960, established that about one-third of offenders were known to their victims and that less than 30 per cent of rapes were reported to the police. Nineteen per cent of rapes were judged to be victim precipitated, using as a definition of this the victim having agreed to, or having invited sexual relations but then retracting before the act of sexual intercourse. Using a similar definition, Curtis (1974) found only 4 per cent of rapes in a seventeen-city aggregate, including Philadelphia, to have been victim pre-cipitated in the year 1967. It is clear from studies such as these that the norms and expectations surrounding male/female interactions are the necessary context in which sexual offences by men against women must be viewed.

Both Amir (1971) and Curtis (1974) highlight the influence of the black poverty sub-culture in the USA, commenting on the findings that most rapes in their samples were committed by blacks on blacks. In the Curtis study, 60 per cent of cases were blacks raping blacks, 30 per cent whites raping whites, 10 per cent blacks raping whites and an insignificant number of whites raping blacks. This, of course, introduces questions of how far victims of different races perceive the predominantly white police and justice systems, and of how police attitudes might vary with offenders and victims of different races. A black woman may simply feel that the odds are too greatly stacked against her to report to the authorities that she had been raped by a white man. Curtis (1976) concludes that there is no single, simple explanation of the effects of cultural and sub-cultural factors on rape and its reporting. Summarizing a number of studies, she concludes that whilst the institutionalized exploitation of women must be a central theme in any consideration sexual crime, this is in ever-changing interaction with a variety of other sub-cultural factors.

In a comprehensive, prospective study, Gibbens and Soothill (1977) reported data on all men charged with rape in London in 1951 and 1961. Offenders fell naturally into three groupings, aggressive rapists for whom the sexual assault was part of a general pattern of aggression (20 per cent of the sample), paedophilic rapists whose victims were aged 14 years or less (30 per cent) and a third group comprising individuals for whom the offence was a relatively isolated incident (50 per cent). The results of this study are interesting in two respects. First, Gibbens and Soothill found that, of the 22 per cent of their sample who were acquitted of rape in 1961, almost as many (14 per cent) were convicted of subsequent sexual offences as was the case for the originally convicted group, sexual re-convictions in this group being 20 per cent for the aggressive rapists, 20 per cent for the paedophilic rapists and 3 per cent for the third group. The second point of interest in this study was that the paedophilic rapists had more previous and subsequent sexual convictions (37 per cent and 20 per cent respectively) than the aggressive rapists (17 and 20 per cent respectively). The aggressive rapists, on the other hand, were notable for their high rates of previous and subsequent violence offending (39 per cent and 66 per cent, respectively) when compared with the paedophilic rapists (14 and 15 per cent, respectively).

Cohen et al. (1971) studied over 800 sexual offenders referred to a Massachusetts treatment centre. Four groups of rapists were distinguished. The first group comprised men for whom the act of rape was primarily aggressive. It often followed conflict with a female relative or friend and appeared to serve the function of harming or degrading the victim. In the second group, offence motivation was predominantly sexual. Only sufficient force necessary to achieve sexual intercourse was used and the offender remained in a high state of sexual arousal throughout. Offenders in this group often reported the belief that the victim would find the experience pleasurable. In the third group were men in whom sexual and aggressive motives appeared to be linked, sexual arousal only being achieved by the infliction of harm upon the victim. The extreme example of this group was the sadistic murderer. The fourth and final group comprised men who had carried out the offence of rape in an impulsive and opportunistic way, often doing so in the context of some anti-social act.

Mohr et al. (1964) assessed all fifty-five paedophiles referred to a Toronto psychiatric clinic between 1956 and 1959. There were three age peaks of offender, puberty, mid to late thirties and mid to late fifties. Paedophilia was defined in terms of an expressed desire for sexual activity with a prepubertal child appropriate to the age of that child, that is immature sexual behaviour. However as Feldman (1973) points out, since 54 per cent of the homosexual paedophiles in Mohr et al.'s sample carried out acts such as masturbation, fellatio and intercourse, their behaviour could hardly be regarded as immature and inappropriate to the age of their child victims.

In a descriptive study of 150 rapists and paedophiles incarcerated in Canadian penitentiaries, Christie *et al.* (1978) compared the two groups on a number of biographical and psychometric parametres. Both groups were, on average, in their late twenties. Sixty-two per cent of the paedophiles and 46 per cent of the rapists had previous sexual convictions. Both groups tended to be problem drinkers and to have been drinking prior to their offences. Seventy-one per cent of the rapists and 57 per cent of the paedophiles were judged to have physically abused their victims to an unnecessary degree.

Mohr *et al.* (1964), again at their Toronto clinic, described fifty-four exhibitionistic referrals. Exhibitionism was defined as exposure of the genitals where this did not lead on to an aggressive act. A distinction was made between exhibitionism which formed part of a recognized disorder, such as dementia, and obsessional exhibitionism. The age of offenders peaked between 20 and 30 years but the age of victims varied considerably. The offender and victim were usually unknown to each other. The exhibitionistic acts varied from partial exposure to open masturbation, and victims reactions also varied considerably, this presumably biasing Mohr *et al.*'s sample in the direction of offenders who had exposed themselves to the victims most likely to report the behaviour to the police.

In a pre-sentence study of 500 sexual offenders in the USA, Pacht and Cowden (1974) compared those recommended for treatment as 'sexual deviates' and those dealt with under the criminal code. The sexually deviated group comprised older men with histories of sexual offending and psychiatric treatment. They tended to have had closer, more long-standing relationships with their victims and to have offended less often under the influence of alcohol than the 'criminal' group. A three-way comparison between rapists, paedophiles and passive non-assaulters, mainly exhibitionists, indicated that the rapists tended to have negative attitudes towards women, to have come from 'mother dominated' families and to have premeditated their offences to a lesser degree than the other groups. In a comparison of extreme assaulters and non-assaulters, the former tended both to have offended with the least degree of victim precipitation and to express the least concern for their victims in interviews. High victim provocation in turn correlated with the offender's expressed concern for the victim, low levels of previous aggression and general 'emotional stability'.

Assessment and treatment procedures used with sexual offenders

Treatment programmes for sexual offenders have taken place in a variety of contexts and have employed a wide range of assessment and treatment methods. Three general distinctions emerge from the literature. The first is the degree to which treatment programmes are integrated within other systems through which the offender passes, for example police, court and probation agencies. Secondly, and linked to the first point, is the extent to which all potential treatment candidates are screened by a particular programme, in other words its referral system. The third distinction deals with the extent to which a programme attempts to deal with the complete spectrum of offender's problems, that is the degree to which it approaches the 'broad based' approach advocated by, amongst others, Crawford (1979).

Perkins (1981) has noted that the reliability and validity of assessment procedures used with sexual offenders cannot be divorced from the purposes of these procedures and the situations in which they are undertaken. For example, an offender being assessed for early release from custody will clearly perceive and approach a particular procedure differently from a similar but unincarcerated offender voluntarily seeking treatment. Verbal and psychometric assessment methods are particularly vulnerable to the kinds of distortion which can occur when offenders fear the consequences of assessment. Procedures involving behavioural observation are less susceptible to such distortion, particularly where they are concerned with measures of acquired skills, such as conversational competence. Psychophysiological assessments of sexual interest, although at first sight likely to be immune from conscious influences, are, as we shall see, also susceptible to distortion under some circumstances.

Psychometric assessment

Of the psychometric measures which have been used with sexual offenders, one method of particular interest is the repertory grid (Bannister and Mair, 1968). This technique involves subjects making comparisons between concepts such as people, behaviour and situations with which they are familiar. With offenders, their offences and victims might also be included. From these comparisons the major bipolar constructs with which the subject views the world can be derived. In a study of repetitive rapists and paedophiles in an English Special Hospital, Howells and Steadman-Allen (1977) established that a common precursor to rape was anger stemming from the offender's feelings of social failure and personal rejection. There was, however, considerable variability in the offenders studied and Howells and Steadman-Allen concluded that similar sexual acts can be mediated by a wide variety of emotional states. Howells (1979) used the same technique to assess ten heterosexual paedophiles in an American State Hospital and a control group of ten non-sexual offenders. Focussing on the nature of the social interactions between the offenders and their victims, Howells established that the paedophiles tended to view other people in terms of a construct of dominance-submission and, at the interpersonal level, found children attractive because of their passivity. It was also found that paedophiles tended to be preoccupied with the physical characteristics associated with small body build. Both the paedophile and the non-sexual offenders viewed women more than men in terms of physical charact̲

perceptions of women in general.

Bancroft (1974), reviewing evidence on psychomᴗ.

deviant individuals, concluded that the approach is generally ᴜᴄ

nor valid than simply asking the individuals concerned for their views. This ᵢˢ

to say that self-reports are themselves accurate, simply that failure to update, or

the absence of suitable normative data, renders of dubious value most of the

psychometric methodology used with sexual offenders.

Behavioural assessment

At the behavioural level of assessment there is a relative scarcity of research with sexual offenders, partly perhaps because of the difficulty of making naturalistic observations, or of setting up analogues of relevant situations. Reporting on social-skills training with sexual offenders, Crawford and Allen (1979) in an English Special Hospital and Perkins (1977) in a prison and out-patient setting noted the difficulties of generating the necessary information on which to judge what are the appropriate heterosexual social skills for offenders from different walks of life.

Barlow *et al.* (1977) developed a check-list of heterosexual social skills which proved capable of differentiating between socially inadequate, sexually deviant individuals and socially adequate, non-deviant individuals. The assessment was based upon 5-minute videotaped interactions with a female stooge. The degree and type of affect displayed and the form of conversation which ensued proved to be the most important factors differentiating the two groups. Whilst this approach provides some valuable leads as to the characteristics of successful social interaction, it is constrained by both the artificiality of its role plays and the predetermined behaviour of the female stooges.

In more of an ethological vein, Gordon *et al.* (1977) examined the social interactions of naive pairs of subjects in naturalistic settings. The verbal and non-verbal classifications empirically derived from these observations were used subsequently to assess the social performance of sexually aggressive offenders. In contrast to the analogue studies of social skills, Gordon *et al.* were able to begin moving towards the much more desirable arrangement in which the social skills to be trained were defined by what actually happens between men and women in relevant situations rather than by what therapists believe happen on the basis of their own social backgrounds and experiences, these often being quite different from those of their patient groups.

Psychopysiological assessment

The psychophysiological investigation of sexual arousal patterns is the third important area of assessment. Zuckerman (1971) demonstrated that the penile response is the most valid measure of sexual interest in the male. Many studies have been carried out using predominantly penile volume or circumference measures (Abel and Blanchard, 1976a) in response to representations of sexual objects (children, adults etc.) or sexual acts (transvestism, sadism etc.). Psychophysiological investigations fall broadly into two groups. The first, characterized by the work of Freund (1963, 1965, 1967 etc.), has used large groups of subjects to standardize procedures for diagnosing sexual orientation by means of small penile responses. The second group of studies, of which the work of Abel and his collaborators is an example (Abel *et al.*, 1973, 1975 etc.), has used the single subject experimental design to investigate the penile responses of individual offenders to visual and auditory material related to their offences.

Freund (1963) was 99 per cent accurate in differentially diagnosing co-operative homosexual and heterosexual subjects using penile responses to rapidly presented slides. When subjects were instructed to fake their responses, however, diagnostic accuracy dropped to 50 per cent for the homosexuals and 74 per cent for the heterosexuals. Similar results were obtained in the differential diagnosis of homosexual and heterosexual paedophilia. Diagnostic accuracy was high with co-operative subjects (Freund, 1965 and 1967) but when a comparison between 'admitting' and 'non-admitting' paedophiles was made (Freund *et al.*, 1979), misclassification rose from 5 per cent for the admitters to approximately one-third for the non-admitters.

Precisely how penile measures of sexual arousal operate is still not fully understood. Bancroft (1971) has noted the importance of cognitive mediational factors in both the inhibition, and enhancement of penile responses. Laws and Rubin (1969), presenting erotic films to four heterosexual subjects, demonstrated reductions in their penile responses from about 80 per cent to 20 per cent full erection by instructions to inhibit responding by 'mental means'. Henson and Rubin (1971) produced similar results with four homosexual subjects. Geer (1974) used a dichotic listening task to test the effects on the penile responding of the level of attention being paid to erotic material. While volunteer subjects listened to an erotic description presented to one ear, they were required to process increasingly complex information presented to the other ear. As predicted, penile responses to the sexual material decreased as a function of the complexity of the information-processing task.

In contrast to this group-based research, and of particular relevance to the treatment of sexual offenders, are the studies of individual sexual arousal patterns. Abel *et al.* (1975) used audiotaped descriptions of rape scenes and consenting sexual intercourse to assess the penile response patterns of individual rapists. The rapists who reported high levels of rape behaviour and fantasy tended to respond to the rape, but not to the consenting sexual intercourse tapes. A second, less rape-preoccupied group of rapists responded equally to both types of tape. Barbaree *et al.* (1979), again using audiotaped descriptions, compared the penile responses of ten rapists and ten students to material depicting rape, consenting sexual intercourse and violent non-sexual assault on a female. Whereas the students responded most to consenting sexual intercourse, the rapists responded to both rape and consenting material but not to violence alone. Barbaree *et al.* postulated that, for their rapist group, it may be insensitivity rather than arousal to the violent aspects of rape which is the crucial factor in mediating their offence behaviour.

The single subject methodology of these studies has tended to utilize audiotaped descriptions of deviant acts. Although audiotaped material of this type is generally less potent than equivalent visual material such as movie film in eliciting penile responses (Abel and Blanchard, 1976a), it has two distinct advantages. First, it can be used to represent the most idiosyncratic activities, some of which would be either technically or ethically impossible to represent on film. Secondly, it enables the selective refinement of the original stimulus tape according to how the offender responds on first testing. Abel *at al.* (1975), for example, described case studies in which the most potent aspects of subjects' initial descriptions of their deviant behaviour were elaborated into second- and third-generation tapes which were gradually able to focus onto the most crucial aspects of the deviant behaviour.

Treatment approaches

Treatment methods used with sexual offenders parallel the range of assessment procedures and have approached the problem at the levels of modifying sexual arousal patterns, training socio-sexual skills and tackling the more elusive components of thoughts, attitudes and feelings. Pacht (1976) makes the point that many therapeutic procedures used with sexual offenders have been adapted to, rather than specifically designed for, that purpose. Taking a behavioural stance, it could be argued that, since most sexual offending is better understood in terms of the circumstances of the offence rather than the personal characteristics of the offender, then society's major response to sexual offending should be at the socio-political, rather than the psychological level. In other words, interventions directed at modifying social and sexual attitudes and in relation to the design of the environment would, if practicable and effective, deal with a larger part of the problem than treating the minority of sexual offenders who persistently re-offend. Having said this, the fact that sexual recidivism does exist, with some individuals persisting in seriously assaultive behaviour over many years, makes individual treatment an important component of any sexual offender policy.

The particular treatment procedures described in the sexual-offender literature can be classified in terms of their underlying methodology; medical, behavioural, psychoanalytic etc, or in terms of their aims; reducing deviant sexual arousal, enhancing non-deviant arousal, controlling deviant behaviour, improving socio-sexual skills etc. The anti-libidinal medical procedures will be considered separately from the psychological procedures, the latter falling naturally into a number of sub-divisions related to their therapeutic aims.

Castration and anti-libidinal medication

Stürup (1968, 1972) reported a 1 per cent re-conviction rate for 900 sexual offenders followed up for 30 years after castration. Marshall *et al.* (1977) criticized this work on four counts. First, the fact that early release was offered to, and subsequently achieved by, offenders who underwent the operation raises serious doubts as to their alleged 'voluntary' status. Secondly, castration was, on the basis of Stürup's own data, needlessly carried out on 750 offenders who were unlikely to re-offend whether treated or not. Thirdly, on the basis that low self esteem is a key area for intervention with certain categories of sexually aggressive offender, castration in such cases is likely to prove counter-productive. Fourthly, the side effects of castration, which can include breast and hip enlargement and unpleasant physical sensations, lead many castrated offenders to report dissatisfaction with their post-operative condition (Langelüddeke, 1963).

Because of the various disadvantages of castration, considerable effort has been devoted to the development of effective anti-libidinal drugs. Where the effects of such preparations are reversible, a number of the more serious ethical problems of castration can be overcome. Neverthless, it is the exception rather than the rule that anti-libidinal medication alone will meet the treatment needs of most sexual offenders. Some offenders, elderly recidivists for example, may be seeking nothing more than a total removal of sexual feelings and in such cases medication can provide the most effective answer. In most other cases, suppression of the offender's sexual drive is helpful primarily by providing a period of sexual quiescence during which other, more constructive forms of treatment can be introduced. The two forms of medication in most common use are the anti-androgen cyproterone acetate and the tranquillizer Benperidol (Bancroft, 1977), the former being regarded as the drug of choice at the present time.

Psychological treatment

The non-medical treatments of sexual offending have stemmed from a number of theoretical models. Although a distinction is often made between behavioural and psychodynamic forms of treatment, and indeed their theoretical bases and traditions are very different, close examination of the actual procedures employed indicates that there is a good deal of overlap (Abel *at el.* 1976b). The major distinction between the behavioural and psychodynamic approaches lies in the rigour with which they specify objectives, report the details of therapeutic practice and evaluate outcome effectiveness. The importance of recognizing that there is a grey area between different therapeutic schools is that it acknowledges the potential which may lie outside the therapist's own frame of reference and, hopefully, militates against the kinds of scientific prejudice which can lead to practitioners from one school blocking from consideration whole areas of potentially relevant work from other schools.

Modification of sexual arousal

Under this heading are procedures aimed at decreasing deviant sexual arousal and increasing non-deviant arousal, the latter usually being adult heterosexual interest. *Aversion therapy* is one of the most well-known procedures designed to inhibit arousal. Developing originally from conditioning principles, the procedure has been varied according to the paradigm employed (classical conditioning, anticipatory avoidance conditioning etc.) and the types of sexual and aversive stimuli used. Essentially the procedure sets out to modify the arousal potential of particular thoughts, images or acts by associating these with unpleasant stimulation of some kind (mild electric shocks and noxious smells being two commonly reported examples). There is good evidence (reviewed by Hallam and Rachman, 1976) that aversion therapy does have a powerful effect in suppressing sexual arousal to deviant material as measured by penile responses and subjective ratings. There is also evidence that it sometimes has the effect of increasing non-deviant arousal.

Early attempts to explain the effects of aversion therapy, including the enhancement of non-deviant arousal, looked to the conditioning principles upon which the procedure was originally based. *Aversion relief* is an example of one such hypothesis. It was supposed that the relief experienced by subjects at the termination of aversive stimulation, such as electric shocks administered during the presentation of deviant material, became associated with the subsequent presentation of non-deviant material. In this way sexual arousal to non-deviant material was assumed to be generated. Barlow (1973), reviewing the literature on procedures designed to enhance sexual arousal, noted that aversion relief was the most common procedure in use at the time of his review. However, in the few instances where its effects had been tested separately from other procedures, notably aversion, it proved to be ineffective. Hallam and Rachman (1976) concluded that the reasons for aversion therapy's success are of much greater complexity than that assumed by the original conditioning analysis. The fact that aversion therapy neither follows the course predicted by conditioning theory nor leads to the kinds of conditioned anxiety which would be predicted lead Hallam and Rachman to conclude, amongst other things, that it is a phenomenom in which cognitive mediational factors are likely to play an important part.

There are a number of variations on the theme of aversion therapy. *Covert sensitization* (Cautela, 1967) is a procedure in which both the deviant material and its aversive consequences are imaginal. Typically the subject is instructed to imagine a sexual scene of relevance to his problem, following which he imagines unpleasant consequences of his behaviour in that scene, for example illness or arrest. Callahan and Leitenberg (1973) found the procedure to be effective with a mixed group of exhibitionists, homosexuals and a paedophile. So too did Barlow *et al.* (1969) with one homosexual and one paedophile. However, Christie *et al.* (1978) reported a failure of the procedure to modify the fantasies of sexually aggressive offenders. It was hypothesized that this group may either be poor in imaginal ability or immune to the imagined aversive consequences of their behaviour.

Shame aversion therapy (Serber, 1970) also falls broadly within the aversion paradigm. The procedure involves the offender acting out his deviant behaviour, for example exhibitionism, in front of therapist aides who are instructed to ridicule or behave disapprovingly towards him. These unpleasant consequences of the deviant behaviour, it is argued, reduce its probability of repetition. Serber and Wolpe (1972) reported the successful suppression of deviant activity at a 6-month follow up with seven out of ten sexual offenders treated by shame aversion therapy. The procedure is not widely reported and it may be that for many sexual offenders it would prove either impracticable or counterproductive.

Approaches to *increasing non-deviant sexual arousal* have been reviewed by Barlow (1973) and Abel and Blanchard (1976a). Evidence for some procedures which had originally shown promise has not been forthcoming. *Penile bio-feedback* (Herman and Prewett, 1974; Barlow *et al.*, 1975) and *classical conditioning* of non-deviant sexual interest (Rachman and Hodgson, 1968; Marshall, 1974) are two notable examples. *Fading*, used by Barlow and Agras (1973) in the treatment of three homosexual patients is another. The fading procedure involved a heterosexual slide being superimposed on a homosexual slide to which the patient had produced a penile response. By gradually fading in the heterosexual, and fading out the homosexual slide, it was found that the patient's penile erection could be maintained. Laws (1974) described an automated version of the procedure used with two paedophiles. Even after fourteen sessions, the treatment effect was lost at follow-up.

Masturbatory conditioning is a procedure based on the positive reinforcement of non-deviant arousal. Linked etiologically to McGuire *et al.*'s (1965) finding that early sexual experiences appeared to be crucial in determining subsequent patterns of sexual arousal and behaviour, the procedure involves patients replacing their deviant masturbation fantasies with fantasies related to the sexual behaviour they wish to acquire or develop. Marquis (1970), using the term 'orgasmic reconditioning', described the successful modification of homosexual interests using the procedure. Abel *et al.* (1973) reported similarly positive results for a patient with sadistic fantasies. Marshall *at al.* (1977), working with incarcerated offenders, advocated masturbatory conditioning as the first line of approach in modifying sexual arousal patterns since it is a means of building in adaptive repertoires before removing maladaptive ones.

Systematic desensitization and variations on this have been used to increase non-deviant sexual behaviour by a process of gradually exposing the patient to any anxiety arousing aspects of the non-deviant sexual object or behaviour. Positive results have been reported in the treatment of homosexuals by Bieber *et al.* (1963) and Bancroft (1970).

Cole (personal communication) has used *surrogate therapy*, a form of *in vivo* desensitization to heterosexual behaviour, with sexually anxious and in-experienced males and females. In Cole's programme for male patients, suitably trained female surrogate partners help the men achieve satisfactory sexual intercourse by gradual guidance and encouragement. Cole reports that the enhancement of patients' confidence following the achievement of satisfactory sexual intercourse is often sufficient to result in the achievement of satisfactory socio-sexual relationships following treatment. Where such consolidation of treatment effects do not occur, patients' confidence is reported to decline. Unlike Kohlenberg (1974), who reported the successful use of this procedure in treating a homosexual paedophile, Cole's only sexual offender patient, a heterosexual paedophile, did not benefit from the approach.

Sex education is a therapeutic element often present in treatment programmes for sexual offenders. Its effects have rarely been tested separately from other forms of intervention. Where this has been done, as in the cases of Crawford and Howells (Crawford, 1981) and Woodward (1980), working with incarcerated adults in a special hospital and borstal boys respectively, sex education proved to have a demonstrable effect on reducing sexual anxiety and increasing sexual knowledge and self-esteem.

A simple procedure, which is again often present in some form in other types of treatment, is *exposure* to erotic material. Herman *et al.* (1974) reported increases in four homosexual patients' levels of arousal to heterosexual material following exposure to a 10-minute erotic film.

Modification of socio-sexual behaviour

Approaches to the suppression of deviant behaviour and the development of repertoires of non-deviant behaviour have focused on each of the cognitive, attitudinal and behavioural response systems. Abel *et al.* (1976b) noted the importance of *empathic therapeutic relationships* in facilitating attitude and behaviour change with sexual offenders. The precise mechanism and effects of therapeutic relationships are still far from clearly understood but it is a fact that most therapeutic work with sexual offenders makes some reference to the importance of the therapeutic relationship, often in terms of facilitating self expression and increasing self-esteem.

The rapid growth of *social skills training* in clinical practice is also reflected in work with sexual offenders. Bozer (1975) regarded the establishment of social competence with females as so crucial to her treatment programme for rapists in a USA State Hospital that she employed all female staff. Crawford and Allen (1979) similarly noted the need for social skills training with their English Special Hospital sexual offender group. Using the social skills training elements of instruction or coaching, rehearsal and feedback, Crawford and Allen demonstrated significant improvements in the social behaviour of their patients which were maintained at a 2-year follow up.

Cognitive behaviour modification (Meichenbaum, 1976) and related approaches (for example Mahoney, 1974; Beck, 1976) are becoming of increasingly recognized value in clinical practice generally. The approach, which involves intervening directly at the level of patients' self statements, rationalizations and attributions, is one to which little direct attention has been paid in the sexual offender literature. Having said this, elements of the cognitive approach often appear in accounts of other procedures as well as in explanations of their effects: an example of the latter was given in relation to aversion therapy. Like 'empathic therapeutic relationships', therefore, cognitive behaviour modification tends to be pervasive and non-specific in the reported literature.

The Birmingham sexual offender treatment programme

Background

In 1974 a feasibility study was set up in the use of psychological treatment methods with sexual offenders at Birmingham Prison. Sexual offenders were identified as an appropriate group with whom to begin examining treatment possibilities for three reasons. First, although sexual offences comprise only 1 per cent of crime known to the police in the West Midlands, Birmingham Prison's catchment area, a significant minority of sexual offenders either attract heavy sentences or else frequently offend. This group therefore constitutes an important treatment and management problem. Secondly, repetitive sexual offenders emerged from a pilot study as a group particularly likely to view their offending in terms of personal abnormality rather than as a function of circumstances. Partly as a result of this perhaps, they were more likely than other groups to express a desire for treatment. This was in contrast to non-repetitive sexual offenders who tended to justify their behaviour in terms of the immorality of their victims or of having misinterpreted ambiguous social cues. In such cases responsibility for their behaviour was attributed to the victim or to the circumstances of the offence. Thirdly, those sexual recidivists who appeared to be suitable candidates for psychological treatment presented behaviour problems of which certain aspects, for example sexual arousal patterns and socio-sexual skills, could be examined whilst they were still in prison. Fourthly, it was argued that if the proposed treatment programme proved to be successful, the relatively small numbers of sexual offenders compared with other groups requiring treatment would ensure that the programme was not immediately flooded by its potential population of treatment candidates.

Authorization to proceed with the programme was given on three conditions. First, it should be primarily a therapeutic service rather than a research project. Secondly, it should rely primarily on procedures the value of which had previously been established. Thirdly, evaluation should be built in to the degree possible without violating the first condition. From the outset it became clear that, in working with imprisoned sexual offenders, a variety of ethical and 'political' issues required attention. For example, the nature of informed consent arose, centering on the possibility that offenders might perceive pressures on themselves to take part in treatment for other than 'a genuine desire to change'. Taking a behavioural view of this issue, speculation about how far offenders may or may not be expressing 'a genuine desire for change' is less relevant than analysing the relationship between their behaviour, including verbal behaviour of this type, and their circumstances. Put crudely, a behavioural analysis will acknowledge that all of us act in relation to our past and present circumstances and it is this relationship rather than the reasons people give for their bahaviour which are of particular importance. Having said this, the problem remained: on what basis should the therapist conduct himself with regard to the offender to ensure that ethically defensible procedures ensure? All along our view was that offenders should, as far as possible, be free from negative consequences for declining or leaving treatment and from inducements to take part, such as the possibility of enhancing their parole possibilities. To this end we operationally defined the 'voluntary' nature of the treatment programme in terms of three principles. First, all treatment and non-treatment options known to us were explained to offenders seeking or being offered treatment. Secondly, we made it clear to those opting for treatment that they would be free to opt out at any stage. Thirdly, we stated our intention to be involved as little as possible in prison decision-making such as the preparation of parole reports.

Between October 1974 and June 1975 all convicted sexual offenders whom it was possible to see were interviewed, psychometrically tested and assessed for suitability for psychological treatment. Links with medical and probation colleagues in the prison ensured both that duplication of involvement with offenders and inter-professional problems were minimized. On the basis of interview and record information, offenders were classified into two groups, those judged to be suitable for treatment (38 per cent) and those not (62 per cent). The first group subsequently became divided into those who received treatment (treatment group) and those for whom treatment options were not finalized before their removal from the prison (quasi-control group). Most of the cases assessed as suitable for treatment involved indecent assaults, mainly against children, and exhibitionism. The offenders concerned were predominantly single (64 per cent) and in their mid-twenties. They had an average of 2.7 previous sexual convictions, were serving about 2 years imprisonment and, by their own accounts, had been offending on average over twice a month during the 12 months prior to imprisonment. The majority of treatment candidates described sexual (71 per cent) and/or social anxieties (62 per cent) which they described as having stood in the way of their developing socially acceptable alternatives to ofending. About a half of those in the original treatment group displayed deviant sexual arousal patterns on psychophysiological testing but, for various reasons, not all offenders in this group had been so tested.

Assessment and treatment of the initial sample of twenty-seven offenders within the prison led to a number of developments. Referrals from other departments within and outside the prison increased and were, in some cases, encouraged. The need to follow treatment through into the post-release period coincided with referrals of out-patient offenders who were on probation and/or under psychiatric care. These two factors were complementary and an out-patient clinic was established within the community, primarily within the psychiatric hospital adjacent to the prison. The period from mid-1976 until 1980 saw the programme become integrated within the forensic, psychiatric and probation services. Cross-referrals and collaborative treatment became commonplace and our own position was formalized within the National Health Service as well as the Prison Department.

The trend for the programme to move more into the natural environment was a consequence first of having begun exclusively within the prison setting: had we begun exclusively in the community we might well have needed to develop some prison involvement. Secondly, it was a consequence of attempting to get to grips with the problems of generalization. Only modification of the most specific and all pervasive behaviours will be maintained in the offender's transfer from one environment (the prison or out-patient clinic) to the natural environment. For complex behaviours, generalization has to be built into treatment from the outset. One of the best ways of doing this is simply to operate in the natural environment from as early on in therapy as possible. The question of offenders' motivation to change proved to be as important an issue as that of generalization. Like generalization, motivation proved to be best viewed in terms of the circumstances of treatment rather than as some internal characteristic of the offender.

The treatment process

The operation of the Birmingham programme over the last 6 years has highlighted a number of issues. The first concerns the relationship between assessment and treatment. Although the psychological treatment literature tends to distance itself from the medical model, a number of over-simplifications about how treatment proceeds are fostered by quasi-medical notions that three distinct stages, assessment, treatment and evaluation, are clearly discernible in each case.

Offenders seeking help to change need, in our experience, ongoing assessment of problems and discussion of therapeutic goals. The effects of any interventions are fed into this assessment and discussion process. Assessment and treatment often merge into each other. Evaluation is less often an isolated event that an ongoing monitoring and guiding of the therapeutic process.

Linked to this point is the question of offender motivation. It is not uncommon for offenders to seek and attend sessions both inside and outside the prison with the aim of avoiding further offending. In our experience, however, this is not usually sufficient to bring about behavioural change. At least three additional components to motivation appear to be required before therapeutic success is possible, specifically that the offender takes some responsibility for the process of change, that he recognizes the relationship between presenting problems and proposed interventions and that he carries through agreed strategies for change into the natural environment.

The last of these three points leads naturally onto the question of generalization. Offenders in treatment often derive immediate pay-offs from the therapy sessions themselves, for example a sympathetic hearing of their problems and a feeling that some positive action is being taken. This is particularly evident with the more concrete and directive forms of treatment such as aversion therapy and social-skills training in which a good deal of the onus for action falls on the therapist. The periods between sessions during which offenders carry out tasks independent of the therapist is the truly testing time. Failure to apply strategies from social-skills training, self-control and cognitive interventions, for example, and failure to apply instructions concerned with desensitization and masturbatory conditioning, for example, are neither uncommon nor necessarily related to any failure of offenders to co-operate in the treatment sessions themselves. Applying change strategies in the natural environment is, in many cases, simply not sufficiently rewarding in the short term to be carried out.

Two offender patients

The way in which treatment operates in the present programme has, over the last few years, gradually approximated to a broad-based, community-centred approach and is illustrated by reference to two offender patients. John was 32 when first seen in the prison 8 years ago. He was convicted of numerous indecent assaults on young girls and expressed a desire to stop offending, mainly through fear of further imprisonment.

He was of low intelligence, socially anxious and socially unskilled. On repertory grid assessment, he viewed his child victims with affection and saw them as both kind and interested in sex. At one level, John saw no harm in his behaviour and his motivation to change was correspondingly limited. John's history indicated that sexual involvement with children had developed in parallel with unpleasant and anxiety arousing sexual experiences with women of his own age: on the repertory grid he saw these women as unkind and 'showing him up'. He had never achieved satisfactory sexual intercourse. A vicious circle had developed of anxiety and avoidance of adult heterosexuality, sexual involvement with children, deviant sexual interest in children and a decreasing desire to change.

Therapeutic intervention was directed first at John's deviant sexual interest. Covert sensitization, aimed at decreasing the potency of deviant sexual interest, proved ineffective, and masturbatory conditioning was of only limited value because of John's forgetfulness or unwillingness to apply the procedure regularly. Social skills training was carried out to help overcome his shyness and lack of social competence, particularly with females of his own age. This proved very effective in terms of pre- and post-training measures but improvements did not generalize into John's natural environment. The reasons for this were apparent when visits to John's home and social situations were made; the social-skills training had failed to address itself to the very particular situations and subculture in which John operated. One effect of social skills training, which had involved sessions with female volunteers, was a decrease in John's fear of adult heterosexuality. Further improvements in this sphere followed from sex education and systematic desensitization to John's phobic reactions to adult female sexual characteristics. At the end of contact with John, which had lasted over 2 years in all, he had achieved satisfactory adult heterosexual intercourse on one occasion, which had improved his confidence and self-esteem. He had also refrained from seeking out children for sexual purposes. However, deviant sexual fantasies persisted and his social life had never really improved significantly. After 5 years out of prison, he has not been re-convicted.

The second offender patient, David, was also in his early thirties when first seen 6 months ago. Unlike John, he was seen exclusively in the community under the terms of a probation order with a condition of treatment. His offences involved indecent exposure to young girls which had occasionally escalated into indecent assaults. David had been married twice, on both occasions to teenagers who had become pregnant by him. He had two sons, one by his present wife and one by his previous wife. David wished to cease offending both in terms of avoiding imprisonment—he had served one prison sentence previously—and because he feared that he might one day 'go too far' and rape a child. David described himself as over-sexed and said that he had occasionally had extra-marital affairs with women and teenaged girls. David's wife did not wish to be involved in therapy as she saw the problem as his alone.

Intervention with David was directed first at ascertaining the precise nature of his sexual interest in children, teenagers and women. This was achieved by means of monitoring penile responses to, and subjective ratings of visual and auditory material. David's masturbation fantasies when he was first seen were approximately 50 per cent in relation to deviant activity with children and 50 per cent sexual intercourse with young women. Masturbatory conditioning was advised and David applied this successfully. Interestingly, the gradual progress made with this procedure was suddenly accelerated to the point of complete success, in that child fantasies disappeared and only young women fantasies remained. At this time he had begun seeing a young woman with whom he anticipated that an extra-marital affair might develop. Interviews with David indicated that extra-marital affairs had in the past had the effect of decreasing child fantasies which somehow 'seemed dirty' at such times. Shortly after this, two things happened; David obtained a job in which many children were present and his relationship with his young woman friend came to an end. He reported being surprised that he was not using sexual fantasies of the children at his place of work. He attributed to himself a degree of 'responsibility' and 'self-control' the presence of which he had not previously been aware. This led him, independently of therapeutic intervention, to 'test himself' when a young niece, to whom he had previously exposed himself, visited the family home. He set himself the task of not exposing himself and succeeded. David continues in his marriage but with the possibility of extra-marital affairs always present. This poses a moral dilemma for him, particularly as affairs are associated with a diminution in his deviant sexual interest. It remains to be seen if his newly acquired 'cognitive shift' and self-control will be maintained and he continues in treatment.

A number of important differences are evident in the cases of John and David. David was under greater pressure to attend out-patient sessions because of his probation order. This could of course have helped or hindered treatment in that attendance, although regular, may have been attributed by him to external pressure rather than a desire to change. Of greater importance, however, seemed to be David's recognition of possible negative consequences of his offending (raping a child) and his greater understanding of the links between problems and suggested solutions. The two cases described reflect a difference of therapeutic approach. John underwent treatment the results of which it was hoped would generalize into his normal environment but which, failing to take account of his very particular circumstances, often did not. With David, on the other hand, the naturally occurring consequences of his behaviour in the real world were the focus of attention and these were constantly reviewed and capitalized upon as therapeutic interventions proceeded.

Evaluation

Two of the most important questions about treatment programmes such as this concern cost and efficacy. As far as cost is concerned, demand for the service from our various referral sources has, over the last 4 years, remained constant and limited to the equivalent of 2 psychologist days per week. The question of efficacy is more complex.

Since the Birmingham programme began, over a hundred sexual offenders have undergone some form of psychological intervention and these have been followed up for varying lengths of time up to 5 years. Evaluation of the effectiveness of the programme is complicated for two reasons. First, and in line with the broad-based treatment strategy outlined earlier, we have attempted to draw on whatever procedures appear to be relevant for each offender. Each has therefore had an individualized therapy programme. Consequently, the most powerful, control group, evaluation has not been possible for particular treatment methods or treatment combinations. The second complication involves the evaluation of the programme in terms of its effects on re-offending. Since treatment proceeds in the offender's natural environment and since we as the treatment agents are linked directly to community-based agencies, we are in a very real sense, and for reasons essential to the operation of the programme, drawn into the decision-making process surrounding sentencing and, to a lesser extent, prosecution. The possibility exists, therefore, that the re-conviction and sentencing of our treatment group is biased to the degree that we advocate continued treatment in the community.

With an awareness of these difficulties, our evaluation has proceeded in three ways. Where pre- and post-intervention assessments of one treatment or treatment combinations have been possible, these have been carried out. Two examples showing the clearest and most significant results involve the effects of electrical aversion therapy on penile responding and the effects on social skills training on self-reports of social anxiety and competence, and on independent ratings of patient behaviour and videotaped role-play performance. The second form of assessment involves evaluating the extent to which offenders' treatment targets have been met, for example achieving a fuller social life, being able to cope with previously anxiety-arousing situations and engaging in non-deviant, rather than deviant sexual behaviour. Data on the achievement of therapeutic goals, which involves the range of assessment methods previously described, are currently being analysed by computer in relation to offenders' previous histories and type and duration of treatment. The third method of evaluation rests on an analysis of re-conviction rates for offenders from the treatment and quasi-control groups. The first five treated patients released from custody for over 5 years were compared with the quasi-control group in early 1980. There were significantly less re-convictions of all types for the treatment group but the difference for sexual offences alone just failed to attain statistical significance. At this stage of evaluation, and as would perhaps be expected, it appears to be the case that the impact of therapeutic intervention is clearest in terms of the direct and immediate effects of particular treatments. The longer-term effects of treatment in terms of offenders' achievement of life goals and the lowering of re-conviction rates are less clear. The data currently being analysed will bear on this.

Conclusions

The sexual offender literature which has been reviewed illustrates the wide range of relevant theoretical models and available methods of assessment and treatment. Experience with the Birmingham programme suggests that the situation in which an offender is seen for treatment is an important context to that treatment, having relevance to the ethical viability of intervention, the offender's motivation to change and the generalization of treatment effects.

A theoretical continuum could be said to exist from those offences for which an environmental or circumstantial explanation is most relevant to those in which internal tendencies of the offender are of greater importance. Since behaviour is not static but develops with time, there is an ever changing relationship between the internal tendencies, such as sexual interests and social skills, and external factors such as the nature of a work situation or the responses of friends and relatives. Many sexual offenders in our programme have illustrated a spiral of negative influences in the development of offence behaviour, for example an unpleasant sexual experience leading to social isolation, leading to the use of deviant imagery, leading to a seeking out of opportunities for deviant behaviour.

Conversely, offenders who successfully change often illustrate the reverse. A change in one aspect of functioning as a result of direct intervention, for example a change in sexual interest patterns, can lead on to changes in some other aspect of the offender's environment, for example greater social responsiveness from those close to him. This kind of effect can often be unpredictable and, it is argued, it is the role of the therapist to capitalize on the naturally occurring positive consequences of interventions rather than to blindly proceed with a package of measures set up at the outset of treatment. It is, after all, in the natural enviornment that any changes will ultimately have to be maintained.

References

Abel, G. G., Barlow, D. H. and Blanchard, E. B. (1973) Developing heterosexual arousal by altering masturbatory fantasies: a controlled study. Paper presented at the Association for Advancement of Behavior Therapy, Miami, December 1973.

Abel, G. G., Blanchard, E. B., Barlow, D. H. and Mavissakalian, M. (1975). Identifying specific erotic cues in sexual deviations by audio-taped descriptions, *Journal of Applied Behavior Analysis*, **8**, 58–71.

Abel, G. G. and Blanchard, E. B., (1976a). The measurement and generation of sexual arousal in male sexual deviates, in *Progress in Behavior Modification*, Vol. 2 (Eds M. Hersen, R. M. Eisler and P. M. Miller), Academic Press, London.

Abel, G. G., Blanchard, E. B., and Becker, J. V. (1976b). Psychological treatment of rapists, in *Sexual Assault* (Eds M. J. Walker and S. L. Brodsky) Lexington Books, Lexington, Mass.

Amir, M. (1971). *Patterns in Forcible Rape*, University of Chicago Press, Chicago.

Bancroft, J. (1970). A comparative study of aversion and desensitization in the treatment of homosexuality, in *Behaviour Therapy in the Seventies*, (Eds L. E. Burns and J. L Worsley) Wright, Bristol.

Bancroft, J. (1971). The application of psychophysiological measures to the assessment and modification of sexual behaviour, *Behaviour Research and Therapy*. **9**, 119–130.

Bancroft, J. (1974). *Deviant Sexual Behaviour: Modification and Assessment*, Clarendon Press, Oxford.

Bancroft, J. H. J. (1977). Mongol sexuality, *The Practitioner*, **218**, 341.

Bannister, D. and Mair, J. M. M. (1968). *The Evaluation of Personal Constructs* Academic Press, London.

Barbaree, H. E., Marshall, W. L., and Lanthier, R. D. (1979). Deviant sexual arousal in rapists, *Behaviour Research and Therapy*, **17**, 215–272.

Barlow, D. H. (1973). Increasing heterosexual responsiveness in the treatment of sexual deviation: a review of the clinical and experimental evidence. *Behavior Therapy*, **4**, 655–671.

Barlow, D. H., Abel, G. G., Blanchard, E. B., Bristow, A. R., and Young, L. D. (1977). A heterosexual skills behavior chicklist for males, *Behavior Therapy*, **8**, 229–239.

Barlow, D. H. and Agras, W. S. (1973). Fading to increase heterosexual responsiveness in homosexuals, *Journal of Applied Behavior Analysis*, **6**, 355–366.

Barlow, D. H., Agras, W. S., Abel, G. G., Blanchard, E. B., and Young, L. D. (1975). Biofeedback and reinforcement to increase heterosexual arousal in homosexuals, *Behaviour Research and Therapy*, **3**, 45–50.

Barlow, D. H., Leitenberg, H., and Agras, W. S. (1969). The experimental control of sexual deviation through manipulation of the noxious scene in covert sensitization, *Journal of Abnormal Psychology*, **74**, 596–601.

Beck, A. T. (1976). *Cognitive Therapy and the Emotional Disorders*, International Universities Press, New York.

Bieber, B., Bieber, I., Dain, H., Dince, P., Drelick, M., Grundlack. R., Kromer, M., Wiber, C. and Bieber, T. (1963). *Homosexuality* Basic Books, New York.

Boozer, G. (1975). *Offender treatment: programming (workshop)*. Paper presented at the Sixth Alabama Symposium on Justice and the Behavioral Sciences, University of Alabama, Tuscaloosa, Alabama, January 1975.

Burnham, D. (1974). Federal surveys to gauge crime levels in big cities, *New York Times*, 27 January 1974, p. 1.

Callahan, E. J. and Leitenberg, H. (1973). Aversion therapy for sexual deviation: contingent shock and covert sensitization, *Journal of Abnormal Psychology*, **81**, 60–73.

Cautela, J. (1967). Covert sensitization, *Psychological Reports*, **20**, 459–468.

Christie, M. M., Marshall, W. L. and Lanthier, R. D., (1978). *A Descriptive Study of Incarcerated Rapists and Pedophiles*. Unpublished monograph, Dept. of Psychology. Queen University, Kingston, Ontario, Canada.

Cohen, M. L., Garotalo, R., Boucher, R. and Seghorn, T. (1971). The psychology of rapists, *Seminars in Psychiatry*, **3**, 307–327.

Crawford, D. A. (1979). Modification of deviant sexual behaviour: the need for a comprehensive approach, *British Journal of Medical Psychology*, **52**, 151–156.

Crawford, D. A. (1981). Treatment approaches with pedophiles, in *Adult Sexual Interest in Children* (Eds M. Cook and K. Howells), pp. 181–217, Academic Press, London.

Crawford, D. A. and Allen, J. V. (1979). A social skills training programme with sex offenders, in *Love and Attraction: Proceedings of an International Conference* (Eds M. Cook and G. Wilson), Pargamon Press, Oxford.

Curtis, L. A. (1974). *Criminal Violence: National Patterns and Behavior*, Lexington Books, Lexington, Mass.

Curtis, L. A. (1976). Present and future measures of victimization in forcible rape, in *Sexual assault* (Eds M. J. Walker and S. L. Brodsky), Lexington Books, Lexington, Mass. 61–68.

Ennis, P. (1967). *Criminal Victimization in the United States in a Report of a National Survey*. Field surveys II, President's Commission on Law Enforcement and Administration of Justice, Washington, DC, February 1967.

Feldman, M. P. (1973). Abnormal sexual behaviour—males, in *Handbook of Abnormal Psychology*, 2nd edn (Ed. H. J. Eysenck) Pitman, London.

Freund, K. (1963). A laboratory method of diagnosing predominance of homo- or hetero-erotic interest in the male, *Behaviour Research and Therapy*, **1**, 85–93.

Freund, K. (1965). Diagnosing heterosexual pedophilia by means of a test for sexual interest, *Behaviour Research and Therapy*, **3**, 229–234.

Freund, K. (1967). Erotic preferences in pedophilia, *Behaviour Research and Therapy*, **5**, 339–348.

Freund, K., Chan, S., and Coulthard, R. (1979). Phallometric diagnosis with 'non-admitters'. *Behaviour Research and Therapy*, **17**, 451–457.

Geer. J. H. (1974). Cognitive factors in sexual arousal—toward on amalgam of research strategies. Paper read at the American Psychological Association, New Orleans, September 1974.

Gibbens, T. C. N. and Soothill, K. L. (1977). Behavioural types of rape, *British Journal of Psychiatry*, **30**, 32–42.

Gordon, A., Marshall, W. L., Loeber, R. and Barbaree, H. E. (1977). *Toward a definition of social competence in sexual aggressors.* Paper presented at the first Annual Conference on the evaluation and treatment of sexual aggressors, Mamphis, Tenn, April 1977.

Hallam, R. S. and Rachman, S. (1976). Current status of aversion therapy, in *Progress in behaviour modification.* Vol. 2 (Eds M. Hersen, R. M. Eisler and P. M. Miller) Academic Press, London.

Henson, D. E. and Rubin, H. H. (1971). Voluntary control of eroticism, *Journal of Applied Behavior Analysis*, **4**, 37–44.

Herman, S. H., Barlow, D. H. and Agras, W. S. (1974). An experimental analysis of exposure to 'elicit' heterosexual stimuli as an effective variable in changing arousal patterns of homosexuals, *Behaviour Research and Therapy*, **12**, 335–345.

Herman, S. H. and Prewett, M. (1974). An experimental analysis of feedback to increase sexual arousal in a case of homo- and heterosexual impotence: a preliminary report, *Journal of Behavior Therapy and Experimental Psychiatry*, **5**, 271–274.

Howells, K. (1979). Some meanings of children for pedophiles, in *Love and Attraction: Proceedings of an International Conference* (Eds M. Cook and G. Wilson) Pergamon Press, Oxford.

Howells, K. and Steadman-Allen, R. (1977). *The emotional mediation of sexual offences.* Paper presented to the annual conference of the British Psychological Society, Exeter, April 1977.

Kohlenberg, R. J. (1974). Treatment of a homosexual pedophiliac using *in vivo* desensitization: a case study, *Journal of Abnormal Psychology*, **83**, 192–195.

Langelüddeke, A. (1963). *Castration of Sexual Criminals*, Walter de Gruyter, Berlin.

Laws D. R. (1974). Non-aversive treatment alternatives of hospitalized pedophiles: an automated fading procedure of alter sexual responsiveness. Paper presented at the American Psychological Association. New Orleans, September 1976. New Orleans, August 1974.

Laws, D. R. and Rubin, H. H. (1969). Instructional control of an autonomic sexual response, *Journal of Applied Behavior Analysis*, **2**, 93–99.

McGuire, R. J., Carlisle, J. M., and Young, B. G. (1965). Sexual deviations as conditioned behaviour, *Behaviour Research and Therapy*, **2**, 185–190.

Marquis, J. (1970). Orgasmic reconditioning: changing sexual object choice through controlling masturbation fantasies, *Journal of Behavior Therapy and Experimehtal Psychiatry*, **1**, 263–271.

Mahoney, M. J. (1974). *Cognition and behaviour modification*, Ballinger, New York.

Marshall W. L. (1974). The clinical conditioning of sexual attractiveness: a report of four therapeutic failures, *Behavior Therapy*, **5**, 298–299.

Marshall, W. L., Williams, S. M. and Christie, M. M. (1977). The treatment of rapists, in *Perspectives on Rape* (Ed. C. B. Qualls) Pergamon, New York.

Meichenbaum, D. (1976). Cognitive behavior modification, in *Behavioral Approaches to Therapy* (Eds J. T. Spence, R. C. Carson and J. W. Thibaut) General Learning Press, New York.

Mohr, J. W., Turner, R. E. and Jerry, M. B. (1964). *Pedophilia and Exhibitionism* University of Toronto Press, Toronto.

Pacht, A. R. (1976). The rapist in treatment: professional myths, in *Sexual Assault* (Eds M. J. Walker and S. L. Brodsky) pp. 91–98, Lexington Books, Lexington, Mass.

Pacht, A. R. and Cowden, J. E. (1974). An exploratory study of five hundred sex offenders, *Criminal Justice and Behavior*, **1**, 13–20.

Perkins, D. E. (1977). Development of a treatment programme for sexual offenders in a prison setting. Paper presented at the annual conference of the British Psychological Society, Exeter, April 1977.

Perkins, D. E. (1982). Assessment and treatment of dangerous sexual offenders, in *Dangerousness: Problems of Assessment and Prediction* (Ed J. Hinton), George Allen and Unwin, London. (In press.)

Rachman, S. and Hodgson, R. J. (1968). Experimentally induced 'sexual fetishism': replication and development, *Psychological Records*, **18**, 25–27.

Serber, M. (1970). Shame aversion therapy, *Journal of Behavior Therapy and Experimental Psychiatry*, **1**, 217–226.

Serber, M. and Wolpe, J. (1972). Behaviour therapy techniques, in *Sexual Behaviours* (Eds H. L. P. Resnick and M. E. Wolfgang) Little, Brown Boston. 239–254.

Stürup, G. (1968). *Treatment of Sexual Offenders in Herstedvester, Denmark: the Rapists*, Munksgaard, Copenhagen.

Stürup, G. (1972). Castration: the total treatment, in *Sexual Behaviour*, (Eds H. L. P. Resnick and M. F. Wolfgang) Little, Brown, Boston.

Woodward, R. (1980). Brief report on the effects of a sex education course on borstal trainees, *Home Office Prison Department Psychological Services DPS Reports*, Series II, No. 78, July 1980.

Zuckerman, M. (1971). Physiological measures of sexual arousal in the human, *Psychological Bulletin*, **75**, 279–329.

Development in the Study of Criminal Behaviour
Volume 1: The Prevention and Control of Offending
Edited by P. Feldman

9

Overview

Philip Feldman

Introduction

This is the first volume of two on recent developments in the study of criminal behaviour. We have collected together several reports of recent British programmes which apply the principles and methods of social learning theory to the problems of diverting young offenders from a track which so often leads from a relatively minor offence through police contact and court disposal, to repeated periods in prison for more serious offences. One chapter deals with the application of social learning principles to a special group, sex offenders. The choice of programmes concerning juvenile and sex offenders was a deliberate one: these are the two groups where the aims of 'clients' and 'therapists' are most likely to be in harmony and a change of behaviour more likely as a result. They are also the areas in which much the greatest volume of behavioural research into offender care is under way. Although the programmes described are British in setting they all draw on American research findings, both in basic and in applied psychology.

The five chapters describing programmes of behaviour change were preceded by three which set out the broader context which both makes such programmes necessary and which either helps or hinders their conception and execution. Once again, much of the material described is British in origin but it is interwoven with American sources and the same conclusions apply on both sides of the Atlantic. Those working directly with young offenders do so within a political framework concerning public policy towards offenders which has both formal and informal aspects. Both traditional and innovative police attempts to prevent and deter crime are expensive and so far relatively ineffective. Institutions for juveniles run on traditional lines are generally unsuccessful. It is far too early to claim that social learning based programmes will succeed where so much else has failed, but the five chapters concerned with practical programmes of *intervention* with offenders allow a limited degree of optimism.

This overview chapter also briefly discusses the possible *prevention* of offending by a variety of planned social policies which range from making it harder to get at money, goods or other targets by illegal means, to the deliberate encouragement of pro-social attitudes and behaviours.

215

The context

The political setting

Norman Tutt describes the twists and turns of British social policy towards juvenile offenders during the past decade. The Children and Young Persons Act (1969) aimed to shift the emphasis from 'punishment' by exposure to the criminal justice system to 'diversion' both by an increased use of police cautioning and by treatment in the community. By the end of the decade the pendulum had swung back from concern with the personal problems of the young offender to the need to protect the community. At the same time, it is recognized that institutional detention is both expensive and relatively ineffective. Such contradictory pressures, combined with the lack of a coherent underlying philosophy in the present juvenile offender system, have resulted in a split between a punishment- and a treatment-oriented approach, with the latter currently losing ground.

The riots in many British cities in the summer of 1981 resulted in the arrest and detention of hundreds, even thousands, of juveniles. This will inevitably increase the pressure for short-term responses emphasizing punishment rather than the more patient long-term attempts at the social rehabilitation of young offenders. At the same time, the scale of the riots and the widespread media publicity which resulted, may assist large-scale programmes aimed at reducing the environmental conditions which set the scene for the riots (and the massive associated looting of stores and other business premises). Whatever the outcome of the resulting political debate, which is going on as this chapter is being written, the message from Tutt's chapter for professionals working with juvenile offenders is clear: observe, understand and seek to influence both the policy makers and the general public; you cannot operate in a cosy and separate professional world.

The police

Conventional policing methods attempt to prevent crime and to apprehend offenders—and so deter future crime. Mike Hough and Kevin Heal present ample data to indicate the limited success of such methods as preventive patrols and formal detective work. Indeed the most important impact of such traditional police activities may be to reassure the public that they are being protected and to encourage them to cooperate with the police, both by reporting crimes and by assisting the police in their work of prevention and detection. Certainly, there is no simple relationship between assigning additional financial resources to the police and a real reduction in crime. The use of specialized, rather then conventional, patrols may have a short-term impact but they are very expensive, and may simply encourage offenders to displace their activities to easier targets. They may even increase police–juvenile tension—and hence result in a longer-term increase in crime and a reduced degree of police-public cooperation. Such research results have led thoughtful policemen to explore more community oriented preventive approaches rather than the conventional deterrent approach to policing (Alderson, 1979). Community policing involves the patient cultivation and maintenance of police-public relationships and may involve the police in the training of juveniles in pro-social attitudes and behaviours.

Conventional institutions for juvenile offenders

The history of attempts to reform, rather than punish, juvenile offenders is a lengthy one and is largely, but not wholly, disappointing. Ian Sinclair and Roger Clarke pull together a great deal of British work on institutional care. Irrespective of the nature or objectives of the regimen, it is crucial to prevent absconding (which re-exposes the juvenile to anti-social influences) and to operate a clear and consistent policy within an overall framework of sympathetic concern. However, even the best designed institutional regimen will fail unless full provision is made for bringing back the juvenile to the outside world. Consequently, it is better to avoid the 're-entry problem' by carrying out change programmes within the community to which the juvenile eventually will have to return. Best of all is a much greater emphasis on prevention—particularly by reducing opportunities for crime.

Current behavioural programmes

Community approaches

Mary Anne Preston gives a detailed account of the development of community care programmes for British young offenders and the concept of 'treatment' implied in these programmes. Despite a shift in venue from institutional to community settings (and irrespective of the details of the particular programme) the main emphases have been on good adult–child 'relationships', regarded as ends in themselves, rather than on planned attempts to alter particular target behaviours. The main British development has been that of 'Intermediate Treatment' (IT). Programmes grouped under this heading have varied widely but share several common, and undesirable, elements—a lack of shape in conception and execution, and little or no emphasis on assessment and evaluation at any stage. Moreover, formally designated IT programmes still cater for only a minority of young offenders and there is a crying need for a coherent national policy. In contrast, deincarceration has proceeded with great vigour in the USA and has been linked with the rapid rise of behavioural approaches both to personal and to broader social problems. For example, Achievement Place has been followed by over thirty-five other American group-home programmes which combine the behavioural approach and the family teaching model.

Preston emphasizes the '3 Rs' if young offenders are to be helped effectively: *relevant* training environments, *relevant* target behaviours, and *relevant* reinforcers. The environment in which training occurs should be that in which the offender has been living, and will continue to live. The exception is the occasional need for very secure accommodation (this is discussed below under Institutions). Eugene Ostapiuk's report of the Shape programme exemplifies the use which can be made of local community resources, both formal and informal.

Relevant alternative target behaviours are again those appropriate to the offenders themselves, rather than those believed appropriate by care staff, which means that the former must make the selection. Such alternatives include basic everyday activities, both common to all juveniles such as job finding and holding as well as those more specific to 'known' offenders such as encounters with the police. Sue Spence provides much evidence for the importance of selecting and matching social skills both to the people who will use them and the settings in which they will be used rather than teaching a blanket set of skills for all persons and all settings.

Likewise, relevant reinforcers are those considered rewarding by the clients themselves rather than by those who work with them.

So far as results are concerned, we cannot at the moment use a stronger term than 'promising' either for the extensive American behavioural programmes, or the sparser British ones, exemplified in this book by those described by Preston and Ostapiuk. The '3 Rs' are far from the only requirements for success, whether in community or institutional settings. Others are discussed following a brief look at institutional care.

Institutions: young offenders

Shifts in public opinion influence public policy concerning the more 'troublesome' or 'disturbed' young offenders (exactly which term is fashionable is a significant indicator of current public opinion). As Ian Reid makes clear, there are effects both on what happens in the institution, on the criteria for selecting the young trainees, and even on the physical design of the buildings. Ideally, large-scale public policy decisions should be based on carefully designed and executed pilot studies carried out over several years by specially trained staff. Instead, political considerations often result in programmes which owe little or nothing to well-established findings, and everything to the current emotional and social climate.

Reid's detailed account of the Glenthorne Youth Treatment Centre also demonstrates that even the most carefully planned behavioural programme is far from sufficient. It must be carried out by a trained staff, directed by a management cognisant of the relevant professional knowledge, and able to select, train and monitor the staff executing the programme. Even then, there are enormous difficulties in transferring newly acquired skills from the inevitably artificial setting of the institution to the eventual home environment of the trainees. If all the other elements mentioned previously are present, a programme can still fail unless the transition is planned and executed with the same detailed control as the training phase. Real life caretakers—often parents—are much less easy to train and manage than are care staff. However, *if* they can be personally involved, they may contribute even more in the way of dedication and sustained effort. Often figures in the host community, such as employers, local police and other officials, are also of great importance in ensuring successful re-entry. Provided that their co-operation can be gained, then special programmes can be constructed which will ensure that they behave in the same consistent manner as the care agents in the institution.

It is clear that there are very many links in the chain from entry through institutional training to going back into the outside world. Failures (defined by the legal authorities as re-offending and reconviction) can result from deficits in planning or execution at any point in the sequence, or simply from a lack of mutual co-operation.

Thus success comes harder from an institution-based programme than from one based in the community. Ideally, it might be best for all programmes to be carried out in the community, which has been done already in the United States in Massachusetts. The County of Kent in Britain has also made a serious attempt in that direction. Nevertheless, we can ignore neither public opinion or the genuine existence of a small number of adolescents with a record of individual or repeated serious acts of violence who require removal from the community and placement in secure accommodation. The challenge is making sure that those few who are locked away will at least not deteriorate even further, and eventually will be rehabilitated.

The institution: sex offenders

Serious sex offenders continue to be imprisoned for many years. As Derek Perkins' chapter makes clear they form a small but important group, both because of the increasing research information which strengthens the possibility of effective help and sustained behaviour change, and because a significant proportion of such offenders do seek help voluntarily. Relevant components of treatment 'packages', which vary in specific composition for each client, include accurate information on sexual anatomy, physiology and behaviour, reducing arousal to sexually deviant stimuli and intensifying it to alternatives agreed by client and therapist, and training in heterosexual social skills. The training programme at Birmingham Prison begins within the institution, near to the known date of discharge, and continues into the community in cooperation with probation officers.

Once again we see that failure may result from a deficiency in planning or execution at any one of a number of steps in a lengthy sequence.

Some key issues

Targets and criteria of change

It is striking that both psychotherapeutic and behavioural programmes have concentrated on the troubles experienced by the offender rather than the problems caused by the offender to others. Psychotherapists appear to assume that the offender steals or assaults because of some form of personal inadequacy or distress; their targets for change involve them in building 'maturity' or 'ego strength'. Behaviour therapists seem to make the same assumption of some personal deficit in the offender, a typical area of emphasis being lack of educational skills. The implication is that if only he was fluent in reading, or has some kind of job skill he would not 'need' to offend. Conversely, it is rare to find a direct attempt to change the behaviour which led to a conviction. The indirect approach is in very sharp contrast to the behavioural stance in the clinical field, in which the emphasis has been on the problem behaviour itself, rather than on some correlate or supposed 'cause'.

The agents of the legal system and the politicians and civil servants who formulate penal policy, regard reconviction as the crucial, indeed often the sole, criterion of success. Both psychotherapists and behaviour therapists give equal weight, and sometimes pride of place, to other indices, whether these are educational and occupational skills or less easily defined variables such as maturity. In the view of those who pay the piper, however much a convicted young offender improves his educational skills or his scores on measures of ego strength, these will be of much less importance than a demonstrated reduction of further offending. The acid test is a change in the behaviour which brought the offender into contact with the system in the first place.

The programmes reported in this volume include both targets intended for the offender—through the acquisition of personally relevant social, educational and occupational skills—and those which will benefit society at large through a reduction in, and preferably the total cessation of, offending by the person concerned. However, with the exception of Perkins' sex offender programme, whereas the former target is aimed at *directly*, by carefully planned and executed programmes of training, the latter is sought indirectly, as a hoped-for consequence of the acquisition by the offender of behaviours alternative to offending. It will be surprising if it proves totally unnecessary to include a direct attempt to change the offending behaviour itself. To do so will require analyses of both setting events and the reinforcers for the commission of criminal behaviours, and the design of appropriate alternative behaviours and rein-forcers. Clearly this will be the most difficult part of the task.

There is a further problem. Whereas it is becoming a common practice for therapists to ask clinical clients what they would like to achieve, this appears unheard of in the world of care for young offenders, whether community or institution based. There is no systematic evidence that the recipients of care share the aims of those providing it, other than a common desire for a quiet and well-run institution or community programme with neither side causing difficulties for the other.

The question of common aims comes up sharply in the context of psychologically-based programmes for offenders. Such programmes are derived from methods developed for those who have sought help for problems from which they lose much and benefit little, either materially or in terms of social or self approval. Most important of all, the client has often sought help voluntarily and is usually pleased when his problems cease or ease. On the other hand, the performance of criminal behaviours is directly damaging to those carrying them out only when they are caught and convicted.

Recruiting, training and managing care staff

Several of the authors in this volume refer to the well-known problem of counter-control by the peer group. A number of studies (e.g. Buehler *et al.*, 1966) have shown how institutional groups of offenders not only value different behaviours from those approved of by the staff, but also are more consistent in reinforcing such behaviours by one of their number than are the staff in reinforcing examples of their own preferences.

Less well known, but equally important, is the lack of cooperation between veteran staff with enthusiastic newly-appointed behaviour therapists. Such difficulties may be overcome either by carefully planned and voluntarily accepted training programmes for existing staff or by the development of completely new facilities, such as Achievement Place or Shape, in which the staff is committed from the beginning to carrying out the programme concerned. Staff must share common objectives and pursue them systematically. Whether or not clients will share them is, as indicated above, quite another matter. Those who *volunteer* to take part in change programmes are obviously much more likely to do so; examples in this volume are provided by the Birmingham Sex Offender study (Perkins) and by the Shape programme (Ostapiuk).

Ian Reid sets out in detail the need for a behavioural programme to be the responsibility of a designated specialist at every stage, from design through execution to evaluation. The specialist must be able to take and implement decisions at each step of the sequence, rather than merely advise management. Responsibilities must include the recruitment, selection and training of care staff. Very few of those currently working in programmes for young offenders have had training in behavioural methods. The inevitable conclusion is that special programmes must be established to provide theoretical and practical training in the behavioural approach to young offenders. Mary Anne Preston illustrates the difficulties of grafting the behavioural approach on to existing broadly-based programmes. By contrast, the Shape programme was designed from the beginning on exclusively behavioural lines.

Effective staff training must be followed by equally effective staff management. The behavioural approach, as outlined by Ian Reid, emphasizes definite criteria for effective job performance, feedback of actual performance and the provision of specific corrective measures, and positive reinforcements for achieving agreed targets. It is most important here to define what exactly constitutes 'effective' performance.

Economic costs and criteria

A public policy issue of great and increasing importance is the financial cost of training programmes of all kinds, and most specifically the relative cost of successful and unsuccessful clients. The Shape programme report by Eugene Ostapiuk is one of the first to make a serious attempt at the difficult task of providing such information. It is noteworthy both for relatively good results in terms of reconviction rates at follow-up, and for the low costs of the programme in comparison with the alternatives.

Future developments

Intervention

The reports in this book and elsewhere are hopeful enough to suggest the desirability of well planned and executed behavioural programmes with young offenders, particularly in community settings, using specially selected and trained care staff. In addition to the increased provision of formal programmes for convicted young offenders, several legal and social agencies might also contribute to reducing re-offending.

The police. Wolfgang *et al.* (1972) found that 46 per cent of young offenders in their Philadelphia study stopped after the first offence and 35 per cent more after the second. They concluded that formal intervention involving custodial care should be delayed until after the third offence, with a consequent financial saving and reduced exposure to the criminogenic setting of a penal institution.

There is also evidence that both the appearance of the suspect and his general demeanour contribute, together with the seriousness of the offence and the (police-perceived) likelihood of effective parental control, to the decision to arrest or to caution a juvenile (Piliavin and Briar, 1964; Werner *et al.*, 1975). The latter found that juveniles may be trained to display behaviours acceptable to the police. It would probably be more practical to train the police in managing their side of police-juvenile encounters. Toch (1969) found that the police who were most prone to use violence in the course of their duties used strong verbal threats very early in a confrontation with a suspect. This increased the likelihood of a similar response by the suspect and hence of an arrest, irrespective of whether or not he committed the offence that led to the encounter. Goldstein *et al.*, (1977) report a training course for police officers in the non-violent handling of aggressive suspects. Even more important, there is a strong suggestion (Stumphauzer *et al.*, 1977) that some police officers found pursuit and arrest more reinforcing than prevention. These authors suggest that changes in police training (and presumably promotion practices) will be needed in order to change this. The chapter by Hough and Heal indicates that some police forces are beginning to shift from more conventional approaches to community policing which may increase effective prevention.

The courts. The courts make widespread use of 'time sentencing', for example 6 months following theft. Yet the two events seem only very loosely related. Wright and James (1974) have suggested replacing this with 'task sentencing', based on behavioural principles. For example, a youth convicted of shoplifting might be sentenced to work in the store from which he stole, literally 'repaying' the shopkeeper.

Probation officers tend to use very loose contingencies such as 'stay out of trouble or else'. Stumphauzer (1974) notes that programmes have been started to train probation officers in behavioural principles. Their success depends, as does that of all other such approaches, on the acceptance of re-education throughout the department concerned. Moreover they will need to be linked with carefully planned and monitored programmes in the offender's natural environment. At present the offender visits his probation officer in an office. There is no more reason for continuing this practice than for self-referring clients to be seen in consulting rooms rather than in the social settings in which problems develop and are maintained.

Fostering. An important current trend is to place young offenders with foster parents rather than in institutions. Foster parents are provided with some training and are paid at a level markedly greater than the cost of keeping the child. They thus receive recompense for their skill and efforts in much the same way as do the professionals employed in residential institutions. Nevertheless, the costs per child are very much less than those in institutions. Furthermore, because only one or two children are placed with each family, the problems of criminalization and of group opposition to staff norms are avoided. In addition, the children have an opportunity both to learn and to practice relevant social skills in real, as opposed to artificial, environments. Major examples of such schemes are those in the State of Massachusetts in the USA and the County of Kent in Britain. Systematic data on their long-term effects are still to be published.

Prevention

Several developments, both already in existence or of obvious potential, might help to prevent some young offenders starting on the track which leads them into the pool of adults who spend many years in and out of prison, forming a 'revolving door' population.

Reducing opportunities by social planning and design. Clarke (1977, 1980) gives several examples of how relatively straightforward measures have reduced particular forms of crime: the British Post Office has virtually eliminated theft from telephone kiosks through the fitting of steel coin boxes; the West Germans have dramatically reduced car theft by compulsory steering locks in all vehicles, and theft of motor cycles was unintentially cut in Britain by the law requiring motor cyclists to wear crash helmets. There is much evidence that a more deliberate use of the surveillance role of employees primarily employed in service capacities and who are in frequent and regular contact with the public would cut down both theft and property damage—the two most frequent offences. For example, apartment blocks with doormen are less vulnerable to burglary and car parks with attendants suffer less auto crimes.

On a large scale, O'Donnell (1980) has reviewed evidence that social networks are related to crime control. Crime rates are higher in transient neighbourhoods where people are less likely to know each other, possibly resulting in a reduced natural surveillance of every day activities, including criminally related ones. O'Donnell and Lydgate (1980) found zoning and land use to be related to crime rates and argued that zoning ordinances might be used to lower them. For example, housing developments could be required to include those social facilities known to increase social networks, hence increasing surveillance.

Community persuasion. McGuire (1980) has described large-scale and successful community programmes, such as the Stanford project which used a mass-media campaign to persuade people to reduce cardiac risk factors by decreasing smoking and shifting to more appropriate diets. The design of these programmes drew on many years of social psychological research into persuasive communications. Such a programme might well be developed in the interests of crime prevention. It would include the following elements: reducing the opportunities provided by open doors and windows and poorly lighted and isolated public places; avoiding danger spots completely or entering them only in groups, the desirability of helping the police, victims and potential victims. As indicated above, crime-prevention exercises should extend to the design of buildings and public places.

The mass media might also be used to model pro-social behaviours. Whereas a great deal of attention has been focussed on the potentially harmful effects of televized violence; little is known of the possible uses of television as a *beneficial* influence and empirical research provides only a few scattered clues (e.g. Leyens *et al.*, 1975). However, there is ample experimental and field evidence that just as antisocial behaviours can be modelled, so can their pro-social counterparts (see Bar-Tal, 1976 and Feldman, 1977 for reviews). In the present context, pro-social behaviours would include assisting victims, or potential victims, and not taking advantage of the latter when the opportunity arises.

Training parents and teachers. There are several attempts to help parents of young offenders to cope with them more effectively. Results vary from considerable success to ineffectiveness, depending on such factors as cooperation by the parents and the extent of counter-control by peers. More certain success might be achieved by helping parents first to acquire effective methods of child management and then using them to promote the development by their children of pro-social behaviours and relevant associated skills *before* offending begins. Such possibilities are discussed in detail by Herbert (1980).

There is much to be learned from the success of some adolescents in keeping out of trouble even while living in the very high crime areas which provide many highly visible models of repeated and often successful offending. Stumphauzer and colleagues (e.g. Stumphauzer *et al.*, 1977; Aiken *et al.*, 1977) are engaged in a long-term programme of research in the very high crime rate *barrios* of Los Angeles. They have found that the relevant 'trouble-avoiding' behaviours include appropriate interactions both with gang members and the police and having a repertoire of rewarding alternative behaviours to crime, including car repairing and other skills. Older brothers, with trouble-avoiding behaviours already in their repertoire, model them to younger brothers who in turn keep out of trouble.

Just as family members may learn to be more effective in developing pro-social behaviours in children, so may *teachers*. However, there seem few planned attempts to train teachers either in child management in general or in the development in children of pro-social behaviours in particular. The literature on behaviour modification now includes many examples of the training of teachers in the more effective classroom management of children already known to be 'difficult'. It should not be a major extrapolation to help teachers develop pro-social behaviours in children before they become difficult. More effective teachers (and more positively reinforcing school activities) might be expected to cut down truancy—there is evidence that many children begin offending at this point—and so reduce the exposure of some children to social models of offending. Improved leisure-time facilities (those sought by children—not assumed by adults) are also relevant to the provision of alternative behaviours to criminal activities.

Professionals and policy makers

As indicated throughout, involvement in policy formulation and decision-making is crucial if psychologists are to make a more effective contribution than has been the case to date in the care and control of young offenders. If the more promising developments are to be of real benefit, they must inform policy-making rather than remain in the pages of professional journals. The policy-makers, rather than scattered professionals, or academic departments, must initiate and monitor experiments. The achievement of this mutual interaction, between social policy and socially relevant research, must be the next step forward for applied psychology in general not only for the care of young offenders.

References

Aiken, T. W., Stumphauzer, J. S. and Veloz, E. V. (1977). Behavioural analysis of non-delinquent brothers in a high juvenile crime community, *Behavioural Disorders*, **2**, 212–222.

Alderson, J. (1979). *Policing Freedom*, McDonald and James, Plymouth.

Bar-Tal, D. (1976). *Pro-Social Behaviour*, Hemisphere, Washington DC.

Buehler, R. E., Patterson, G. R. and Furniss, J. M. (1966). The reinforcement of behaviour in institutional settings, *Behaviour Research and Therapy*, **4**, 157–167.

Clarke, R. G. V. (1977). Psychology and crime, *Bulletin, British Psychological Society*, **30**, 280–283.

Clarke, R. G. V. (1980). Situational crime prevention—theory and practice, *The British Journal of Criminology*, **20**, 136–147.

Feldman, M. P. (1977). *Criminal Behaviour*, Wiley, Chichester.

Goldstein, A. P., Monti, P. J., Sardino, T. J. and Green, D. J. (1977). *Police Crisis Intervention*, Behaviordelia, Kalamazoo, MI.

Herbert, M. (1980). Socialisation for problem resistance, in *Psychological Problems: The Social Context* (Eds M. P. Feldman and J. Orford), pp. 139–72, Wiley, Chichester.

Leyens, J. P. Camino, L., Parke, R. D. and Berkowitz, L. (1975). Effects of movie violence on agression in a field setting as a function of group dominance and cohesion, *Journal of Personality and Social Psychology*, **32**, 346–360.

McGuire, W. J. (1980). Communication and social influence processes, In *Psychological Problems: The Social Context* (Eds M. P. Feldman and J. Orford), pp. 341–366, Wiley, Chichester.

O'Donnell, C. R. (1980). Environmental design and the prevention of psychological problems, in *Psychological Problems: The Social Context* (Eds M. P. Feldman and J. Orford), pp. 279–310, Wiley, Chichester.

O'Donnell, C. R. and Lydgate, T. (1980). The assessment of physical resources and their relationship to crimes, *Environment and Behaviour*, **12**, 320–331.

Piliavin, I. and Briar, S. (1964). Police encounters with juveniles, *American Journal of Sociology*, **70**, 206–214.

Stumphauzer, J. S. (1974). *Six Techniques of Modifying Delinquent Behaviour*, Behavioural Sciences Tape Library, Leonia, NJ.

Stumphauzer, J. S., Aiken, T. W. and Veloz, E. V. (1977). Eastside story: behavioural analysis of a high juvenile crime community, *Behavioural Disorders*, **2**, 76–84.

Toch, H. (1969). *Violent Men*, Aldine, Chicago.

Werner, J. S., Minkin, N., Minkin, B. L., Fixsen, D. L., Phillips, E. L. and Wolf, M. M. (1975). 'Intervention package': an analysis to prepare juvenile delinquents for encounters with police officers, *Criminal Justice & Behaviour*, **2**, 22–36.

Wolfgang, M. E., Figlio, R. M. and Sellin, T. (1972). *Delinquency in a Birth Cohort*, University of Chigago Press, Chigago.

Wright, J. and James, R. (1974). *A Behavioural Approach to Preventing Delinquency*, Charles T. Thomas, Springfield, Illinois.

Author Index

229

Subject Index

Absconding, 51, 53, 60, 61, 63–67, 70
Achievement Place, 82, 84, 112
  teaching parents, 101
Aggressive behaviours, 91
American Bar Association, 20–22
Approved schools, 51, 53, 57–58, 63–67, 69, 72
Assertive training, 117
Assessment, 180, 181
Assessment of sex offenders
  and heterosexual social skills, 197
  and individual arousal patterns, 198
  and naturalistic observations, 197
  and penile response measures, 198
  and psychometric testing, 196
  and psychophysiological assessment, 197
  and reliability and validity, 197
  and the repertory grid, 196
Aycliffe School, 140

Behavioural contracts, 95, 176, 181
Birmingham sex offender treatment programme
  and cognitive factors in therapy, 209
  and descriptions of offender-patients, 205
  and evaluations, 209, 210
  and generalization into the natural environment, 206, 207
  and indecent assaults on children, 207
  and indecent exposure, 208
  and links with other agencies, 206
  and masturbatory conditioning, 208
  and modifying deviant sexual interest, 208
  and offender motivation, 207, 210
  and reconviction, 210

and relationship between assessment and treatment, 206
  and repertory grid assessment, 207
  and selection of offender-patients, 204, 205
  and social skills training, 208
  and terms of reference, 204, 205
Borstals, 51, 52, 53, 58, 72
Boys' Town, 82, 84

Caning, 64
Care Orders, 12, 15, 16
Centre for Community Youth Development and Achievement
  Tucson, 84
Chelfham Mill School, 139, 82
Children and Young Persons Act 1969, 1, 2, 3, 79, 167, 168, 171, 178
Community Homes with Education, 2, 12, 13, 17, 20, 72, 120
Community intervention, 187
Community policing, 40–43, 46
Community programmes
  in UK, 144
  in USA, 145–148
  public acceptance, 156
  relevant reinforcers, 158
  utilizing limited resources, 155
Community projects, 175, 177, 178
Conversation skills
  training of, 112
Crime
  and criminal investigation, 35
  detection of, 35
  displacement, 44
  geographical distribution of, 37
  increases in, 30
  juvenile rates of, 27, 28

235

legislation, 167, 168
prevailing attitudes, 136
Police, 216, 222–223
and ethnic minorities, 39, 41, 43
and fast response to calls, 33
and juveniles, 29, 38, 39, 43, 108, 112, 222–223
community constables, 41
community involvement departments, 41
community relations, 34, 39
crime prevention officers, 44, 45
criminal investigation, 35
econometric studies of, 31
foot patrol, 32
increases in manpower, 30, 36, 46
mobile patrols, 32
schools liaison, 43
specialized patrols, 33, 34
strikes, 35, 36
sub-divisional organization, 27, 28
team policing, 42
work of uniformed branch, 28, 29
Probation, 51
hostels, 51, 59–63
Psychotherapy, 135–136

Rape
and classifications of rapists, 194
and motives of rapists, 194
and preconvictions and reconvictions of rapists, 194
and sexual arousal patterns of rapists, 198
and sub-cultural factors, 193
and victim precipitation, 193
Reconviction
and personality, 54, 67, 68
environmental effects on, 51–52, 54–56, 61, 62, 67, 68, 69
family effects on, 51, 52, 54, 57, 62, 68, 73
prediction of, 51, 52, 53, 54, 55, 56, 67, 69
Rehabilitation of offenders
behavioural approach, 137
psychotherapeutic approach, 135
relevant behavioural targets, 156–158
street corner research, 138
traditional approaches, 135
Rehabilitation Research Foundation, 138

Reinforcement, 52, 142
application to society, 142
and offenders, 158

St. Charles Youth Treatment Centre, 84
Security
definition of, 105
Self esteem, 121–122
Self government, 98
Self-reported offending, 122
Sentences, 8–13, 223
and cautioning, 9
and juveniles, 8–13
Sex offences
and community surveys, 192
criminal statistics of, 192
legal definitions of, 192
models of, 191
and reconvictions, 192
and attitudes towards victims, 195
and definition of sexual deviation, 195
Shape Project, 89, 148–154
accommodation scheme, 149
efficacy, 153–154
offence behaviour, 152
self government, 149
work experience scheme, 152
Single-case methodology
limitations of, 113
Social learning theory, 51, 52, 65, 67–72
Social skills
and young offenders, 107–108, 109–111
definition, 107
offenders versus non-offenders, 109–111
Social skills training
approaches, 109
community programmes, 129
criticisms of studies, 125–128
efficacy with young offenders, 128
group design studies, 116–120
long term, generalized effects, 120
influence of ongoing regime, 122–123, 127
limitations of research, 116
prevention of offending, 130
single-case design studies, 112–116
research methodology, 111
with cognitive therapy, 129
with token economy systems, 129